The Complete Idiot's Reference Card

Yoga Goes with the Flow

Sun Salutations!

The sun is the center of our solar system, and without its energy and warmth, we wouldn't be able to exist on this planet. Yoga's sun salutation is devotional: offering thanks and greetings to the sun that sustains us. As a *vinyasa,* or continuous flow of yoga postures, sun salutations balance and center your awareness while energizing, strengthening, and toning all the major muscles and organs in your body. As you breathe through the postures, you are in tune with the rhythm of the life force itself, something yoga calls *prana.* Try starting your day with an invigorating practice of sun salutations, performed at sunrise, out-of-doors, facing east. Good morning, yoga-style!

alpha books

We're All Yogis! Yes, Even YOU!

Yoga is for *everyone* and *everyone* who practices yoga is a yogi.

Yoga, thousands of years old, is timeless—transcending cultures, eras, and philosophies. A lot of people think yoga is a religion, but it's not. Yoga is a *path*. When you begin a yoga practice, you start to learn how to connect and focus both your body and your mind. In fact, yoga means *union* and *discipline*. Following the yoga path means getting in touch with yourself; it means exploring your own spirituality. Reach up; you have the sun and the moon within you!

The sun and the moon with standing figure.

Yoga's Guidelines for Living

Incorporating these yoga guidelines for living into your yoga practice will enhance your success—in yoga and in life!

Yoga Don'ts: Yamas	*Yoga Do's:* Niyamas
Do No Harm (*Ahimsa*)	Be Pure (*Shauca*)
Tell No Lies (*Satya*)	Be Content (*Santosha*)
No More Stealing (*Asteya*)	Be Disciplined (*Tapas*)
Cool It, Casanova (*Brahmacharya*)	Be Studious (*Svadhyaya*)
Don't Be Greedy (*Aparigraha*)	Be Devoted (*Ishvara-Pranidhana*)

THE COMPLETE IDIOT'S GUIDE™ TO

Yoga

*by Joan Budilovsky
and Eve Adamson*

alpha books

A Division of Macmillan General Reference
A Simon & Schuster Macmillan Company
1633 Broadway, New York, NY 10019

©1998 Amaranth

All right reserved. No part of this book shall be reproduced, stored in a retrieval system, or transmitted by any means, electronic, mechanical, photocopying, recording, or otherwise, without written permission from the publisher. No patent liability is assumed with respect to the use of the information contained herein. Although every precaution has been taken in the preparation of this book, the publisher and authors assume no responsibility for errors or omissions. Neither is any liability assumed for damages resulting from the use of the information contained herein. For information, address Alpha Books, 1633 Broadway, 7th Floor, New York, NY 10019-6785.

Macmillan Publishing books may be purchased for business or sales promotional use. For information please write: Special Markets Department, Macmillan Publishing USA, 1633 Broadway, New York, NY, 10019.

THE COMPLETE IDIOT'S GUIDE name and design are trademarks of Macmillan, Inc.

International Standard Book Number: 0-02-861949-8
Library of Congress Catalog Card Number: 97-073163

99 98   8 7 6 5 4 3 2

Interpretation of the printing code: the rightmost number of the first series of numbers is the year of the book's printing; the rightmost number of the second series of numbers is the number of the book's printing. For example, a printing code of 98-1 shows that the first printing of the book occurred in 1998.

Printed in the United States of America

This publication contains information based on the research and experience of its authors and is designed to provide useful advice with regard to the subject matter covered. The authors and publisher are not engaged in rendering medical or other professional services in this publication. Circumstances vary for practitioners of the activities covered herein, and this publication should not be used without prior consultation from a competent medical professional.

The authors and publisher expressly disclaim any responsibility for any liability, loss, injury, or risk, personal or otherwise, which is incurred as a consequence, directly or indirectly, of the use and application of any of the contents of this book.

Joan Budilovsky, yogi and co-author of this book, demonstrates the yoga poses depicted in the photographs.

Alpha Development Team

Publisher
Kathy Nebenhaus

Editorial Director
Gary M. Krebs

Managing Editor
Bob Shuman

Marketing Brand Manager
Felice Primeau

Senior Editor
Nancy Mikhail

Development Editors
Phil Kitchel
Jennifer Perillo
Amy Zavatto

Editorial Assistant
Maureen Horn

Production Team

Book Producer
Lee Ann Chearney, Amaranth

Production Editor
Stephanie Mohler

Copy Editor
Laura Uebelhor

Cover Designer
Mike Freeland

Cartoonist
Judd Winick

Photographer
Saeid Lahouti

Illustrator
Wendy Frost

Designer
Glenn Larsen

Photo Editor
Richard H. Fox

Indexer
Chris Barrick

Layout/Proofreading
Angela Calvert, Cindy Fields, Daniela Raderstorf, Megan Wade

Contents at a Glance

Contents

Foreword

The world-famous violinist Sir Yehudi Menuhin said about yoga that it is "a technique ideally suited to prevent physical and mental illness and to protect the body generally, developing an inevitable sense of self-reliance and assurance." Yoga did not make him a musical genius, but has given him energy, balance, and a sense of well-being for the past four decades, allowing him full expression of his great talent.

Yoga can do the same for anyone. Old or young. Male or female. Busy or super busy. In fact, yoga in one form or another is practiced by several million people today. It has been part of the kaleidoscope of our Western culture for over a century now and has proven incredibly effective in the maintenance of a sound body and mind and even the restoration of one's health. This is why several progressive insurance companies are now including yoga in their alternative therapies coverage.

Yoga is a tradition that looks back upon at least 5,000 years of experience and experimentation. Although it was created in India in a different cultural environment, the basic insights and laws on which it is based are valid anywhere in the world. Of course, there is much more to yoga than its potency as a system of health care. But this is for you to discover.

In this book, you will be gently but persuasively guided into the beginnings of yoga practice. The authors serve as knowledgeable and cheerful friends, motivating you all the way. Within these pages you will find no lack of encouragement, and everything is explained step-by-step. So, please, take the leap into what you will discover to be a rewarding and healing experience.

—*Georg Feuerstein, Ph.D., M. Litt., director of the Yoga Research Center; author of* Shambhala Encyclopedia of Yoga *and* Shambhala Guide to Yoga; *editor of the* Yoga World *newsletter; and a contributing editor of* Yoga Journal.

Introduction

Imagine waking up one morning to find that all stresses in your life have been replaced with total joy. Yes, joy—the kind of pure joy you felt as a child when it was summer and the sun was shining and you had nothing to do but explore the whole world. Now, imagine possessing a strong, flexible body over which you have complete control. To top that off (literally!), imagine a mind free of chaotic thought, confusion, and uncertainty. Imagine pure health, pure consciousness, and pure bliss. These are the goals of the yogi.

And that yogi is you! Even if you don't attain your goals tomorrow, or the next day, you will soon be on an amazing journey. We have each traveled down our own paths a little way. We've looked ahead, peeked over the horizon of the next few hills, and now we'd like to give you some hints about how to make the most of what's in store for you on your journey into yourself. Yoga is a process of self-discovery and everyone's discoveries will be different, but we hope to steer you toward the potential "you," the perfect "you," the "you" waiting to be set free.

And it won't be difficult. Yoga is beautifully simple. In fact, we think you're gonna' love it!

How to Use This Book

This book is divided into six parts, each bringing yoga into your life in a different way.

Part 1: "Let's Get Into Yoga" eases you into the concepts of yoga. We talk about why this ancient Eastern system of health is great for modern Westerners, and how yoga can improve all aspects of your fitness, including your performance in other sports. We'll introduce you to your body, yoga-style, and reveal what yoga can do to improve your mental state as well as your physical condition.

Part 2: "Let's Get Spiritual: Growing with the Tree of Yoga" includes a little history, just to put yoga in context, then explains the various types of yoga. Next, we talk about the "rules" (yoga's guidelines for living), the importance of breath control, and the finer points of *Hatha Yoga,* the most popular form of yoga in the West.

Part 3: "Starting Your Yoga Practice" will help you do just that. We offer advice on how to find a yoga class and teacher, how to practice yoga at home, what to wear, how to overcome any mental stumbling blocks, when to practice, how to squeeze yoga into a busy day, and how to craft your own, personalized practice. This section will help you to make yoga your own.

Part 4: "Energize: Postures to Build Strength and Endurance" is the first section of exercises. We show you outstanding standing postures, beautiful backbends, terrific twists, and inversions, including the famous headstand posture. We'll also talk about *vinyasa,* dynamic combinations of postures that will have you breaking a sweat.

Part 5: "Calming Down: Postures to Quiet the Body and Mind" is the section of calming and centering postures, including sitting and meditative poses, forward bends, and a detailed discussion of *shavasana,* or the corpse pose. You'll learn how to let go of your mind, and you'll discover how great stress management can feel.

Part 6: "Living Your Yoga" is about specific aspects of the yoga lifestyle. We tell you the best foods for a yogi to eat, how yoga can address certain physical problems, and how to practice yoga with a partner. Next, we show you how yoga is great for all the stages in a woman's life, from PMS to menopause. We explain why guys will love and benefit from yoga, how to introduce yoga fun to your kids, and how seniors can find renewed energy and health through yoga. This section extends yoga beyond exercise, into the rest of your life.

Yoga Jewels

Throughout this book, we'll be adding four types of extra information in boxes, for your enlightenment:

Wise Yogi Tells Us

These special boxes will offer you tips and advice for living your yoga.

Know Your Sanskrit

These boxes will give you definitions for Sanskrit (the classical language of India) terms and correct pronunciations, too, so you can talk the talk.

Ouch!

These cautionary boxes contain information about how to avoid potential problems.

A Yoga Minute

These boxes are full of fun anecdotes and trivia about the fascinating world of yoga.

Acknowledgments

Far more people than can ever be mentioned here have, directly or indirectly, helped to make this book what it is. We'll name a few, but we send sincere and grateful energy out to all of you: Joan's dear friend and Webmaster Kathie Huddleston, who convinced her that she needed a yoga Web site on the Internet, and who consequently created the most beautiful YOYOGA! Web site (http://www.yoyoga.com). All Joan's students, who have taught and continue to teach her so much, and to all her teachers. Eve's husband, Todd (even though he'll never be a yogi in this lifetime). Joan's future husband (although she's not sure in which lifetime he'll appear). Eve's 2-year-old son, Angus, who considerately facilitated the writing of this book by taking lots of lengthy naps. Dr. Georg Feuerstein, for his invaluable advice and counsel. Saeid Lahouti, the photographer for this book, who has shared at least a few lifetimes with Joan (the photos for this book alone took several!). Wendy Frost, for her beautiful illustrations. Lee Ann Chearney at Amaranth, our book producer, for always giving us "all the best." Witty and charming Gary Krebs, for finding Joan on the Internet and for persevering in the frustrating game of phone tag. William Hunt, for walking his talk, and for his high-caliber tech review. Eve's good friends, Caitlin Scott, whose layperson yoga viewpoint was invaluable, and Kathy Streckfus, for pointing the way. Joan's friend, Chuck Reiter, whose simultaneous nostril breathing and continual encouragement are each appreciated in their own way. The many wonderful bookstores (the people in them, really) that have encouraged both of us as writers. Joan's parents, John and Leona, and Eve's parents, Richard and Penny. And to our families and friends who have been there or are there to lend an ear, a hand, a good thought, the right words, or whatever it takes—offering yet another view of the "many limbs" of yoga.

Special Thanks from the Publisher to the Technical Editor and Packager.

The Complete Idiot's Guide to Yoga was reviewed by an expert in the field who not only checked the technical accuracy of what you'll learn here, but also provided insight to help us ensure that this book tells you everything you need to know about yoga. Our special thanks are extended to William Hunt.

William Hunt is a certified yoga instructor, ordained priest, and the director of the Hatha Yoga teacher's training program at the Temple of Kriya Yoga in Chicago. He also co-teaches with Dr. Bruno Cortis, cardiologist, in wellness seminars.

This book would not have been possible without the expert vision and editorial guidance of Lee Ann Chearney of Amaranth. The team at Alpha is immeasurably grateful to her for her hard work and diligence. Thanks, Lee Ann!

Part 1
Let's Get Into Yoga

Part 1 is an introduction and more, filling you in on why the ancient and venerable system of living called yoga is so relevant to our modern, Western world. If you want to get in better physical, mental, emotional, and spiritual shape, yoga is the key. No matter what your fitness level, no matter what your personal philosophy, no matter what your religion or lack thereof, yoga can make a positive impact on your life.

We'll go on to help you get more familiar with your body and what yoga can do for it in terms of strength, flexibility, balance, grace, and muscle tone. Do you know which bone is your coccyx, which muscle is your sartorius, or the difference between a tendon and a ligament? You will after reading Chapter 3. Learn how to chant a mantra *and gaze at a* mandala, *and why you would want to do either one (or both!).*

Chapter 4 ends this part with a little mind power. Learn how yoga can make your mind as toned, strong, sharp, and effective as it makes your body strong and supple. Learn what yoga's true and original purpose has always been, and how this ultimate objective can lift you to a new level of personal achievement. Best of all, learn how yoga can set you free to feel and enjoy pure, unadulterated bliss.

Why Practice Yoga?

When it comes to yoga, idiots just don't exist. Banish the thought that yoga is too esoteric to understand, too mystical, or on the fringe. Forget about the notion that yoga is only for double-jointed people who've been able to fold themselves into a suitcase since birth, or for perpetual '60s flower children who sit around and chant all day. Negative thinking and stereotypes are contrary to the philosophy of yoga; yoga is user-friendly. Anyone—at any fitness level, and with a wide range of personal and fitness goals—can benefit from beginning a yoga practice. Even you.

Maybe you want to try yoga because you've never been able to touch your toes and you'd like to do it before you retire. Maybe you're seeking a quiet place to center yourself, to meditate by taking your mind somewhere far away from the house, the kids, the office, and the million nagging details of everyday life. Maybe you're an athlete who wants to learn yoga breathing for the advantage gained by stronger lungs and better circulation. Or maybe you've heard that yoga is great for migraine headaches, relief from chronic lower back pain, or good physical therapy after an injury or during an illness. It's all true.

Know Your Sanskrit

Yoga (pronounced YOH-gah) is derived from the Sanskrit root "yuj," meaning to yoke or join together.

Know Your Sanskrit

Prana (pronounced PRAH-nah) is a form of energy in the universe that animates all physical matter, including the human body. *Prana* is the soul of the universe. Doing yoga maximizes your body's flow of the universal life force, giving you better health and increased vitality.

But the ancient and venerable art of yoga is neither a "sport" nor a "religion"; it's a journey of the body and mind. When you do yoga, you nurture the movement of *prana*—the life force. You'll read a lot of Sanskrit words in this book because yoga terminology originated thousands of years ago in this ancient language. But there's nothing ancient about the concept of *prana: prana* is the life "force." May the force be with you as you begin your yoga practice.

Yoga is a system of techniques that reflects real and proven scientific concepts. Many things Western scientists understand about the body have actually been known by yoga practitioners for centuries. Yoga "sees" the body from a different perspective than traditional Western medicine, but the basic principles are the same. What we Westerners call nerve plexus, yoga calls *chakras* (although these don't coincide precisely—*chakras* include psychospiritual energy). What we Westerners call spinal alignment, yoga accomplishes through various poses or exercises designed to do what many of us pay chiropractors to do. The human body is in a constant state of flux, continually adjusting internally to the influence of a changing external environment. Western medicine calls this process "homeostasis." Yoga's "five sheaths of existence"—in essence, the body, the breath, the emotions, the intellect, and happiness—reflect the same need for balance between internal and external forces. The terminology may be different, but the concepts are universal.

Yoga is a fun activity that can produce powerful results. Yoga will wake up your body, sharpen your mind, and clarify your spirit. Yoga doesn't hurt, is only as difficult as you make it, and allows you to proceed at an individualized pace. Yoga can be a tiny part of your life, or you can incorporate its theories, rituals, postures, diet, and philosophy into every aspect of your life. You control how deeply yoga touches you. But if you begin a steady practice, be assured that yoga will transform the way you look, feel, move, breathe, and interact with friends, family, and coworkers.

Yoga Is Occident Insurance

Life in the West (the Occident, as opposed to the Orient) is no picnic. Sure, it's exciting, even exhilarating, but after all the pressures, stresses, responsibilities, frustrations, resentments, choices, temptations, and obsessions the average Westerner has faced by the end of a typical working day, it's no wonder we are a culture eagerly searching for ways to simplify our lives.

So how can yoga help? In the face of a daily existence that is so vibrant it almost vibrates us apart, yoga is an oasis. Yoga teaches the frantic mind to settle and find peace, and it helps the ravaged body to heal itself by building physical confidence and emotional well-being. Yoga removes scattered energy, replaces depleted energy, and keeps your body, including all its internal systems, toned and in good working order.

So…what are we getting at here, you ask? Yoga is the best life insurance policy there is. It helps you slow down, center yourself, and get the most out of your life so that every day is precious. By holding the body in a series of yoga postures that stretch and strengthen your muscles, loosen your joints, focus your breathing, and tone your internal organs, you'll find a new friend in your body. While you continue to hold each posture, your mind will learn how to tune out the distractions of life and hone in on how things are for you in this moment of living. Doing yoga makes you *listen* to how you feel—physically and mentally. This newfound power of concentration will carry over into every aspect of your life. Signals you once ignored—that crick in your neck or your obsessive worrying over a detail that keeps you from seeing the forest for the trees—are instantly acknowledged and seen for what they are: warning signs that you are heading down the wrong path. Yoga can help you regain your sense of self-fulfillment and joy, ensuring a more satisfying, not to mention fitter, existence.

Yoga Is a Great Stressbuster

Stress is a simple fact of life on Earth in the 21st century; stress is so common that countries all over the globe are incorporating the English word "stress" into their own languages: *"Que stress. ¡Me siento agobiada/o!" ("What stress. I am totally overwhelmed!").* If you've never been under stress, we'd like to know your secret. (It's probably yoga!)

Yoga tackles stress on many levels. The postures, or *asanas,* help you control your wayward body, making it stronger, more flexible, better functioning, and, consequently, more resistant to disease and other

Know Your Sanskrit

Chakras (pronounced TSHAH-krahs) are centers of energy that are located between the base of your spinal column and the crown of your head. Each *chakra* has a corresponding color, sound, perception, and biological function. Note that the actual spelling of *chakra* is "cakra," but this spelling isn't commonly used.

Ouch!

Yoga doesn't hurt and isn't about unnatural contortion. Sure, accomplished yogis may be able to move into seemingly impossible positions, but these postures are for people who have progressed to a level where such positions are possible and helpful. Some bodies are born more flexible than others. Each person has to find his or her own edge—the point just before discomfort occurs—and grow into it at a comfortable pace. We're all working the same edge, just in different places!

physical problems. Practicing the *asanas* trains your body to do exactly what you tell it to do. Your doctor knows that moderate exercise, deep breathing, and relaxation are all great ways to relieve stress—yoga accomplishes all three. Yoga's breathing exercises, or *pranayama*, consciously channel the flow of the life force, *prana,* into and out of the body. Physiologically, deep, regular breathing sends a signal to each cell of your body to relax. Yoga meditation calms your racing thoughts and exercises your ability to master your own mind, rather than letting your mind master you.

Yoga is a physical, mental, and spiritual way of life that puts reality into perspective. Yoga doesn't change your stressful circumstances, but it will teach you how to react to them without neglecting or even injuring yourself.

Yoga Promotes Whole Body Fitness

Maybe you're an accomplished athlete, or maybe you're a couch potato. Exercise to you may mean breezing through a five-mile run in the morning and a requisite visit to the gym three times a week, or it may mean getting up to look for the remote control. Either way, yoga is perfect for you!

Because yoga combines so many different fitness elements and is so easily tailored to the individual, it can be practiced with great benefit at the beginner level as well as at the most advanced level. Whether you're a beginning or advanced practitioner, yoga will slowly, gently, and easily open up your body. You'll feel taller, breathe easier, and move about more comfortably.

Non-athletes also might be attracted to the idea that yoga isn't competitive. In fact, a sense of competitiveness is in direct opposition to the yoga frame of mind. Your yoga practice is personal and has nothing to do with anybody else. Plus, yoga will give you so much energy and such an improved self image that you may find exercise isn't as bad as you thought.

Yoga is designed to work all your muscles, not just a few isolated major muscle groups. Many of the postures, such as the twists and inversions, stimulate particular internal organs or release energy from stress-prone areas such as the lower back or neck. Yoga's fine-tuning exercises are the ultimate full-body workout. Other exercise programs tend to develop only one part of you—cardiovascular fitness, leg strength, or fat burning, for example. Yoga does it all.

Wise Yogi Tells Us

If you are overweight or have a problem with overeating, yoga is the perfect exercise for you because it's gentle on the out-of-shape body, stiff joints, and heart. You'll feel better about your body as you begin to lose weight, and you can achieve an inner peace and confidence that will help you avoid compulsive overeating.

Although many different types of yoga exist, *Hatha Yoga* is the branch of yoga that concentrates on the body and the form of yoga most emphasized in this book and practiced by Westerners. *Hatha Yoga* is an excellent fitness program, but it's also more. *Hatha Yoga* is based on the idea that gaining supreme control over your body is the key to control of your mind and freedom of your spirit. Through postures (*asanas*), breathing exercises (*pranayama*), and meditation, *Hatha Yoga* exercises, tones, and strengthens the whole person—body, mind, and spirit. Even if you start with the physical exercises alone, however, *Hatha Yoga* will quickly begin to work its magic.

Fitness today means more than a healthy body. Our culture is experiencing a growing trend toward things spiritual. With a growing passion for holistic health alternatives, we are a society looking for balance in a world that is out of balance. Holistic fitness is quickly becoming a mainstream concept, and yoga fits comfortably into this trend. Yoga is the answer to the spiritual seeker's *and* the athlete's search for physical excellence because it's the best all-purpose, all-person, whole-self, individualized fitness program—time-tested over centuries.

Know Your Sanskrit

Hatha Yoga (pronounced HAT-ha YOH-gah, not HATH-ah YOH-gah, as it is frequently mispronounced) is the type of yoga most commonly practiced in Western culture. *Ha* means "sun" and *tha* means "moon," so *hatha* is a combining of complementary forces. *Hatha Yoga* is the branch of yoga that transforms the human body via physical strengthening and purification, to make the body a worthy vehicle of self-realization.

Yoga Is Healing Power

Yoga is a boon to the healthy body, but it can also be of supreme benefit to the body in need of healing. Of course, the best route for a healthy person to take is one of prevention. Healthy habits, maintenance of the body, peacefulness of mind, and calmness of spirit will go a long way toward protecting you from

A Yoga Minute

According to the World Health Organization, an estimated 691 million people worldwide suffer from high blood pressure.

compromised health. Yoga is great preventive medicine because it keeps all of you—body, mind, attitude, outlook, immune system—in top form. Your spine, the "Grand Central Station" of your body, is stretched, loosened, and aligned by yoga—postures are designed to allow energy to flow freely through your spine and entire body. Many holistic health practitioners and even traditional practitioners argue that if the spine is aligned, the entire body works better, feels better, and fights disease more effectively.

Yoga aids:

➤ circulation

➤ digestion

➤ respiration

➤ reproduction

Yoga also:

➤ tones your organs

➤ improves your posture

➤ frees your breathing

➤ is cleansing

Yoga helps your body purge itself of toxins that can negatively affect your health, both by releasing negative energy and, more directly, removing obstacles to the proper stimulation of the body's lymphatic system. The lymphatic system, the centerpiece of the immune system, protects and maintains the body's internal fluid environment, both filtering toxins and transporting nutrients to the blood. Lymph is pumped through the body by movement—when we breathe, contract or release our muscles, or even with the motion of our beating hearts or of our digestive systems as we process food we've eaten. Yoga helps our bodies go with their natural flow. Even if you're not very mobile, yoga can be practiced with eye exercises, simple stretches, and conscious rhythmic movements Take your fitness personally and craft a yoga fitness plan that is all your own.

If you're sick, injured, or bothered by nagging health complaints, yoga can be a therapeutic addition to your physician's treatment plan. Of course, yoga should *never* be used in place of competent medical care. Ask your doctor or physical therapist about how yoga can be helpful in alleviating your specific health problems or concerns.

My Yogi, Myself

Once you've created your yoga plan and have begun to practice, guess what you are. Healthier? Sure. In better shape? Of course. But you're something else, too—you're a yogi! (A female yogi is actually called a *yogini*—pronounced YOH-gee-NEE—but let's be contemporary and say we're all yogis.) Anyone who practices yoga is a yogi—that's what "yogi" means. You needn't be wise, you don't have to wear a loin cloth, and you certainly don't need to practice for 10 hours every day. Even if you start with just a little yoga, you're a yogi. Of course, the more yoga you practice, the more you'll gain, and the wiser a yogi you'll become.

Yoga is practiced to varying degrees around the world, but some exuberant practitioners who have devoted their lives to the practice of yoga have achieved amazing control over their bodies. Although, according to yoga, such feats aren't important to the goal of spiritual enlightenment (self-realization), yogis have been known to:

➤ Stop their own hearts (then start them again, of course).

➤ Live to be well over 100 years old.

➤ Suspend their breath for an hour a day or more.

➤ Stand on one foot for several years (don't ask us why).

➤ Lie comfortably on a bed of nails.

➤ Eat razor blades without harm (we prefer a nice salad).

Below are a few more incredible feats that border on the supernatural, but these we'd have to see to believe:

➤ Become invisible at will.

➤ Remain suspended in mid-air (handy when all the chairs are taken).

➤ Move through space at the speed of light (saves on gasoline).

It doesn't matter why you approach yoga, whether for fitness, for stress relief, for enlightenment (self-realization), or for healing. It doesn't matter how advanced you are, whether you are out of shape and inflexible or an athlete extraordinaire. It certainly doesn't matter how much you already know about yoga. If you let yoga help you, it will help you in whatever way you require.

If you're intrigued but still need just a little more convincing before you're ready to assume pretzel-like contortions or begin *dhyana,* your daily meditation, read on for 10 great reasons to practice yoga:

➤ Yoga will tone your muscles and trim excess weight. It may even change your attitude about your body for the better.

➤ Anyone can do yoga. It's just a matter of starting at the appropriate level and remembering that you aren't competing with anyone.

➤ Yoga doesn't hurt. You go at your own pace, do what feels good, and stop before you feel pain. What could be better?

➤ Yoga will give you the gift of boundless energy.

➤ The increased energy and vitality you receive from regular yoga practice will make you feel as if hours have been added to your day.

➤ Yoga lets you dare to be different. Anyone who teases you about doing yoga doesn't understand what you're doing—explain it to them!

➤ You can do as much or as little yoga as you like. Start with the postures and you may find your interest in breathing, chanting, and meditation develops later—or not at all, which is fine, too. It's all up to you.

➤ Yoga is definitely not about guilt! You can benefit the most from regular yoga practice, but practicing the postures whenever you have time is still beneficial and certainly better than no yoga at all.

➤ Contrary to popular belief, yoga isn't a religion. It's a method for life that can complement and enhance any religious system of beliefs, or it can be practiced completely apart from religion.

➤ Yoga will help ease your aches, pains, and stiffness. You'll feel like a kid again.

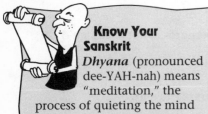

Know Your Sanskrit

Dhyana (pronounced dee-YAH-nah) means "meditation," the process of quieting the mind to free yourself from preconceptions and illusions. The result is a clearer vision of the truth about yourself, your life, and the world.

But don't take being a yogi lightly just because you've become one without too much effort. Your body, your mind, and your happiness are *your* responsibility. Your yoga program is a great start, but you need to have the right yoga plan. Learn as much as you can about yoga, and consider taking a yoga class. The best way to learn yoga is with a teacher who can help you with the finer points of the postures, answer your individual questions, and guide you in finding a sequence of postures that best suits your needs and personality.

Even before you find a teacher, though, reading and learning about yoga can start you on your way. The more you know about yoga, the more you can focus on how it can help you. This book is a great start in your search for the perfectly personalized program. Apply everything you learn to your own journey. How can each new piece of information improve the personal program you are creating for yourself? Think about what you've learned already. Are you beginning to see how yoga might fit into your life? Yes? Then you are wiser already.

Yoga Sets You Free

Perhaps you're flirting with the idea of yoga because you imagine it's an interesting fitness plan, but perhaps you're looking for something more. People have been practicing yoga for thousands of years, not because they want to be "in shape" (a fringe benefit), but because they are seeking meaning in life. Yoga can be a fitness program, but it can also be a path to greater self-knowledge and, ultimately, self-actualization. Yoga helps you reach the fullness of your human potential. You will be more confident, stronger, healthier, and more at peace with who you are. You will make better decisions, set and achieve worthwhile goals, and become the person you want to be.

The ultimate goal of the yogi is to achieve the experience of truth, which may mean different things to different people but which is, to some degree, a consistent experience for all—a clarity of vision, supreme focus, and a feeling of oneness with the earth, even the universe. This ideal state is called *samadhi* and involves consciousness to such a heightened degree that individual ego falls away and oneness with the universal force of love and goodness, or *brahman,* is achieved. It is the state of pure bliss.

A few rare and diligent yogis have been able to maintain this state for extended periods, but for most of us, *samadhi* is an elusive experience. We may get occasional glimpses of it, or sudden rushes of bliss that fall away but become imprinted in our memories. After all, we do have to live in the world, which is often a less than blissful place. On the other hand, you and your world are what you make them, and yoga can help you optimize yourself, your experience, and your all-important perception of the world around you. Yoga is fitness plus peace and fitness plus joy.

Know Your Sanskrit

Samadhi (pronounced sah-MAH-dee) is the goal of yoga. It's when the yogi finally becomes aware of nothing but *brahman* (pronounced BRAH-mahn)—the all-pervading Supreme Self, or God—everywhere. It's a state of absolute bliss and may be transitory or, ideally, perpetual.

The Least You Need to Know

➤ Yoga reduces stress and improves concentration.

➤ Yoga is a great workout at any fitness level.

➤ Yoga helps prevent illness and keeps the systems of the body in order.

➤ Yoga increases energy and vitality, promoting well-being.

➤ Anyone who practices yoga is a yogi!

Chapter 2

Yoga Fitness Power: Beyond Stretching

In This Chapter

➤ Yoga as a body/mind workout

➤ Yoga as your ultimate fitness power source

➤ How yoga enhances your sports performance

Yoga is more than stretching. No matter what your fitness level, yoga can be a challenging exercise program that builds superior strength and endurance. You'll even break a sweat! Yoga involves a level of mental and physical concentration that results in greater flexibility, increased muscle power, refined balance, improved cardiovascular function, increased lung capacity, toned immune and digestive systems, and improved functioning of internal organs. If you're looking to yoga for body/mind fitness power, you've come to the right place.

Yoga Means Connection

Yoga taps into your inner power, connecting your body with your mind. It's easy to fall into a pattern of associating fitness with the body alone. We run, do aerobic dance, bicycle, and perform sit-ups and push-ups all for our bodies. What does your mind have to do with it? But the yogi will soon see the absurdity of this notion. Body and mind are one, and although they can become isolated and dissociated from each other, yoga brings them back together where they belong. Everything works better when all the circuits are connected. Your mind can boost your physical performance to new heights, and control over your body is training for control over your mind.

Are You Off-Balance?

Perhaps you've been feeling "scattered" lately. Do you lose things easily? Forget appointments or information? Are you overwhelmed by the buzz of activity in your life? Maybe you think you don't have the time to slow down and get "centered," but you must know this: You don't have the time *not* to get centered. If you're feeling out of balance, you're wasting your days, your energy, and your power. You're like a house with the heat on and all the windows open. Yoga can help you close the windows (or turn off the heat) and center on making the most of each precious moment of your day.

Sometimes stress is a good thing. It can give you the power to escape from a dangerous situation. It can help you succeed in life, both in your physical pursuits (say, running a marathon) and in your intellectual challenges (say, passing a test). Too much stress, however, wreaks havoc on the body. When experiencing stress, the brain stimulates the adrenal glands, resulting in certain telltale symptoms:

➤ Your heart rate speeds up.

➤ Your blood pressure rises.

➤ Your breathing quickens and becomes more shallow.

➤ Your pupils dilate.

➤ Your muscles tense.

➤ You sweat.

➤ Your senses become heightened.

➤ Blood flows to your muscles and brain.

Too much of this kind of activity will wear out anyone's system. Yoga's body/mind fitness power can channel stress more efficiently, helping you instead of hurting you.

Mind Meet Body, Body Meet Mind

Beginning to practice yoga is like introducing your body and your mind for the first time. Sure, they have resided in close proximity your entire life, but do they really know each other? If you want to be truly fit, you must introduce your body to your mind, and your mind to your body. *Hatha Yoga*, the yoga that concentrates on strengthening and purifying the physical body, is the perfect introduction.

Practicing *Hatha Yoga* means finding the balance in the union of your body, mind, and spirit. *Hatha Yoga* is truly a holistic exercise (body + mind + spirit = holistic) because it involves the activation, control, and mastery of every part of your body. Fitness is the inevitable result—so is restful sleep, improved health, and tranquillity of mind. *Hatha Yoga* gives voice to what the body knows: All its parts are one.

Coming Back to Center

Just like any other sport, yoga requires a warm-up period. Haphazardly practicing may build your strength to a small degree, but you won't get the benefits of yoga's body/mind discipline. Centering is a mental warm-up to go along with your physical warm-up. As you practice your beginning poses, consciously focus your mind on your body. Notice how your body feels and what it's doing. Commit to your yoga practice for the next 10, 15, 30, or however many minutes you have allotted yourself. The more often you make a habit of consciously centering your mind on what your body is doing, the more you'll notice a feeling of calm, of being centered in your daily life. Your yoga fitness power is showing!

> **Ouch!**
> If you already have a medical condition, such as chronic back pain, yoga can be great therapy. A yoga teacher can show you which postures will benefit and strengthen your particular weak area. But be careful. The postures should feel comfortable, not painful!

Tapping into Your Yoga Power Source

So how does all this "centering" and concentration get you in shape? Because your mind and your body are so intricately connected, a centered mind with the power of concentration works directly on the body, allowing each yoga posture to accomplish the maximum possible benefit. Don't be misled into thinking the "mental" parts of yoga can be ignored because you aren't in it for the "enlightenment." Perhaps getting in shape is priority one for you. That's great! But the key to yoga's fitness power is in the synthesis of everything you are—your body, your mind, your spirit—each part working together to make the whole stronger, healthier, and more alive. Remember, a healthy body means more than just a strong body. As any doctor will tell you, a positive attitude toward life is central to the body's natural healing powers. Yoga stimulates your body/mind power source, channeling your positive mental energy into your physical workout, and vice versa.

Bend Without Breaking

If you've always been athletic but haven't concentrated on maintaining your flexibility, you may be nervous about trying yoga. You may ask yourself: "Don't I have to be able to sit in that lotus pose all day?" Of course not! Endurance isn't necessary for the beginning runner—you attain endurance by running. Yoga is the same way. If you're about as flexible as a steel pole, start slowly and only go as far into a posture as you can. Every week of practice will take you further. Before you know it, your joints will loosen, your muscles will stretch, and your body will take on a smoother, more pleasing shape.

Know Your Sanskrit

The **lotus pose**, also called *padmasana* (pronounced PAHD-MAH-sahn-ah) is a yoga sitting pose in which the left foot lies upturned on the right thigh, and the right foot lies upturned on the left thigh. It is meant to resemble the perfect symmetry and beauty of the lotus flower.

Perhaps you've always been naturally flexible. Don't think yoga will be simple! There's always the next posture waiting for you.

As you accomplish postures you couldn't begin to achieve when you started, you'll understand flexibility in a new way. The achievement of a yoga posture is like winning a marathon without anyone else losing—pure triumph!

Balancing Acts

You probably take your ability to balance for granted. You get up in the morning, walk around all day without incident, and lie back down at night. Balancing wasn't always so easy, however. In fact, during one illustrious period of your life, learning to balance took up most of your waking moments.

Through yoga, balancing once again captures your attention. Balance is challenging. Yoga balance postures take keen muscle control and strength, mental centering, and lots of practice. Once you've refined your balancing act, you'll discover that the walking you take for granted is even easier than before. Balancing is control, both in stillness and in motion.

Strength from the Gut

Everybody knows lifting a heavy weight takes strength. But balancing takes strength, too. So does holding a posture for an extended time. Yoga strength training is *isometric* (a form of exercise in which muscles are tensed in opposition to each other or to an immovable object). After assuming each yoga pose, you hold it for as long as you can hold it correctly. Talk about a way to wake up muscles you never knew you had! Yoga's isometric action is easier on your muscles than the weight-bearing and pounding of other sports, yet extremely effective for building strength. What's more, each yoga position in a well-structured workout includes a posture and its opposite, so your body will stay physically centered, never developing any side or particular body part out of proportion to the others.

Yoga positions are entered and held by the body in order to find the peace within—the point where sustaining the pose is easy, natural, and feels "right." The more difficult the pose, the harder it is to find peace. Yoga postures mirror life. When things are easy, it's easy to feel good. But feeling good when things aren't going your way—whether it's a bad hair day or a more serious tragedy—is a challenge. Yoga is a journey through the poses, working with each pose until you find that peace, then progressing to the next level. This progression combines the building of physical strength with the toning of the mind.

This might surprise the Western athlete even more: Strength is compounded when the body, mind, and spirit are exercised together. Strength will mean more to you, once you've practiced yoga, than it did before.

Keeping the Faith

"But I know it will be just like that aerobics class," you may be thinking. "I'll be all excited for the first week or two, then I'll get bored and quit." In any given day, probably just as many people quit a fitness program as start one. Why should yoga be any different?

The benefits you'll soon feel from your yoga practice are so comprehensive, you may well find you'd rather give up coffee, doughnuts, or pepperoni pizzas than give up your daily yoga "therapy." Beyond the more obvious benefits of increased flexibility, balance, and strength, yoga has thousands of less dramatic (though no less important) rewards. Yoga feels different than other fitness programs because each posture is specifically designed to activate your body in minute ways, adjusting here, stimulating there, stretching here, strengthening there, compressing, releasing, expanding, reaching—with all this internal maintenance, you can't help but enjoy increased health and a vibrant sense of well-being.

Wise Yogi Tells Us

Yoga is great for teenagers, who already tend to be strong, flexible, and energetic. Teenagers are frequently surprised at how challenging yoga can be. The mental focus, physical control, and spiritual development that come along with yoga are wonderful therapies for adolescents whose hormones are raging and who may feel depressed, out of control, or angry without knowing why.

Yoga vs. Other Exercise

Most Western forms of exercise emphasize stress on the muscles combined with quick, harsh movements. Yoga avoids such movements, which tend to trigger lactic acid production in muscle fibers, leading to pain. In addition, yoga's emphasis on breathing delivers more oxygen to muscles to further lessen the effects of lactic acid production. You needn't give up your favorite sport, however. Just add yoga to the program. But first, read on to see how yoga compares to your favorite fitness activity.

17

Yoga can enhance your performance in all your favorite sports.

Awesome Aerobics

Aerobic dance can be a lot of fun, especially for those who like music. Aerobic dancers who also do yoga are more graceful, have more fluid movements, are better able to keep up, and are more flexible. Like running, aerobic dance is primarily a cardiovascular activity; although low-impact aerobics are kinder to your body than high-impact, aerobic dancers still experience a lot of stress on their muscles and joints. Aerobics is energizing and is great for people who need the motivation of a class and an instructor. Yoga is a great complement because it balances aerobic dance's frenetic energy by inducing a sense of calm and inner control.

Rockin' Running

"But I *know* yoga won't give me the cardiovascular strength and endurance that running gives me!" you may be protesting. Consider this: Runners rely on strength and balance. Flexible runners get injured less often. Runners also tend to have shallow, hard breathing patterns; they hyperventilate. Yoga's deep breathing exercises increase your lung capacity, getting more oxygen to your brain and increasing your endurance.

Yoga is kinder to your body than running, so it makes a great alternate workout to give your body a rest from the constant pounding and joint stress runners experience.

Runners frequently injure their feet, ankles, knees, and hips. You can use yoga postures to build strength in these same body parts! In fact, the New York Road Runners club promotes an official yoga program called "Power Yoga."

Super-Charged Stretching

Most of us have had basic stretching exercises drilled into us since grade school gym class. Bend down and touch your toes, reach to the right, reach to the left, roll your head from front to side to side. The difference between this type of stretching and yoga is that yoga stretches are specifically designed not only to lengthen your muscles, but also to stabilize your joints, stimulate your organs, balance your endocrine system, and strengthen your muscles as you hold the stretch. It's still a good idea to do basic stretches before engaging in strenuous exercise, such as running or swimming, but if you also add yoga to your fitness program, stretching will soon be a breeze.

> **A Yoga Minute**
> According to the National Sporting Goods Association, exercise walking was the number one fitness activity in 1996, with 73.3 million participants. The sport that grew in popularity the most? Snowboarding.

Superior Swimming

Swimming is an excellent exercise because it works your muscles and your heart without putting stress on your body. Swimming is essentially a cardiovascular exercise. You move through the water and increase your heart rate. If you're a swimmer, you'll find yoga a great addition to your fitness program because the increased flexibility and strength gained through yoga make swimming easier. Also, the breathing practice in yoga is of exceptional benefit to swimmers, who must have good breath control.

>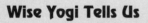
> **Wise Yogi Tells Us**
>
> End every yoga session with a few minutes of complete and total relaxation. Don't move, don't think; practice sitting absolutely still. Simply feel your body. This little space at the end of your yoga workout is an important part of bringing mind and body together, grounding your awareness and allowing your body to make the most of your workout.

Uplifting Weight Lifting

Lifting weights adds bulk to muscles but decreases flexibility. Many weight lifters are "muscle-bound." Weight lifters can benefit dramatically from yoga because while weight training builds bone, muscle mass, and strength, yoga will lengthen the muscles and keep them flexible. Weight lifters also benefit from the breathing exercise and balance training of yoga. Yoga is really a form of weight lifting. You aren't lifting barbells, but in many of the poses, you are lifting your own weight. Think about how much you weigh—wouldn't it be quite an accomplishment to lift that weight easily?

Ecstasy: Yoga Union

The Western approach to yoga tends to be more fitness-oriented, while the Eastern approach to yoga is based on the idea that a healthy body makes it easier to progress spiritually. Either approach benefits both body and mind, however. If you're interested in yoga for its physical benefits, you can consider the spiritual "centeredness" you achieve a splendid bonus. Or, if you tend more toward the Eastern way, consider fitness the icing on the cake of spiritual growth. Either way, yoga fitness power means self-confidence, self-control, and inner peace. Whatever your fitness level, let yoga challenge you.

It's All in Your Mind!

Everyone knows that a good percentage of athletic performance is mental. We've all seen our favorite team in a pressure situation get psyched out—suddenly, they can't do anything right. Think about the last time you played your favorite sport. Was there ever a time when you suddenly slipped into "the zone"? Your performance becomes flawless and you're able to exceed your normal abilities.

Because yoga unites body and mind, it teaches you control over your mental state as it teaches you control over your body. What happens to you really is "all in your mind," so let your mind be your instrument—learn how to "play" it in the zone of peak performance.

Maximize Your Performance

One of the goals of yoga is to attain a state of oneness with the universe. Surprisingly, this goal has endless practical applications. When your mind and body are one, and one with the power of the universe, the sense of tranquillity and control you can achieve makes everything clearer and simpler. Everything you do will be affected. Do you have a big presentation at work? You are calm, confident, and empowered. Do you have a championship tennis match? You are strong, flexible, buoyant, and the ball seems to go exactly where you will it to go. Do you have a really difficult test? Your mind is so uncluttered that all your studying comes back to you effortlessly.

Of course, such power doesn't come easily. A week of sitting in the *lotus* position for five minutes a day won't be enough to send you permanently into "the zone." Yoga is a process. Your body and your mind need to learn new habits and a new way to communicate with each other. But if you're persistent and follow the yoga path, you'll quickly perceive the changes blessing your life. You'll feel peace of mind, even the ecstasy of oneness with the life force. And you will be in the best shape you've ever been, too.

So what are you waiting for?

The Least You Need to Know

➤ Yoga is about personal progress, not competition.

➤ Yoga uses mind power to build body power.

➤ Yoga's isometric action is easy on the body.

➤ Yoga makes you a better runner, dancer, swimmer, weight lifter, and all-around great athlete!

How Comfortable Are You in Your Body?

You know the types who are comfortable in their bodies. You've seen them gliding through life. Are you comfortable in *your* body? Are standing, sitting, and lying down easy, or do you feel your clothes binding, your stomach sagging, your back aching, and your knees cracking? Can you spring up from a sitting position on the floor like a child, or is hoisting yourself to a stand always accompanied by grunts, long sighs, and various strange popping noises from assorted joints?

The truth of the matter is that most of us aren't comfortable in our bodies. Why? Because we don't maintain them. Fitness expert Jack LaLanne once said that if more people treated their bodies with the same care and upkeep they give to their most precious possessions—their houses and their cars—everyone would be fitter and healthier. Isn't a little maintenance worth the effort?

A Self-Test for the Yoga-Challenged

Are you yoga-challenged? In other words, are you so far out of touch with your body that yoga seems like an impossibility? Take this test to find out how in tune you are with your body. Choose the one best answer for each question.

1. The longest amount of time I can sit on the floor without feeling some sort of pain and discomfort is:

   A. 30 minutes or longer.

   B. 15 minutes max.

   C. Maybe 2 minutes.

   D. Why the heck would I want to sit on the floor? Why do you think couches were invented?

2. My back:

   A. Never hurts.

   B. Hurts 24 hours per day.

   C. Hurts after I've been sitting for too long.

   D. Hurts when I don't exercise regularly.

3. My coccyx is:

   A. The vertebrae at the base of my neck.

   B. My kneecap.

   C. A small, triangular bone at the base of my spine.

   D. I'm quite sure I don't have a coccyx!

4. I get sick (cold, flu, gastroenteritis, etc.) or injured (sprained ankle, twisted knee, back went out, etc.) at least:

   A. Once a year.

   B. Once every few months.

   C. Once every few weeks.

   D. I hardly ever get sick or injured.

5. My vision is:

   A. Excellent (20/20 or better).

   B. Pretty good. I have glasses or contacts, but my prescription isn't a very strong one.

   C. Terrible. I can't see well at all without my glasses or contacts.

   D. I'm sorry, I couldn't quite make out the question. It's too blurry.

6. Whenever I feel a cold coming on, the first thing I do is:
   A. Push fluids, get more sleep, go in late to work, and drag myself through the day.
   B. Try to talk myself out of it or ignore it. I don't have time to get sick!
   C. Go to work, but whine and complain that I'm getting sick while sneezing and coughing all over my coworkers.
   D. Rest, bundle up on the couch with some herbal tea with lemon and honey, increase my vitamin C intake, and stay home so I can get better.

7. The difference between tendons and ligaments is:
   A. Tendons connect muscles to bones, while ligaments connect bones to bones or hold organs in place.
   B. Tendons connect bones to bones or hold organs in place, while ligaments connect muscles to bones.
   C. Tendons and ligaments are both those things I'm always pulling and tearing, after which my doctor says, "There's nothing I can do."
   D. Huh?

8. The way I feel about my body can best be described as follows:
   A. I dislike certain parts of my body, but other parts are pleasing. I'm good at disguising my faults with my clothing.
   B. My body is okay, but I don't pay much attention to it.
   C. I love my body. I think it's beautiful, and it feels good to be in it. I take good care of it so it will stay that way.
   D. I practically have a heart attack every time I look in the mirror, so I just don't look in the mirror.

9. I can do the following:
   A. Bend down and touch my toes easily.
   B. Bend down and touch my knees easily.
   C. Fold completely in half, bending forward, hugging my calves with my arms, and resting my head and entire upper body against my legs.
   D. If I look down, I can almost see my feet.

10. My muscles are visible:

    A. In a lot of places if I flex—I can see the line of my calf muscle if I stand on my toes, and I can see my biceps and triceps if I flex my arm.

    B. All the time. I can see my thigh muscles, calf muscles, biceps, triceps, deltoids, and abdominal muscles, even without flexing them. I am truly buff!

    C. My muscles might be visible on an X ray—that is, if X rays show muscles.

    D. Every now and then, especially when I'm at a lower weight, but mostly I just see smooth, rounded surfaces with some bumpy cellulite here and there.

Now, score your test by giving yourself the correct number of points, as indicated below, for each answer. Add up your points, then check the following section to see what your score means.

1. A. 3	2. A. 3	3. A. 2	4. A. 2	5. A. 3
B. 2	B. 0	B. 1	B. 1	B. 2
C. 1	C. 1	C. 3	C. 0	C. 1
D. 0	D. 2	D. 0	D. 3	D. 0

6. A. 2	7. A. 3	8. A. 2	9. A. 2	10. A. 3
B. 1	B. 2	B. 1	B. 1	B. 2
C. 0	C. 1	C. 3	C. 3	C. 0
D. 3	D. 0	D. 0	D. 0	D. 1

Your score: _____

What Your Body Is Telling You, and Whether It's Good News

So, how'd you do on the quiz?

If you scored 25–30 points: Are you already a yogi and just reading this book for fun? You have a wonderful awareness of your body. If you aren't doing yoga, you'll probably love it.

If you scored 16–24 points: There are a few things you don't like about your body, but at least you pay attention to it. As you work through yoga's exercises and meditations, your bad habits will eventually disappear on their own. You won't need willpower because treating your body well will feel so good!

If you scored 8–15 points: Yoga can help you become more aware of your body and improve your self-image. You'll discover feelings, muscles, positions, and energies you never imagined you had in you. If you don't pay attention to your body, it'll break down faster, and you don't want that!

If you scored 0–7 points: Talk about somebody who needs yoga! You're barely aware of your body at all, either because you ignore it or because you dislike it so much that you want nothing to do with it. Yoga can gently coax you into a new relationship with your body, one based on respect and appreciation.

Most of us have many illusions about our bodies. Unfortunately, these illusions affect not only our feelings about our physical appearance, but also our self-esteem and our relations with others. Be aware that the following italicized statements about your body are *not true:*

➤ *Your body is without consciousness, and your mind is separate from your body.* Many of your organs and tissues have properties similar to your brain, sending out messages, receiving information, reacting accordingly, and letting you know when you're being abusive or kind to your body. Your entire body is awake, alive, and aware.

➤ *You can't change your body.* Not only can you change your body profoundly through your actions and thoughts, but your body continuously changes itself: All your cells are replaced every five years. Your body is supremely mutable.

➤ *Your body is solid.* Actually, at the atomic level, your body consists of vibrating atoms with lots of space in between. You are more energy than matter!

➤ *Bodies are a curse.* Bodies are an opportunity and a tool through which the inner soul can be discovered.

➤ *I am a victim of genetics.* Genetics only reveal the make and model of your body. What you do with that body and that mind and how you care for them can be as powerful as your genes.

> **Ouch!**
> Stop punishing yourself! Hating your body is unnatural; why not give yoga a try? The postures will improve your health, and yoga's meditation will help your mind feel more benevolently toward your body. Life is too short to ignore or berate the primary mechanism that houses your soul.

➤ *People judge you by your body, first and foremost.* Your self-concept is a powerful force that emanates from you and influences others.

Your Body and Yoga 101

No matter how in touch or out of touch you are with your body, everyone has energy cycles. Sometimes your energy peaks, sometimes it lags. Energy cycles can be related to monthly cycles, the weather, lunar cycles, health, diet, and level of exercise.

Yoga helps these energy cycles flow smoothly. Instead of super highs and abysmal lows, you can enjoy a steady stream of controlled energy like an exhalation of air you control by the size of the opening of your lips and the force of your exhalation.

The Muscle and Bone Connection

Yoga postures make more sense if you know a little bit about how your body works. Your particular physical challenges will become more specific to you, too, if you understand your own anatomy.

Your skeleton is your frame. It supports your fat, muscles, and organs. It contains 206 bones. Connecting the muscles to the bones are tendons. Muscles help you bend your joints and perform all sorts of tasks. Strong muscles go a long way toward supporting your frame, making it easier to achieve good posture. Think about how effortlessly an infant curls up and raises its toes to its mouth. Your back and spine are completely loose before you learn to walk. Once walking begins, the spine tightens and flexibility diminishes and diminishes and… Yoga is the caretaker of the spine, lengthening and extending it to release the energy that runs through this neural superhighway.

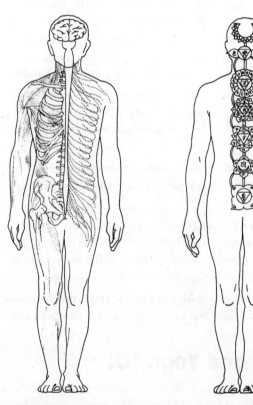

The Western anatomical model of the human body's musculoskeletal and nervous systems (left) is complemented by yoga's seven energy centers, called chakras *(right), which store and release* prana, *the life force.*

Eastern Body, Western Body

That the body and the mind are one is an easy concept for the Easterner. The physical body is merely one of several "bodies." It's a temple to house the spirit, but should be well tended and rigorously cared for because of the importance of what it holds. The *astral* body is the vehicle of the spirit and is maintained through breathing, meditation, and concentration. The *causal* body is the place where the spirit works. The ego is absent from the causal body, and the spirit can know its true potential here. Ideally, the spirit transcends all bodies and becomes pure consciousness, an individual expression of the divine. To the traditional Easterner, the mind/body is sacred, not to be abused, but to be used as a vehicle for the spirit's expression, which results, finally, in enlightenment.

On the other side of the spectrum is the Westerner. Traditionally, the Westerner sees one part of the self at a time. The body is the body. Healthy food keeps it running, and exercise keeps it strong. End of story. Then there is the mind. The mind is the source of intelligence and thought. Activities that stimulate the mind, from philosophical conversations to crossword puzzles, keep the mind active. End of story. Then there is the spirit. The spirit might be nurtured and maintained by going to church or by a personal philosophy or spirituality. In many, the spirit is ignored. End of story.

Westerners have certainly survived—and thrived. So why should we change a system that works? Because it keeps us off-balance. Westerners are movers and shakers, yet many of us exist on the edge of health and sanity, surviving on caffeine, nicotine, and sugar, wracked by stress, and saddled with materialism, ego, desire, and greed. We need something to even us out, calm us down, and get us in touch with ourselves again. Don't believe that this will slow you or make you less effective. Integrating mind, body, and spirit can only make you a better and more effective, productive person—Westerner or Easterner.

Wise Yogi Tells Us

Moderation is the wisest, most peace-inspiring course. Nothing should be so important that it must be had in excess, and nothing should be so important that it must be utterly denied.

Do You Trust Your Body?

Maybe you've never thought of your body in terms of something you should or shouldn't trust, but you have an intimate relationship with your body. It's your vehicle for communicating with the world. Do you trust your body? How many of the following statements do you agree with?

➤ "When I get a craving, I can't control my eating. I'll eat an entire quart of ice cream, a huge steak, a pound of chocolate, candy, a whole pizza, or a pie."

A Yoga Minute
Every *chakra* has a corresponding color:

- ➤ Thousand Petaled Lotus *chakra* is violet
- ➤ Sun *chakra* is indigo
- ➤ Mercury *chakra* is blue
- ➤ Venus *chakra* is green
- ➤ Mars *chakra* is yellow
- ➤ Jupiter *chakra* is orange
- ➤ Saturn *chakra* is red

➤ "I'm accident-prone, especially when I play sports or exercise. I always twist an ankle, jam a thumb, or something."

➤ "I always get sick just when an important event is about to happen. My body betrays me when I need it most!"

➤ "I don't know what to think about myself because what I see in the mirror is totally different than how other people describe me."

➤ "I'm uncomfortable in most of my clothes."

If you agreed with any of the above statements, you have problems trusting your body. Your body is not your enemy, and it's not a stranger. The wonderful thing about yoga is that it reacquaints you with your physical self. You'll get to know your body like never before, and it will begin to respond the way you intend. You'll know what your body is going to do. You'll have more control over your physical being and mental state, so you'll be injured less, be more sure about what you think, and be more self-confident.

What You Need Is to Release Your Chakras

Ouch!
Feeling frazzled and unfocused? Try a pose that awakens your Saturn *chakra*, located at the base of your spine. Angry, hostile, or overemotional? Try a pose that stimulates your Venus *chakra*, located behind your heart. Having a problem communicating? Work with your Mercury *chakra*, located in the throat. Each *Hatha Yoga* posture is designed to awaken different *chakras*, so practicing the right poses can be the best prescription for what ails you.

In yogic thought, the body contains seven energy centers, called *chakras* (literally "wheels"), that store energy, or the life force, *prana*. Westerners would interpret the *chakras* as nerve centers, but they are much more than this. They are centers of psychospiritual energy that don't precisely correspond to any tangible physical structure. The seven *chakras* are as follows (there are other, subtler *chakras*, but these are the most commonly known):

➤ Saturn *chakra*, located just above the anus at the base of the spine, involves elimination and your sense of smell. A coiled energy lies here sleeping, like a serpent. When awakened through yoga, this energy travels up the spine through all the *chakras*.

➤ Jupiter *chakra*, located on the spine near the genitals, involves water, sexuality, passion, the creation of life, and taste.

➤ Mars *chakra,* located on the spine behind the navel, is associated with digestion or "gastric fire," your sense of self, and your actions.

➤ Venus *chakra,* located behind the heart, is the center of your compassion and emotions.

➤ Mercury *chakra,* located in the throat, is the center for communication.

➤ Sun *chakra,* located in the middle of the brow, is also known as the Third Eye, or center of un-clouded perception.

➤ Thousand Petaled Lotus *chakra,* located at the crown of the skull, is the center of self-realization, perspective, unity, and enlightenment.

All *chakras* must be activated or awakened for true enlightenment, which is not an easy process. Awakening your *chakras*—releasing the energy that flows through your spine—can take years, perhaps lifetimes! It's hard work to lighten up (or, to achieve enlightenment).

> **Know Your Sanskrit**
> A *mantra* is a sacred sound used in meditation as the object of focus, meant to resonate within the body and awaken the *chakras*. The word *mantra* is a composite of two Sanskrit root words: the first, *man,* means "continual or constant thinking." The second, *tra,* means "to be free." *Mantra* is a process by which you free yourself from worries or doubts, but not from consciousness.

Mantras: Beyond OM

"I'll do yoga," you say, "but I draw the line at chanting." Okay, so you've been put off by a few OM stereotypes on television and in movies. But bear with us a for just a little bit—it's not as bad as you think, once you understand what chanting is all about.

A *mantra* is a sound or sounds that resonate in the body and evoke certain energies; *mantras* help stimulate the *chakras* by soothing your mind and awakening your senses.

> **Wise Yogi Tells Us**
>
> OM SHANTI SHANTI SHANTI (pronounced OHM SHAHN-tee SHAHN-tee SHAHN-tee) is a great beginning *mantra* to try. Shanti means peace, and when repeated three times, it balances the body, mind, and spirit. It's easy to use and to remember.

OM is a common *mantra* because it's designed to invoke a universal perspective: You see your body/mind in relation to its place in the big picture. In Sanskrit, OM is spelled "aum," and each letter is a sacred symbol:

Know Your Sanskrit
A *mandala* is a circular geometric design used as a center of focus in meditation and meant to suggest the universe's circular motif (from atoms to solar systems) and the spirit's journey. *Mandala* means "circle" or "center."

➤ The "a" represents the self in the material world.

➤ The "u" represents the psychic realm.

➤ The "m" represents indwelling spiritual light.

Chanting OM unifies your perceptions so you can sense yourself as an integral part of the universe. Gradually, the chant helps you shed everything that separates you from the universe—all your negativity, illusions, and misperceptions of yourself and the world. OM is a great *mantra* for anyone. Don't be embarrassed! Give it a try!

Mandalas: Goin' Round in Circles

While a *mantra* is meant to soothe the body and mind through sound, a *mandala* is meant to center the mind through sight. *Mandalas* are beautiful, usually circular, geometric designs that draw your eye to the center. *Mandala* means "circle" or "center," and the designs suggest the circular patterns that exist in so many levels of life, from atoms to solar systems. *Mandalas* represent a pilgrimage to enlightenment. As you focus on the center of the *mandala,* you'll notice the outer parts shifting and changing in your peripheral vision; eventually, your focus will become clear and the center will be all that you see.

Mandalas are a metaphor for the spiritual path of the mind and body. This well-known mandala *appears in the floor of Chartres Cathedral in France. Spiritual pilgrims literally walked through the* mandala *to attain spiritual insight. Get a pencil and try walking the Chartres* mandala *by tracing the path you would take to reach the center and then return from the center to the world again.*

Using *mandalas* and *mantras* together is a wonderful way to meditate because the combination of aural and visual stimulation awakens and clarifies your mind, body, and spirit in multiple ways. Adding color to your *mandala* goes even further toward stimulating the senses. (And you thought meditation would be boring!)

The Least You Need to Know

➤ Yoga helps you feel better in your body.

➤ Body awareness is an important part of practicing yoga.

➤ *Chakras* are related to nerve centers in the spine.

➤ Releasing *chakras* optimizes your neural superhighway.

➤ *Mantras* and *mandalas* channel the body's energy and focus the mind.

Yoga Mind Power: Go with the Flow

Life is not a war, it's not a contest, and it's not a race. Life is *being*. Yoga helps you see this truth and live it each moment. The need to name, label, evaluate, and analyze everything we come into contact with can be debilitating to the spirit. Yoga teaches you to look without classifying, to listen without judging—to learn, simply, how to feel. Everything is subjective. Realizing this will help bring peace to your busily categorizing mind and help you see the truth in difficult situations, people, and even yourself. Labels make perception seem easy, but perception isn't easy, so banish the labels and look harder and closer at yourself and the world. Let yoga show you how.

A Fight-or-Flight World

There's no doubt about it—we live in a stressful world! The human animal has a specific way to deal with stress, and it's called the *fight-or-flight response*. When confronted with a stressful situation, your adrenaline starts pumping. Your muscles tense. Your senses heighten. In essence, your body becomes primed to deal with the stress in two ways:

either fight with the utmost energy and strength or get away as fast as possible. How can fight-or-flight help you? It gives you energy. It gives you a quick reaction time. Your mind is sharper and clearer. If you recognize all this and work with your body, your experience of a stressful situation—say, presenting a new product line at work or teaching a class to a new group of students—will be vibrant and exciting.

The problem with the fight-or-flight response comes when it's engaged too often. Bodies can only take so much stress, and if you're in a constant state of elevated awareness, muscle tension, and excess energy, you're bound to break down. Maybe you'll get sick, collapse from exhaustion, or just plain lose your ability to communicate so others can understand you. The problem with our world is that it constantly bombards us with stressful situations. What's more, our culture rewards those who take on the most stress. Who do you admire more, your colleagues who are always taking on projects and coming up with new ideas, working late every night, and helping everyone else who gets behind? Or the colleagues who relax at their desks talking on the phone, leave at five with over-flowing in-boxes, and never seem in a hurry to get anything done?

We want the overachievers on our team: the high-powered, assertive, I-can-do-anything types. With that kind of pressure, it's no wonder we're all under so much stress.

Enter yoga! In a fight-or-flight world, yoga is like a daily trip to the spa. Not only will it relax you and calm your mind, but it can fine-tune the fight-or-flight response. With yoga, you learn to clear your mind and listen. You learn to focus, concentrate, and tune in. Obstacles that confuse us and prohibit us from seeing clearly are gently washed away with yoga. When the fight-or-flight response kicks in, the yoga practitioner can channel it so that it's as productive as possible. When your muscles tense, you're aware of them and can direct their energy to stand straighter, move more quickly, and react more deftly. As your senses heighten and your thinking sharpens, you'll see how to clear your mind of everything but the task at hand. Answers will come to you. The perfect combination of words will flow effortlessly from your mouth. You'll be able to perceive your situation clearly—the motivations of others, your position in the circumstances, and what should be done. Panic is replaced by confidence. Yoga is the key to making the fight-or-flight response work for you because it gives you control over your physical and mental responses to this instinct.

Concentration, Relaxation, Meditation

Meditation is an important part of yoga. But maybe you aren't interested in meditating. That's fine—just practice the *asanas*. Chances are, however, that the more you progress through the *asanas,* the more interested you'll become in meditation. Meditation can do wonderful things for your mind and your body.

Perhaps you aren't sure what meditation is. Really, it's a simple concept. Meditation is the process of attaining total awareness through the cessation of thought. You begin by relaxing. You concentrate on relaxing. Perhaps you feel like a wave relaxing into the ocean, because that's what you are. You are a part of the universe the way a wave is part of the ocean. In fact, repetition of the mantra OM even sounds like waves on the shore. Soon, your thought waves decrease and become still. The wise Indian sage, Patanjali, says: "Yoga is the cessation of the fluctuations of the mind." We say, still waters run deep.

As you let your mind relax, notice the thoughts that come to you and gently push them away. This is difficult at first. We are so used to having busy minds. Especially if you've never meditated before, you may find it virtually impossible to stop the thoughts racing through your mind. You may think about chores you should be doing, a problem at work, a fight you had with your spouse or child, what to make for dinner, or what you plan to do that weekend. We are conditioned to believe that every minute should count and that we should always be getting as much done as possible. But yoga disagrees with this notion. Yoga says that the mind needs to be stilled occasionally to keep it working at peak efficiency. Face it, you wouldn't leave all the appliances on in your house all day long every day and expect them to work properly for a long period of time. Things would go haywire, burn out, blow out, blow up, or break down.

So why should your mind be any different? It isn't a perpetual motion machine. If you don't learn how to calm and still your mind, it's bound to need some loving care and maintenance. We're not saying that if you don't meditate, you'll go nuts (though it's possible!). What we're saying is that a neglected mind is one that doesn't work as well as it could. Meditation is mental maintenance. Teaching yourself how to relax your mind and release it from the stress of thought for a short period each day keeps it clear and clean. You'll think better. You'll see more accurately and with more insight. You'll be able to concentrate and focus on things like never before. You'll be able to truly relax. In fact, you'll probably be amazed at the mind power you never knew you had.

Know Your Sanskrit

Patanjali was an Indian sage who, thousands of years ago, wrote a text called the *Yoga Sutra*, which recorded concepts that had been passed down orally for many years. This extremely influential text, which consists of a series of aphorisms about how to practice yoga, has helped to define the modern practice of yoga.

Ouch!

Even meditation can be counter-productive. Although you probably won't pull a muscle while meditating, it's possible to stay stressed, or even become more stressed in your efforts to relax! Don't think. Don't worry that you aren't meditating correctly. Feel your body, feel your breathing, and feel who you are. Let your thoughts flow through your mind like pictures on a movie screen, flickering and passing on. Gently, lovingly, let each thought go. Ahhhh!

From Full Mind to Mindfulness

What is stillness? Simply a lack of movement? As you move through your daily life, stillness would probably not be an adjective you would use to describe your mental state. You are busy, you have responsibilities, and you are good at what you do. This takes a full mind, a mind always thinking about what to do next. A mind prepared to deal with conflict. A mind ready to tackle anything, whether it's a toddler's temper tantrum or capturing a multi-million dollar account for your company. Who has time for stillness when you've got so much to *do?*

You do, because stillness will take your full mind, empty it out, give it a good, thorough cleaning, and transform it into a mindful mind. What does that mean? A mindful mind is like a mirror that is meticulously polished. It reflects what is really there and nothing else. When you become mindful, you learn to suspend everything you believe about yourself. Your limits, your shortcomings, your fears, what people have told you that you can and can't do—all these are put on hold. What's left is the real you, and your possibilities are limitless. Mindfulness takes courage. It can be scary to look at the real you. But if you take a good look, you'll have new power. You'll understand who you are like never before. And, as your self-concept expands, so will your concept of the world. Everything is within your grasp. Yet you aren't grasping—you're simply living, achieving, and being the best person you can possibly be.

This involves extending your meditation to your daily life. Once you've made meditation a part of your life, you can gradually learn to carry its principles with you throughout your day. When negative feelings arise, push them away as if they were balloons. If people are unkind, unfair, or judgmental of you, you can learn gently to push these balloons away, too. Meditation in daily life means remembering the peace and stillness you've learned to achieve during regular meditation, then finding that peace and stillness throughout the day. The real you will shine through best when you're in touch with this inner peace.

Wise Yogi Tells Us

To help yourself meditate, think of all the definitions of yourself you know. "I am a teacher." "I am a father." "I am bad at math." "I am shy." "I am lazy." "I am well-meaning." "I am jealous." Now, pretend these phrases are untrue. Just pretend. Then look beyond. What's left is the real you, and you may be surprised at what you see. Surprised—and pleased.

Relax Past Your Boundaries

What are your boundaries? We all have them, and they are all branches of *avidya,* or our false perceptions of life and of ourselves. Boundaries limit us from the truth and from our potential. Some of the boundaries we impose upon ourselves are known as *asmita,* or ego; *raga,* or attachment; *dvesha,* or rejection; and *abhinivesha,* or the survival instinct.

Ego is a boundary difficult for most Westerners to avoid. Your ego is what gives you a sense of who you are to the world. To say, "I am the smartest one in this class," is ego. To say, "I have to win this game," is ego. To say, "I am beautiful," or, "I am right," or even, "I am good at my job," is ego. To most Westerners, some expression of ego seems natural and even productive. Why not be proud of what you do, how you look, or what you've accomplished? You certainly should be proud of who you are. But *asmita* means being proud of the wrong things—the things that limit you, such as material possessions, physical appearance, beating out someone, or being the best, which implies you're better than others. Deep inside, you're a jewel. You're a beautiful soul that's part of a beautiful universe. Getting caught up in the petty and non-lasting aspects of life can only hold you back from your true potential. Maybe you still think you've got to be competitive to "win," but yoga can help you to see winning in a new, more fulfilling light.

Know Your Sanskrit

Avidya (pronounced ah-VEE-dyah) is the word for incorrect comprehension. The opposite of *avidya* is **vidya,** (VEE-dyah) correct understanding. *Avidya* inhibits our perception in many ways—through automatic, learned responses; dependency on habits; and negative self-talk. *Avidya* is like a cloud in front of the sun. Learning to recognize *avidya* and dispel it is one of the goals of yoga.

Attachment is related to ego and involves desire. Do you know what it's like to want a cookie or a piece of cake, not because you're truly hungry but just because you want the pleasure? The desire for pleasure can overcome you, and you can be fiercely single-minded until you get what you want. If you've experienced this feeling, then you know what *raga* is. Attachment also involves material possessions—that sort of "fever" you get when you see something you really want. It can consume your entire mind—the desire for that new dress, a stereo system, or a hot red sports car. Attachment to any material possessions, sensual sensations, addictions, desires, or even an obsessive attachment to another person is a boundary that holds you back from truth and the true knowledge of yourself. Attachment gets in the way of who you really are.

Rejection is like the opposite of attachment and is called *dvesha.* Your spouse left you, so you refuse to get involved in a relationship again. You were thrown from a horse, so you refuse to ride. You were in a car accident, so you vow never to drive another car. All these are *dvesha.* Rejecting experiences, people, or thoughts that have caused you pain in the past blocks you from the future. But *dvesha* needn't be so drastic, and we all experience it. You refuse to try okra because you think it will taste unpleasant. You don't go to a party because you know the social interactions will be

Know Your Sanskrit

Asmita (pronounced ah-SMEE-tah) is the ego, *raga* (pronounced RAH-gah) is attachment, and *dvesha* (pronounced DVEH-shah) is rejection.

stressful and you just don't have the energy. This isn't to say that you can't make the decision not to do certain things, but when you reject things out of a fear of discomfort, pain, or inconvenience, rather than rejecting things simply because you don't want or need them, then *dvesha* has become a stumbling block in your life.

Wise Yogi Tells Us

"Heart breathing" is a technique that can be very renewing. Sit comfortably. Close your eyes. Notice your breathing, but don't try to control it. Feel your chest expanding and contracting. Now imagine the breath is flowing out of your heart with each exhalation and pouring into your heart with each inhalation. Don't think about anything. Just feel the breath flowing in and out of your heart. Imagine the breath is pure love. Do this for 5 to 10 minutes, then slowly open your eyes, get up, and move on. Remember the feeling throughout your day. Then do it again tomorrow!

The final obstacle is the survival instinct, or *abhinivesha*. This instinct may seem to be a positive one at first, but it is actually a stumbling block between you and enlightenment. This intense desire to remain alive is related to the fear of death (although they aren't the same). You probably want to remain you. You may fear death, but you also love your life (for the most part), and so fear any kind of change in your existence. Enlightenment, involving release from the material world and tangible existence, its dissolved ego, is not only terrifying in its mystery but terrifying in its implication that your life as you know it will cease. We are animals, after all. Our instincts are for self-preservation. Moving beyond our instinctual natures into our spiritual selves isn't easy.

Know Your Sanskrit

Abhinivesha (pronounced ah-bhee-nee-VEH-shah) is the survival instinct, or thirst for life. It is the desire to exist and so becomes an obstacle toward enlightenment, which is existence but beyond the personal existence to which unenlightened individuals cling.

Yoga helps dispel *abhinivesha* (the survival instinct), as well as the other aspects of *avidya* (incorrect comprehension) that cloud our perception and inhibit our growth. Sure, you'll probably always have occasional bouts of ego, attachment, rejection, and the instinct to cling to your material existence. But through yoga, you can learn to recognize them for what they are, then blow them out like matches. Yoga helps you relax, think more clearly, and see the inner you that is a part of the universe and all that is good. Yoga helps reveal *avidya* for the impostor it is. And if you can perceive the stumbling blocks in your path clearly and without doubt, you can confidently step around them.

Find the Zone—And Move In!

We've already talked about the *zone*. The zone is that place you go when your skill is suddenly heightened, your mind is sharp, and you can do no wrong. Athletes know about the zone. When an athlete is in the zone, he or she has reached peak performance. The mind is thinking quickly, sharply, and accurately. It's almost as if the other team members or competitors are moving in slow motion. Success is effortless.

Artists know about the zone. It's the place where nothing else exists but the task at hand. A painting seems to paint itself. The words to a novel flow effortlessly. The sculpture emerges, the actor becomes the character, and the dancer becomes one with the dance.

Students know about the zone. It's that rare time when the answers to a test are obvious to you and all the information you've studied seems immediately available. Your brain exceeds itself, the words to an essay write themselves, and the meanings to formulas become suddenly clear.

Another word for the zone in contemporary culture is *flow*. Anyone can achieve flow, but some achieve it more often than others. You have flow when you become completely absorbed in what you're doing. Time stops, nothing else exists, and you become one with your work. During flow, you can accomplish things you never thought you could.

Ouch!
Do not sit awkwardly during meditation. Sitting slumped over with a crooked spine or sitting in a position too advanced for you can cause injury to your body and make you frustrated. It's impossible to truly relax into your meditation if your body is strained or in pain. So stay within your physical limits while meditating and concentrate on your mind, instead.

Wouldn't it be nice to achieve flow whenever you want—to move into the zone and live there all the time? For most, flow comes and goes, seemingly according to its own whim. But for the experienced yoga practitioner, the zone is a place to go whenever you choose. Because yoga uses control of the body to still the mind and control of the mind to manipulate the body, body and mind become integrated not only with each other, but also with the external world. If you're one with your work, your art, or your sport, you've achieved flow. You're in the zone. Yoga is like a key to the secret door into the zone. Open it, and you'll live beyond your limits, finding new productivity, creativity, efficiency, and true delight.

Release Your Inner Delight

Joy, bliss, ecstasy—whatever you want to call it—is yoga's big payoff. Maybe you consider yourself a happy person, or maybe you suffer from depression. Maybe you had a happy childhood, or maybe you've been hurt in the past. It doesn't matter—no matter who you are, no matter what has happened to you in your life, you have the capacity for joy. Deep inside you, bliss waits for you to find it. Yoga will ferret out that joy with relentless persistency. Through yoga, you can find that joy and release it.

A Yoga Minute
The symbolism of the lotus flower is extremely important in yoga. The lotus flower is a beautiful circle of petals that floats on a lake. The lotus's roots, however, are deep in the mud. This mud provides the nutrients to help the lotus grow and achieve its beauty. To yogis, the lotus represents human life. Our lives are submerged in "mud," in the material world, in striving and grasping, in worry and pain. Yet we can use these challenges the way the lotus root absorbs nutrients from the mud—sending up a shoot that will ride to the top of the murky lake and bloom on the surface in perfect beauty.

But make no mistake—it isn't easy to release your inner delight. A body that's undisciplined, weak, and lazy saps all your inner energy to keep it maintained. A mind fraught with chaotic thought is too absorbed on the surface level to delve deep enough to find inner joy. But with persistent yoga practice, the body becomes strong, controlled, flexible, and disciplined. The mind becomes quiet, calm, and tranquil. A restless body that at one time struggled to maintain the lotus position for an extended period and a mind that regularly wandered without purpose now both respond with focus and commitment.

Maybe inner joy isn't what you're looking for. Maybe you don't even believe it's something that's possible for you to find. Don't worry about that—yoga is a journey, and you go at your own pace. Practice the postures. Meditate, if you feel like you're ready. Gradually, as you become prepared, the joy—the inner delight—will come.

The Least You Need to Know

➤ Yoga uses the fight-or-flight response to your benefit.

➤ Yoga teaches mindfulness.

➤ Meditation is simply relaxation for your mind.

➤ Meditation stimulates *vidya,* correct understanding, and dispels negative thoughts, feelings, and actions.

Part 2
Let's Get Spiritual: Growing with the Tree of Yoga

This section begins with a mini-history lesson—yoga has been around for thousands of years and in all that time, it has branched into various types, from studious Jnana Yoga *to active* Karma Yoga *to mystical* Kundalini Yoga. *Learn about how yoga came to the West and why our culture is coming to a point in its evolution where yoga will become a powerful and pertinent tool.*

Next, we'll introduce you to yoga's comprehensive guidelines for living. Far from hard-and-fast "commandments," yoga's yamas *(abstinences) and* niyamas *(observances) point the way along the path that will most enhance your yoga journey. Patanjali's Eightfold Path (of which the abstinences and observances are the first two aspects) is laid out in an easy-to-follow format, explaining the eight important facets of a yogi's life, from keeping the body fit to mastering detachment, concentration, and meditation.*

Controlling the breath keeps body and mind operating at peak efficiency. In Chapter 7, we'll explain the how's and why's of the yoga system of breath control called pranayama. *Chapter 8 goes on to describe the details of* Hatha Yoga, *a system of yoga emphasizing control of the body and the most popular form of yoga in the West.*

OG CALL IT "YOGA".

Chapter 5

Going Back in Time: The Yoga Tradition

In This Chapter

➤ The history of yoga

➤ The nine types of yoga

➤ Yoga for the new millennium

➤ How yoga first came to the West

➤ Non-spiritual yoga: Is it possible?

You don't have to know anything about the yoga tradition to practice yoga. After all, we're not in school and we're not going to give you any kind of history test. But history can be interesting, especially when there *isn't* a test— no pressure! Yoga's history is particularly illustrious and ancient. Understanding the deep and sagacious roots of your fitness program may help you gain a deeper appreciation of yoga's staying power and sacred origins.

People Practiced Yoga in 2500 B.C.

Yoga has been around for a long, long time. How long, you ask? The Rig-Veda is quite possibly the oldest-known text in the world, and it contains definite elements of yoga. Although the only remaining written versions are a few hundred years old, the earliest hymns are believed to be over 4,000 years old. The hymns of the Rig-Veda were passed down via an oral tradition, with great accuracy. Hindu priests were trained to memorize the hymns to the letter. If the Rig-Veda is indeed thousands of years old, its existence may coincide with the existence of the Vedic people who lived along the Indus River and also with the Pyramid Texts, thought to be the oldest written documents in existence.

A Yoga Minute
The Rig-Veda, passed down through the centuries via memorization, contains 1,028 hymns composed in archaic Sanskrit. That's a lot to remember!

But just because yoga is old doesn't mean it's old-fashioned. Yoga is timeless, transcending cultures, eras, and philosophies. They say you never know if something will be a classic until it has stood the test of time. Need we say more?

Yoga Studies All Religions

Yoga may seem like a religion. It offers guidelines for living, spirituality, study of sacred texts, and communion with the "divine." Some branches of yoga seem more religious or mystical than others, but yoga itself isn't a religion.

Yoga is open to all religions and encourages the study of all religious and spiritual texts. Yoga is not biased, prejudiced, or exclusive. You needn't be a Hindu, a Muslim, a Christian, or a Jew, but you may be any of these. Whatever religion you practice, yoga will help you understand your beliefs more clearly and get you in closer touch with your spiritual side.

Wise Yogi Tells Us

The Bhagavad Gita is one of India's most beloved sacred texts. It's widely available and still a good read. (And it isn't even very long!) Pick up a copy and see what the fuss is all about. Read the whole thing, even if it takes a while to get into it. It's a great story, and you'll be wiser afterward.

In Search of the Sacred (Svadhyaya)

Because yoga encourages the study of the sacred (*svadhyaya*), it may be helpful for you to become at least superficially familiar with the major spiritual texts. Reading and studying any or all of them will benefit your yoga practice by expanding your mind to possibilities you may not have considered. Studying the sacred texts of our world, or even just those of your own religion, can help you get in touch with the spiritual journey our species has undergone since we were first able to comprehend the concepts of spirituality, divinity, and the universe. A few of the major sacred texts of India (since that's where yoga really blossomed, and many of these texts directly mention yoga or its concepts) are:

➤ The Rig-Veda, considered the most ancient of sacred texts. Meaning "Knowledge of Praise," it's been orally passed down via sages who memorized it. Consisting of 1,028 hymns, the Rig-Veda is now believed to be over 4,000 years old.

➤ The Upanishads, the scriptures of ancient Hindu philosophy.

➤ The Bhagavad Gita, perhaps the most famous Hindu text and the epic story of Arjuna, a warrior-prince, who confronts moral dilemmas and is led to a better understanding of reality through the intercession of the god, *Krishna.*

➤ The Yoga Sutra of Patanjali, the source of Patanjali's Eightfold Path. Many call Patanjali the father of yoga because of this significant and influential text, but yoga was around long before Patanjali, who only made it more accessible.

➤ *The Hatha-Yoga-Pradipika,* a 14th-century guide to *Hatha Yoga*—everything you always wanted to know about *Hatha Yoga* but were afraid to ask!

> **Know Your Sanskrit**
>
> *Svadhyaya* (pronounced svahd-YAH-yah) means "inquiring into your own nature, the nature of your beliefs, and the nature of the world's spiritual journey." Accomplished by the study of sacred texts, such as the Bhagavad Gita and the Bible, as well as through self-contemplation, *svadhyaya* is one of yoga's observances and one aspect of Patanjali's Eightfold Path, as described in the Yoga Sutra (and further explained in Chapter 6).

Planting the Seeds: Yoga Branches for All Growing Personalities

Up to this point, although we've been focusing primarily on *Hatha Yoga,* we haven't really been distinguishing between all the different types of yoga. Yoga has a unified goal—a state of pure bliss and oneness with the universe—but various methods each emphasize a different way to get to that goal.

> **Know Your Sanskrit**
>
> *Krishna* is a playful and popular Hindu god, and the star of the Bhagavad Gita.

Hatha Yoga: Know Your Body, Know Your Mind

As we've mentioned before, *Hatha Yoga* works under the assumption that supreme control over the body, or the physical self, is one path to enlightenment. *Hatha Yoga* is a sort of spiritual fitness plan in which balance is a key. Attention to the physical is foremost in *Hatha Yoga;* this particular type of yoga involves cleansing rituals and breathing exercises designed to manipulate the body's energy through breath control, in addition to the postures or exercises for which *Hatha Yoga* is commonly known.

Raja Yoga: Know Your Mind, Know the Universe

Raja Yoga, also known as The Royal Path, emphasizes control of the intellect to attain enlightenment. Meditation, concentration, and breath control are paramount in *Raja Yoga,* the yoga of the mind. *Hatha* and *Raja Yoga* work well together; *Hatha Yoga* is often considered a stepping stone to *Raja Yoga* because after control of the body is mastered, control of the mind comes more easily.

> ### Wise Yogi Tells Us
>
> If you're ill, whether you've got a cold, chronic pain, or something more serious, *Hatha Yoga* postures, meditation, and a practice of mindfulness can be of great benefit. Learning to relax, physically and mentally, can comfort you and aid in healing. If you're in physical pain due to illness, however, or find yourself too distracted to even think about meditating, start slow, as little as five minutes a day. Even taking a series of full, deep breaths can be centering to body and mind.

Kriya Yoga and Karma Yoga: Act it Out!

Kriya Yoga and *Karma Yoga* are the yogas of action. *Kriya* means spiritual action, and *Kriya Yoga* involves the practice of quieting the mind through scriptural self-study, breathing techniques, *mantras,* and meditation. *Kriya Yoga* understands that divine energy is stored in the lower part of the body. The study of *Kriya Yoga* breathing and meditation techniques helps to bring this energy up the spine. As the energy builds, the yogi's body (physical and astral) is strengthened.

> ### Know Your Sanskrit
> *Karma* is the law of cause and effect, or "what goes around comes around." Everything you do, say, or think has an immediate effect in the universe and in you. *Karma* is not negative. It is neither bad nor good. It is the movement toward balanced consciousness.

In *Karma Yoga,* the emphasis is selfless action. *Karma Yoga* transcends concerns of success or failure, egoism, and selfishness. What emerges is service to all beings. Because yoga teaches that every person is part of the divine universal spirit, *Karma Yoga* encourages that all beings on this earth be served with the respect deserving of a divine presence. The follower of *Karma Yoga* proceeds through daily life attempting to increase virtue and decrease lawlessness in the world by working for others and foregoing personal desires, resulting in greater empathy for and understanding of the world—and eventually, of course, enlightenment.

Bhakti Yoga: Open Your Heart

Bhakti Yoga places sincere, heartfelt devotion to the divine ahead of all else. *Bhakti Yoga* involves reverence, devotion, and perpetual remembrance of whatever divine presence is meaningful to you. Unsettled minds, intellectual concerns, the material world—all fall away as love takes over and the heart is enveloped in thoughts of the divine. The heart is *Bhakti Yoga's* focus and is cultivated as the primary way to achieve unity with the divine.

Jnana Yoga: Sagacious You

Jnana Yoga is the path of knowledge and wisdom. Inquiring minds are what *Jnana Yoga* is all about, and because all knowledge is hidden within us, *Jnana Yoga's* goal is to inquire deeply into ourselves through questioning, meditation, and contemplation, until we find that knowledge. *Jnana Yoga* involves a radical shift in perception. Everything you know, think, believe, or feel is questioned, temporarily. When everything you know is suddenly untrue, all that remains is you and the universe, which are the same thing. The goal is wisdom, which is far beyond the mere accumulation of information. It's direct knowledge of the divine through the elimination of all that is merely illusion.

Tantra, Mantra, and Kundalini Yoga

Tantra, Mantra, and *Kundalini Yoga* are grouped together here because they are all somewhat different than the other types of yoga. Although they share many practices and ideas, *Tantra, Mantra,* and *Kundalini Yoga* are more esoteric than other forms of yoga. *Tantra Yoga* involves the study of sacred writings and rituals. *Mantra Yoga* is the study of sacred sounds. *Kundalini Yoga* is the study of *Kundalini* (energy) movement along the spine that is released through breath and specific *Hatha Yoga* movements. All three should be learned under the guidance of a qualified teacher and require a degree of emotional, mental, and moral preparation.

Tantra Yoga isn't all about sex, although that's what many people seem to think. *Tantric* thought assumes that we live in a dark age (*kali yuga*) and therefore must use every method possible to boost our spirituality. *Tantra Yoga* also believes in the power of ritual. It is most famous in Western culture for its notion that sexual energy is an important store of energy that can be rechannelled to further you along your way to spiritual enlightenment.

Know Your Sanskrit

Kali yuga (pronounced KAH-lee YOO-gah) is the fourth of four ages (*yuga* means "age"), and the age in which we are now living. The shortest of all the ages, *kali yuga* is 432,000 years long. The other ages are: *satya yuga,* the first age (1,728,000 years); *treta yuga,* the second age (1,296,000 years); and *dvapara yuga,* the third age (864,000 years).

Know Your Sanskrit

Tantra means "technique," and *Tantra Yoga* involves the techniques of ritual and study to eliminate obstacles to enlightenment.

Know Your Sanskrit

Shamanism (pronounced SHAH-mahn-ihzm) is the religion of certain northeast Asian peoples, based on the philosophy that the workings of good and evil spirits can be influenced, but only by *shamans* (pronounced SHAH-mahns), the priests of *shamanism*.

Know Your Sanskrit

Japa is the repetition of a *mantra*.

Know Your Sanskrit

Kundalini is energy that lies curled like a snake at the base of the spine and can be awakened through various techniques and movements, after which it travels up the spine, activating the *chakras*. *Kundalini Yoga* is specifically designed to release this energy and channel it.

Mantra Yoga centers around the principle that sound can affect consciousness. Shamanism, yoga's probable precursor, considered sound an extremely important aspect of the search for spiritual enlightenment, and many religions use singing, chanting, rhythm, and recitation in their rituals, even today. *Mantra Yoga* arose as a result of mystical experiences rather than philosophy. A mantra is a syllable or sequence of syllables designed to clear the mind and encourage spiritual awakening. Sanskrit syllables are often used because they awaken reflexology points in the mouth, which in turn energize the body to higher states of consciousness. OM, which we introduced in Chapter 3, is the most commonly known mantra, and sounds curiously (but probably not coincidentally) like "Amen," the sound that punctuates so many religious hymns and prayers.

Chanting a *mantra* puts you in touch with the vibrational patterns of the world and the universe's ocean of vibration, helping you ascend to a state of oneness with the universe. *Mantra Yoga* is all about vibration and the sonic aspect of the divine.

Japa is the process of repeating a *mantra* over and over for the purpose of clearing the mind. Following are a few *mantras* besides OM that you might like to try:

➤ OM NAMAH SHIVAYA (pronounced OHM NAH-mah SHEE-vah-YAH). To divinity my salutations again and again.

➤ HARI-OM (pronounced HAH-ree OHM). Preserving goodness in all.

➤ OM NAMO BHAGAVATE VASUDEVAYA (pronounced OHM NAH-moh BAH-GAH-VAH-teh VAH-soo-DEE-VAH-yah). I turn to the divinity within the heart of all beings.

➤ AHAM BRAHMASMI (pronounced AH-HAM BRAH-MAHS-mee). I am the absolute.

➤ OM MANI PADME HUM (pronounced OHM MAH-nee PAHD-may HOOM). Enlightened body, enlightened speech, enlightened mind, active compassion.

Kundalini Yoga involves techniques meant to awaken the energy, symbolized as a snake, that "sleeps" at the base of the spine. When released correctly, i.e., when the recipient is properly prepared, *kundalini* energy, sometimes called "serpent power," is potently powerful and results in enlightenment. If released too soon, *kundalini* energy mixes with a person's negative emotionality and can turn into intense and painful experiences. Pure *kundalini* is a balanced and compassionate state of being. A person cannot have a negative *kundalini* experience. If they have a negative experience, it is due to something other than *kundalini*. A *kundalini* awakening is thought to result not only in enlightenment, but also in the ability to control involuntary bodily functions.

To awaken the *kundalini,* you must go through complex mental and breathing exercises that should be practiced only under the guidance of a qualified teacher. Sometimes (though it's rare), a *kundalini* awakening will happen spontaneously; but don't be scared away. *Kundalini Yoga* is, at its heart, searching for the same thing as all other types of yoga. Classes are available in this interesting branch of yoga; with proper instruction, the practice of *Kundalini Yoga* can be enjoyable, energizing, and ultimately enlightening.

Why Practicing Yoga Is So 21st Century

The 20th-century world could accurately be described as materialistic. When people gradually become disillusioned by materialism, discovering that it doesn't bring happiness, they search for a way of life more satisfying and fulfilling. So you've got the Porsche, the penthouse, the beachfront condo, and the three-carat diamond. Now what? Throughout history, priorities change and fashions come and go. The pendulum is swinging back toward spiritual priorities and self-actualization, away from more worldly concerns.

Yoga fits easily and comfortably into these new (or renewed) priorities. Yoga doesn't concern itself with technology, wealth, or sophistication. It's an inner journey toward self-realization and an outer journey toward physical control, holistic health, and confidence that comes not from possessions but from self-possession.

East Meets West

Nineteenth-century America was largely unfamiliar with Eastern thought. Then, in 1893, Swami Vivekananda addressed the Parliament of Religions, causing quite a sensation. He quickly became a popular figure and was followed by a number of other *swamis* who came to the United States to teach and guide Westerners along the Eastern path of yoga. Swami Vivekananda was followed by many other *gurus* who came to the West and profoundly influenced their followers, such as Swami Paramahansa Yogananda, Swami Sivananda, and many more.

The Beatles became interested in Eastern thought and even visited India, befriending Maharishi Mahesh Yoga. George Harrison in particular was fascinated

Know Your Sanskrit

Swami is correctly spelled "svamin," but Westerners say *swami*. *Svamin* is a title of respect for a spiritual person who is master of himself rather than others. *Guru* literally means "dispeller of darkness." *Gurus* are self-realized adepts who initiate others into self-realization.

with Indian culture. He became enamored with the sitar and was the first to bring sitar music into rock and roll. The Beatles, through songs such as "Norwegian Wood (This Bird Has Flown)" and "Within You, Without You," introduced Hindu melodies to modern music and opened Westerners' minds to different sounds and new experiences.

> ### Wise Yogi Tells Us
>
> Maharishi Mahesh Yoga was the inventor of Transcendental Meditation, or TM, which involves the mental repetition of a *mantra*. A *mantra* can either be provided to you by your TM instructor or you can create your own. TM is a great way to achieve deep relaxation, and TM instructors are widely available to teach you the technique.

The Maharishi came to the West in 1959. America's "hippie generation" took to yoga in the 1960s, perhaps because traditional values were being questioned and yoga offered an alternative set of values attractive to spiritual seekers. After a few decades of excessive materialism and a world of violence, drug abuse, broken families, and the notable absence of any firmly held spiritual beliefs, yoga is more popular than ever before. We are seeking the spiritual with new vigor as an answer to a world we can't control.

Can You Do Yoga Without Being Spiritual?

"All right, all right," you may be saying, "I'm interested in yoga, but this whole spiritual angle just isn't *me*." Worry not. You can do yoga without being spiritual, even though yoga is traditionally a spiritual pursuit. The postures, as we've said before, are great for fitness. Breathing exercises have wonderful physiological benefits. Even meditation needn't be spiritual, just a fitness program for the mind.

Yoga is so personal that it's impossible to say what it "should" be for anyone. In fact, yoga is distinctly "anti-should." It involves doing what feels right for you, what you want to do. The purpose of yoga is to maximize your potential—to help the best possible you emerge. Maybe the best possible you has no use for spiritual enlightenment. Whatever your potential, whatever your gifts, yoga will help you find them and make the most of them.

The Least You Need to Know

➤ Yoga is really, really old, but still really, really relevant.

➤ Different types of yoga—*Hatha, Raja, Kriya, Karma, Bhakti, Jnana, Tantra, Mantra,* and *Kundalini*—each emphasize different practices but have the same goal: enlightenment.

➤ You don't have to be spiritual to practice yoga, but if you practice yoga, you'll probably end up a little more spiritual.

Chapter 6

Walking Yoga's Eightfold Path

> **In This Chapter**
>
> ➤ Yoga don'ts
>
> ➤ Yoga dos
>
> ➤ Body and breath control
>
> ➤ Detachment and concentration
>
> ➤ Meditation and pure consciousness

If you're the kind of person who likes a nice, clean set of rules to live by, this is the chapter for you! In Patanjali's Yoga Sutra, the eight limbs of yoga are enumerated. They provide a structure for your yoga practice and your daily life. They are designed to help you along the yoga path. One very important thing to remember about the eight limbs of yoga: They are *not* commandments or laws! They are more like guidelines for living. But if you don't follow the guidelines, it doesn't constitute any sort of "sin." The Yoga Police won't come to your house and arrest you. Success with your yoga practice will simply be easier if you live your life according to Patanjali's suggestions.

However, if you don't want to meditate, give up meat, or even relinquish your materialistic nature, don't pressure yourself. Remember that yoga is not only a practice, but something that happens to you. As you progress and grow, you may find that you're naturally less materialistic, you lose interest in eating meat, or you become drawn to meditation as the next logical step in your journey. Maybe you want to tackle the suggestions one at a time. No hurry!

And for those of you who want some commandments and want them *now*, it's also fine to view Patanjali's Eightfold Path more stringently. It all depends on who you are and what kind of thinking you're most likely to respond to.

Just Say No: Yoga Don'ts (Yamas)

First we'll talk about Patanjali's suggested abstinences. This is a difficult category for a lot of people who want to do yoga but don't want to be bound to any restrictions. Again, the abstinences, or *yamas,* aren't rules meant to limit you. They are suggestions meant to help you grow by purifying your body and mind. You may find you already live by many of them.

Do No Harm (Ahimsa)

The first *yama* is about non-violence. That's an easy one, you say? Well, non-violence means more than keeping yourself from beating up your obnoxious neighbor when he won't turn the stereo down. We can be violent in many ways, often without realizing it.

Ahimsa involves non-violent actions, non-violent words, and non-violent thoughts. Non-violent actions involve the obvious—don't physically hurt people. (No, not even when they hurt you first.) Non-violence isn't exactly about turning the other cheek. It's more like dodging the punch. For some, non-violent action also means vegetarianism because meat was once an animal, bird, or fish and had to be killed. Killing is violence. But if this step is too big for you, don't worry about it for now. Concentrate on eliminating violence in other ways.

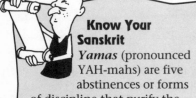

Know Your Sanskrit

Yamas (pronounced YAH-mahs) are five abstinences or forms of discipline that purify the body and mind: *ahimsa* (pronounced ah-HIM-sah) means "non-violence;" *satya* (pronounced SAHT-ya) means "truthfulness," *asteya* (pronounced ah-STAY-yah) means "non-stealing;" *brahmacharya* (pronounced BRAH-mah-CHAR-yah) means "chastity or non-lust;" and *aparigraha* (pronounced ah-PAH-ree-GRAH-hah) means "non-greed."

Non-violent words are also important. Non-violent speech means refraining from words that slander, degrade, or hurt another person. A good rule of thumb is to "honey-coat" your words because you may have to eat them later! But that doesn't mean lying. You needn't tell your Aunt Maude that her polyester pants suit is the most lovely outfit you've ever seen—she may give you one for your next birthday! And what if she asks you what you think about it? "Aunt Maude, that outfit is definitely *you!*"

Non-violent thoughts are equally important. Aunt Maude can't hear you thinking, "If I had taste like that, I would never leave my house!" The trouble with your thoughts, though, is that they pervade your entire being and are notoriously difficult to control. Non-violent thoughts mean refusing to think harm to anyone, even if you really think they deserve it. (Oops! That's bordering on a violent thought right there!) Let your negative thoughts go, wish your enemies well (even in the privacy of your own brain), and your heart will lighten. According to yoga, we are energy and our thoughts can be sensed on an energetic level, so they are impossible to hide completely. People sense what you're thinking, so you're better off transforming your negative thoughts than trying to hide them. The beautiful thing about yoga is that your awareness becomes heightened and you perceive the thoughts of others more clearly.

And one more thing about non-violence: Negative talk and thoughts about yourself ("I am ugly," "I am lazy," "I can't do anything right") are doing violence to yourself. It counts—don't do it!

> **A Yoga Minute**
> Many scientific studies have shown that large groups practicing organized meditation in one location reduce social stress and violence.

Tell No Lies (Satya)

The second *yama* involves truthfulness. But what is the truth? You and I have different truths, so isn't truth changeable? According to yoga philosophy, truthfulness is the result of our mind, speech, and actions being unified and harmonious. According to yoga philosophy, truth does no harm. This results in personal integrity and strength of character.

Are any of the following familiar?

➤ Someone confides in you and you promise you won't tell his or her secret, but then you don't "count" your spouse or your best friend. You've said the words, "I'm not supposed to tell you this, but…".

➤ You receive an extra $10 bill with your grocery change or at the bank and walk quickly away. After all, you need the 10 bucks more than that big corporation!

➤ You occasionally bend the rules just a little on your income taxes.

➤ You tell poor Aunt Maude you aren't feeling well and can't possibly visit her this week, even though you're actually feeling just fine.

Most of us have had at least occasional instances where it seemed more convenient, easier, or even kinder to bend the truth (or just snap it right in two!). It isn't easy to suddenly wake up one morning, vow to act completely truthfully, then stick to your vow. You can start by becoming more aware of what you're doing. Ask yourself, "Is this harmonious with all parts of me? Does this do no harm?" If you aren't sure, maybe you should hold back. Dig deeper for the real truth in your daily life.

Just like everyone around you, you are so much more complex than your outward appearance, your job, the face you show the world, or the opinions of others. What often seems to be the truth—what is obviously the truth, what you know is the truth—is often not the truth at all. Truth is tricky, but it's out there, buried under layers of misrepresentations, grudges, low self-esteem, unfortunate experiences, negative input, and discomforts. Striving for truth and bliss in your everyday life will help those layers fall away. Living truthfully takes some effort, but you can do it!

There are absolute truths that one perceives in the stillness of one's being. We're all searching for truth, and it's within everyone's grasp.

No More Stealing (Asteya)

So you think you don't steal? Just because you've never shoplifted a candy bar or a car radio doesn't mean you don't steal. The concept is simple, even if the implications aren't: If it's not yours, don't take it. (I assume we needn't mention that this *yama* includes no robbing banks or holding up armored cars!) That means no shoplifting, no plagiarizing, and no taking credit for anything anyone else has done or said. Don't interrupt people and steal their center of attention. Don't steal your child's chance to do something on his own by doing it for him. Your actions affect this world—don't forget that.

Cool It, Casanova (Brahmacharya)

Brahmacharya is about chastity. No, don't close the book and toss it aside! This *yama* doesn't mean telling your spouse the fun is over and you now need separate beds. *Brahmacharya* is about virtue and/or sexual abstinence. Many great yogis are householders, which means they are married…with children.

Being virtuous means holding the opposite sex in high esteem. True respect for someone you love doesn't preclude sex, but it helps sex become a spiritual act as well as a physical act. You aren't just joining with your lover physically, you're joining with him or her on a much deeper level. You'll become more like your lover. You'll add his or her life lessons to your own. Virtuous sex is the essence of two people becoming one.

We probably don't have to tell you what the opposite of virtuous sex is—one-night stands, multiple sexual partners, having sex with someone you don't know, obsession, lust. If you don't have someone whom you truly love and respect, abstinence from sex may help clear your mind because clearing and purifying the body clears and purifies the mind. Meaningless physical contact can be confusing and distracting. Avoiding this kind of behavior can help you be more in tune to those out there who could be potential life partners.

Virtuous thoughts are thoughts filled with love and respect, not lust or selfishness. When sex keeps you from becoming your best self, or keeps your partner from doing the same, it's not virtuous sex. But when you and your partner move further toward self-actualization because of the purity of your love, you're having sex the way it was meant to be! (And this may even mean not having sex at all!)

So, not to embarrass you or pry into the intimate nature of your current relationship, but…are you having virtuous sex? You're not sure? Ask yourself three questions:

1. Do I understand the difference between love and lust? (Are my thoughts about my partner more about love than lust?)

2. Do I feel better able to fulfill my potential when with my partner?

3. Am I recognizing and respecting the dreams of my partner?

If you answered yes to all three, congratulations! You're having virtuous sex.

Don't Be Greedy (Aparigraha)

Go to your closet and count how many pairs of shoes are lined up in there—or how many red sweaters or white shirts or ties. Or maybe you can't even open the closet because it's bursting with *stuff*. It isn't easy to abstain from greed in this materialistic world. With television, radio, and billboards continually telling us what we want and what we must have, it's hard not to believe some of it. But are you familiar with the feeling of buying something you've always wanted, then feeling strangely dissatisfied, as if the fun was in the wanting, not in the actual possessing? That is greed's payoff—emptiness. Non-greed means living simply, possessing only what is necessary, and recognizing that possessions are merely tools to use in life. Accumulations, whether material things or unnecessary thoughts, tie you down to this world. Simplify your life as you simplify your thoughts.

Greed can also surface in less obvious ways. Talking too much, interrupting others, and dominating conversations while barely showing a flicker of interest in the participation of others are all ways greed creeps into our lives through language. Think before you speak, and consider how your words will sound and what effect they will have. Practice listening and being truly present in a conversation, absorbing everything other people are saying.

Thoughts can also be a source of greed. How come the Smiths have a swimming pool and a fancy two-level deck, while you have to sit on the back stoop under the sprinkler? Why did your best friend get diamonds for her birthday when you just got a toaster? Envy and jealousy clutter the mind and can become obsessions. How much better it is to turn those feelings around and feel truly happy for the person who has something you don't have! In fact, once you start to be happy for someone else simply because of their joy, you may become so fulfilled by your happiness that you lose your desire for whatever they have. How much simpler your life becomes when you can be happy due to something beyond your own needs!

Yoga Dos: Just Say Yes (Niyamas)

And now for the fun part! *Niyamas* are Patanjali's observances—what to do, as opposed to what not to do. The first *niyama* cleanses the way for all the others.

> **Know Your Sanskrit**
> *Niyamas* are observances or personal disciplines. Again, there are five: *shauca* (pronounced SAH-tshah) means "purity, or inner and outer cleanliness;" *santosha* (pronounced san-TOH-shah) means "contentment;" *tapas* (pronounced TAH-pahs) means "self-discipline;" *svadhyaya* (pronounced svahd-YAH-yah) means "self-study;" and *ishvara-pranidhana* (pronounced ISH-var-ah PRAH-nee-DAH-nah) means "centering on the divine."

Be Pure (Shauca)

Purity is achieved through the practice of the five previous *yamas,* so the *yamas* and *niyamas* work hand in hand. The abstentions clear away negative physical and mental states of being, leading you straight to purity. Purity can apply to various aspects of your life. Cleanliness is very important to yoga. Keeping yourself clean by bathing; dressing in fresh, clean clothes; and keeping your surroundings clean are all part of pure actions.

What you eat is also important. Fresh, natural, and healthy foods are best. Foods obtained through non-violent means are ideal because they can be eaten with full, unadulterated joy; this is why yogis traditionally practice a vegetarian diet. (Of course, if you want to get "yoga-technical," vegetables are alive, too—all life is to be respected, revered, and appreciated, and all life is interconnected—so respect each meal for the life given to sustain another.)

Be Content (Santosha)

Just saying the word *santosha* invokes a feeling of calm. Practicing contentment means finding happiness with what you have and with who you are. Of course, you can always work toward improvement, but that doesn't mean you can't be content while you're improving yourself! Contentment helps you see that you're exactly where you're supposed to be right now. It doesn't mean you'll be happy when you can finally stand on your head, get that promotion, or find a soul mate. It means happiness in this moment, as you are.

Wise Yogi Tells Us

Feeling discontented? Try the following exercise: Make a list of everything that makes you discontented. Then rewrite your list, finding a way to see each source of discontentment in some positive light. For example, rewrite, "I hate my job," to say, "My job has taught me I am more creative than I thought." When you're finished, throw away that first list—you don't need it!

Contentment means learning to reevaluate obstacles as opportunities. Limitations are learning experiences. Easier said than done, we know! If you feel unhappy with your life, you may find it especially difficult to cultivate contented thoughts. Practicing contentment involves taking full responsibility for your life and the situations you're in. Find the positives in life's lessons and choose to grow from them. You're in charge of your own destiny, but that also means not beating yourself up for the "mess" you're in. Thank yourself for it. Laugh! Know that every situation or challenge presented is a doorway to greater growth.

Wise Yogi Tells Us

If the *yamas* and *niyamas* seem like a lot to remember, make yourself an abbreviated version—as plain or fancy as you like (framed calligraphy? computer graphics?)—and hang it up in your bedroom, bathroom, or wherever you'll see it each day. Soon, you'll have them memorized and they'll become a part of you.

Be Disciplined (Tapas)

For all the *yamas* and *niyamas* to be truly effective, you'll need a little self-discipline. Not your strong point? If self-discipline were easy, what would be the point? It would hardly be discipline.

Anyone who exercises daily is showing self-discipline. Dedicating a specific time each day to your yoga practice is self-discipline. But how many times have you started an exercise program, only to abandon it as soon as it got boring or tedious? Learning how to stick to something even when you don't feel like it will build your strength and wisdom. You probably manage the self-discipline to brush your teeth twice every day. Just extend that discipline, bit by bit, to other aspects of your life, one step at a time. Maybe tomorrow, you'll brush your teeth and have a healthy salad for lunch. Maybe next week, you'll be brushing your teeth, eating salads, and doing 10 minutes of yoga. By next year, there's no telling what you can accomplish.

Disciplined words mean speaking gently and sincerely, not angrily or hurtfully. *Act* rather than *react* because you cannot control the actions of others. Self-disciplined thoughts replace the negative with the positive, resentment with forgiveness, violence with peace, and unhappiness with joy.

Wise Yogi Tells Us

Self-discipline is difficult for almost everyone, but changing your attitude may help keep you on track. The best way to do this is to focus on the positive: "I will spend 30 minutes practicing yoga today." "I will relax with deep-breathing exercises tonight before I go to bed." "I will have a soothing cup of herbal tea this morning." Focusing on the positive makes being disciplined more fun. Because really, discipline isn't deprivation, it's self care.

Be Studious (Svadhyaya)

Svadhyaya doesn't just mean you should read a lot of books. It means studying yourself through introspection. Do you act according to your beliefs? Do you say what you mean? Are you walking your talk? Studious action means paying attention to your physical self. How are you sitting, standing, or walking? Do you feel graceful or stilted? Do you look the way you feel? If not, why not? Studious words and thoughts involve the study of various sacred texts—whichever are relevant to you—to inspire and teach you. Through self-study, you can see which thoughts, actions, words, and experiences actually make you happy, and which block your happiness. Dedicated, non-violent introspection will fill your life with clarity.

Be Devoted (Ishvara-Pranidhana)

The last *niyama* involves devotion. Focus on the divine, whatever that means to you—how it is in you and part of you and all around you. *Ishvara-pranidhana* is an observance that works beautifully with any religion. Whether you're devoted to God, Buddha, or the Force, this *niyama* reminds you to relinquish ego and center on your highest ideal. Positive energy will flow from the divine into all areas of your life.

Are You Wearing Your Walking Shoes?: More Yoga Pathways

But what about the rest of the Eightfold Path? Technically, so far we've covered only the first two limbs. The remaining limbs of the Eightfold Path are also important and complete the framework for the modern practice of yoga.

Growing with Yoga's Eightfold Path.

Body Control (Asanas)

We've already talked about body control, or the *asanas,* as both an important part of yoga and the most well-known part. Remember that body control is not the only path, but merely one path yoga offers. Yet, body control is very important and makes a great starting point for any aspiring yogi. *Asana* literally translates as "posture" and is derived from the Sanskrit root *as,* which means "to stay." Patanjali describes an *asana* as having *sthira* and *sukha,* or steadiness and the ability to remain comfortable. Remember these two qualities when practicing your postures, keeping in mind the very important *yama* of *ahimsa,* or non-violence: Never work to the point of pain because that is doing violence to your body.

Breath Control (Pranayama)

Pranayama is another important path. *Prana* refers to the life force or energy that exists everywhere and is manifested in each of us through the breath. *Ayama* means "to stretch or extend." *Prana* flows out from the body, and *pranayama* teaches us to maneuver and direct *prana* for optimal physical and mental benefit. After all, breathing is life. You can go for months without food, days without water, but only moments without breath. Breathing affects all our actions and our thoughts, too. Mastering your breath is an important step toward mastering the rest of you!

Detachment (Pratyahara)

> **Know Your Sanskrit**
> *Sthira* (pronounced STHIH-ra) is steadiness and alertness. *Sukha* (pronounced SOO-kah) means "lightness and comfort." Both are desirable qualities in yoga postures.

> **Ouch!**
> Are you feeling listless, depressed, and under-the-weather? According to ancient yoga texts, you have too much *prana* outside your body. *Prana* is constantly moving and flowing into and out of us, and *pranayama* is a tool for maintaining your health and well-being. Keep yourself healthier and happier by keeping more *prana* inside (where it belongs)!

The fifth limb of yoga is sense-related. *Pratyahara* is the practice of withdrawing the senses from everything that stimulates them. Normally, we live by our senses. We are drawn to look at beautiful or even ugly things. We listen, we taste, we touch, we smell. This is the ordinary state of things, but it's also a state we can temporarily suspend in favor of a deeper awareness. *Pratyahara* cuts off the connection between the senses and the brain. This can happen during breathing exercises, during meditation, during the practice of yoga postures, or during any activity requiring concentration.

Know Your Sanskrit

Pratyahara (pronounced PRAH-tyah-HAH-rah) means withdrawal of the senses; *dharana* (pronounced dah-RAH-nah) means orienting the mind toward a single point; *dhyana* (pronounced dee-YAH-nah) means meditation; and *samadhi* (pronounced sah-MAH-dee) means becoming one with the object of your meditation.

But what is the purpose of detaching ourselves from our senses? Aren't the senses good? They help us appreciate beauty, as when we watch a sunset, or warn us of danger, as when we smell smoke or spoiled food, and they permit us to communicate with each other. Unfortunately, our senses can also become so pleasurable that they control us instead of our controlling them. Maybe you enjoy your sensation of taste so much that you have become a little too obsessed with food. Maybe you love to talk but often talk so much that you forget to listen. Maybe you're addicted to television, caffeine, or sex. *Pratyahara* wipes the sensual slate clean.

Detachment is also a great technique for pain control and an excellent way to deal with uncomfortable symptoms or chronic conditions. Try the following technique for attaining sense withdrawal:

➤ Sit erect. Place your thumbs on your ears, closing them off. Your eyes should be closed. Place your index fingers near your eyelashes to hold them gently shut and prevent movement of your eyeballs (this assists the eyes in staying focused on the sun *chakra* or Third Eye). Each middle finger rests on the nasal passages. Your ring fingers are set on your upper lip and your little fingers on your lower lip.

➤ Take a deep breath and gently press all fingers so your sense organs are suppressed. Turn inward, tuning out the external world. Focus your attention on your sun *chakra*.

➤ When you can no longer comfortably hold your breath, release your fingers.

➤ Exhale slowly. Inhale slowly. Repeat this gentle pressure for deeper reflections.

Concentration (Dharana)

Dhri means "to hold," and *dharana*, yoga's sixth limb, is all about learning to concentrate. Concentration involves teaching the mind to focus on one thing instead of many, as is our usual state of mind. *Dharana* is an exercise that can help with meditation. The goal is to become aware of nothing but the object on which you are concentrating, whether it's a candle flame, a flower, or a mantra you repeat to yourself. The purpose is to train the mind to eliminate all the extra, unnecessary junk floating around, to learn to gently push away superfluous thought. *Pratyahara* (withdrawal of the senses) is often the result when *dharana* is achieved, and both assist with more productive meditation, or *dhyana*.

Meditation (Dhyana)

Concentration is the exercise that leads to the state of meditation, and meditation techniques are, in essence, purity techniques. Meditation occurs when you've actually become linked to the object of your concentration so that nothing else exists. It's keen, heightened awareness, not nothingness. Your mind is completely focused and quiet but awake and aware of truth. Many methods exist to bring you to this state, but oneness with the object of your meditation, and subsequently, oneness with the entire universe, is the objective. And don't forget the wonderful fringe benefit of a calm and uncluttered mind able to think more quickly and see more clearly in all your daily activities!

Pure Consciousness (Samadhi)

All the limbs of yoga lead to *samadhi*, the final limb of the Eightfold Path. *Samadhi* means "to merge," and this state of pure consciousness means just that: a complete and total merging with the object of your meditation. When in a state of *samadhi*, you understand not only that you and the object of your meditation are one, but that you and the universe are one. There's no difference between you and everything else. How does this feel? Like a loss of identity? Yes, identity is meaningless in *samadhi*, but you won't be sorry because *samadhi* is one stage of pure, total bliss.

The Least You Need to Know

➤ Yoga offers guidelines for living.

➤ The five abstentions are non-violence, truthfulness, non-stealing, non-lust, and non-greed.

➤ The five observances are purity, contentment, self-discipline, self-study, and devotion.

➤ Yoga also involves body control, breath control, detachment, concentration, and meditation.

➤ The goal of yoga is a deep, blissful oneness with the universe, which leads to liberation and self-realization.

Can You Breathe?

Of course you can breathe…or can you? Maybe well enough to get by without collapsing, but are you using your breath optimally? Probably not. Most people don't breathe as fully or deeply as they could because it takes practice and concentration. Once you've learned the fine art of breath control, however, you'll certainly feel the difference.

An integral part of *Hatha Yoga* and other forms of yoga is *pranayama,* or breath control. In fact, the manipulation of breath to control the physical manifestation of *prana* is *Hatha Yoga's* realm, while the manipulation of the mental manifestation of *prana* is the goal of *Raja Yoga.*

People in all cultures have learned to manipulate *prana,* either consciously or unconsciously. Faith healers, hypnotists, prophets, shamans, and spiritualists may use *prana,* even if they don't know the source of their power or assign that power to something else.

Yogis learn to use *prana* purposefully to push the mind to a higher state of consciousness. Speech can be charged with *prana,* which is why some people captivate us when they talk.

Prana, the Universal Life Force

In the last chapter we described *prana* as the life force or energy that exists everywhere and is manifested in each of us through the breath, but *prana* isn't exactly the same thing as breath or oxygen. *Prana* exists in all living things. It doesn't have consciousness—it's pure energy. Every cell in your body is controlled by *prana. Prana* animates all matter.

Prana can be a difficult concept to comprehend; it may become clearer if you understand what it isn't.

Once a body completely dies, administering oxygen won't bring it back to life, so, obviously, oxygen doesn't equal life. Life is animated by more than oxygen—it's animated by *prana. Prana* is also not the matter it animates, nor the spirit it propels. *Prana* is universal energy that's in the air, in all matter, and is used by the spirit. You breathe in *prana* along with air, and *prana* regulates your body, from your nervous foot tapping the floor to your thoughts about your weekend plans.

We're now going to turn a little bit of attention to biology— biology according to yoga, that is. But don't get scared off; the concepts are easy to follow. Trust us.

Prana moves through the body along two energy pathways on either side of the spine. *Pingala* is on the right side and represents the sun. *Ida* is on the left side and represents the moon. In the middle is a passageway called *sushumna* that runs through the spinal cord. Just picture a subway. The energy that keeps it running smoothly is *ida* and *pingala.* The *kundalini* is the train sitting at the bottom of this subway waiting to be energized.

Know Your Sanskrit

Pingala (pronounced pin-GAH-lah) is a channel on the right side of the spine through which *prana* moves. *Ida* (pronounced EE-dah) is a channel on the left side of the spine through which *prana* moves. *Sushumna* (pronounced soo-SHOOM-nah) is a hollow passageway between *pingala* and *ida* that runs through the spinal cord, through which *kundalini* can travel once it's awakened. *Nadis* (pronounced NAH-deez) are psychospiritual energy pathways.

The yoga interpretation of the body has a basis in Western anatomy, too. According to physiology, both afferent and sensory nerves exist in the body:

➤ *Afferent nerves* carry messages to the brain and correspond to *pingala.*

➤ *Sensory nerves* carry messages from the brain to the rest of the body and correspond to *ida.*

The spinal cord or center of these two currents (afferent/*pingala* and sensory/*ida*), *sushumna,* also controls the currents that move through the body's nervous system. In yoga, there are 10 currents, called *nadis. Pingala, ida,* and *sushumna* are the major three.

Picturing the physiology (Western-style!) of your thoracic cavity (the cavity containing your lungs and heart) may help you visualize what's happening as you breathe during *pranayama*. When you inhale, your 24 ribs and two lungs expand. Your diaphragm, a large, flat muscle at the base of your thoracic cavity, moves downward to make room for air rushing in. Imagine that it looks a little like an upside-down plunger, helping to pull air in. Deep breathing means filling your lungs from the bottom up. You have a lot of room in there for air!

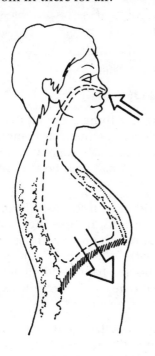 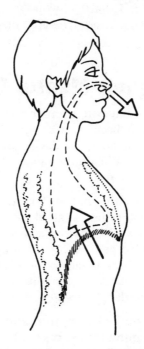

The diaphragm muscle moves downward on inhalation and upward on exhalation. Take a deep breath and feel the muscle in motion!

When you exhale, your ribs and lungs contract. Your diaphragm rises, pushing the air back out, again like a plunger. When you breathe, imagine the breath is flowing deep into your abdomen, then slowly filling up the abdominal cavity, lower thoracic cavity, and, last of all, the chest. On the exhalation, imagine the air flowing out from the chest, the lungs, past the diaphragm, and out of the deepest regions of the abdomen. This is deep breathing!

Try not to move your chest or shoulders when you breathe. All movement should be in your abdomen or lower rib area. Put your hand on your abdomen and try to expand and contract from there. And keep those shoulders still! Rising and falling shoulders are usually an indication of shallow breathing.

Wise Yogi Tells Us

According to wise yogis, the length of life is a matter of the number of breaths, not the number of years. Breath is so important to an accomplished yogi that he or she can get almost all necessary energy from the air. Sleeping? Eating? Minor concerns compared to the breath! That's why yogis have been known to sleep for just a few hours at night. All their energy is replenished through *pranayama* instead—the yogi's beauty sleep!

Breath Control Equals Mental Control

Your breath and your mind have an intimate relationship. Just think about all the ways your breath is affected purely because your mind is experiencing something completely unrelated to breathing. Spend an entire day aware of your breath. Notice how it quickens or slows according to what you're doing, saying, or even thinking? Your breath can be affected merely by who you're near.

Just imagine watching an exciting movie. You're sitting still in your seat eating your popcorn. You aren't doing anything at all to get out of breath. As the opening credits roll, you see the name of your favorite actor or actress and your breath quickens in anticipation. When the movie gets suspenseful, you hold your breath. When the action speeds up, so does your breathing. Your breath responds to the movie's happy ending by becoming steady, smooth, and regular. As the credits roll, if the movie was a satisfying experience, you may even feel winded, as if you have been through a workout.

What our brain perceives, our breath mirrors and our body experiences. Imagine harnessing this power! Just as the mind influences the breath and body, so can the breath influence the mind and body. Controlling the power of breath is the technique of *pranayama*.

There are actually five different manifestations of *prana* that act as vital energy in the body, depending on where they are. Each type complements one of the five nerve centers:

➤ *Prana* (pronounced PRAH-nah) (not the *prana* that is the universal life force, but a sort of "sub-*prana*") rules the respiration process. It manifests in the heart *chakra*, flows into the body through inhalation, and moves up toward the brain.

➤ *Apana* (pronounced ah-PAH-nah) controls excretion, including the kidney, bladder, colon, genitals, and rectum. It's generated in the body by exhalation and flows downward toward the rectum and out of the body, ridding the body of impurities. It manifests through the Saturn *chakra*.

➤ *Samana* (pronounced sah-MAH-nah) governs the digestive system, including the stomach, intestine, liver, and pancreas. It manifests through the Mars *chakra*.

➤ *Udana* (pronounced uh-DAH-nah) lives in the throat and controls swallowing. It also serves as the force dividing the astral body (the vehicle of the spirit) from the physical body at the time of death. It's the vital energy of speech, and manifests through the Mercury *chakra*.

➤ *Vyana* (pronounced vee-AH-nah) flows throughout the entire body, regulating blood flow as well as muscle and joint movements. It's the vital energy of circulation and manifests through the Jupiter *chakra*.

Blow Your Mind

Learning breath control isn't difficult, but it takes concentration. There are many exercises to try. Following are a few techniques. Experiment with each and consider incorporating a few of them into your yoga workout.

OM Exhalation

This technique extends the breath, softens it, and makes quieting the mind easier. Soon you'll feel a oneness drawing you closer to *samadhi*.

➤ Sit in a meditative posture. Close your eyes.

➤ Inhale deeply, taking the breath to the root of spine.

➤ Open your lips and begin to make the OM sound while exhaling slowly.

➤ Envelop your being in the sound.

➤ Spend approximately 30 seconds on the O sound of OM and about 10 seconds on the M sound.

➤ Continue this process several times.

Ujjayi: Drawing Breath

Jaya means "success on the spiritual path," and *ujjayi* means "she who is victorious." The *ujjayi* technique (pronounced oo-JAH-yee) aids in recalling and working with your dreams. It is also cooling to the head, aids digestion, soothes nerves, and tones the body. This breathing exercise produces sound in the throat with the inhalation.

A Yoga Minute
We inhale oxygen and exhale carbon dioxide. Trees and plants inhale carbon dioxide and exhale oxygen. Perfect harmony!

➤ Inhale slowly, keeping the lips closed and closing off the *glottis,* which is the opening between the vocal chords. A soft, humming sound happens, kind of like "hahhhhhhh." You should hear a distinct sound—think "Darth Vader" breathing.

➤ Inhale to the heart. The upper portion of the lungs are used fully. You should feel the passage of the exhale, and you should hear it from the roof of your mouth.

Bhastrika: Bellows Breath

Bhastrika (pronounced bah-STREE-kah) is a powerful technique. Progress with it slowly to make the foundation strong. The bellows breath brings heat to the body and is excellent for weight reduction. It clears energy, purifies the physical body, and opens up restrictions in the spine, permitting a freer energy flow.

(1) The diaphragm muscle pulls the navel in as you exhale deeply and sharply. Breathe rapidly through your nose by forcing air out with sharp movements of your diaphragm (the large muscle at the base of your thoracic cavity which helps to control the breath). Don't hold your breath between breaths. Aim for deep, quick movements of the diaphragm muscle. Soon the inhalation will take little effort as it becomes more of a reflex to the exhalation.

(2) Place your middle and forefingers together and straight under your nostrils (keep a tissue nearby!). You should feel air against your fingers, with full force.

(3) Do 10 cycles, then hold your breath for a few seconds.

(4) Repeat as many times as possible. If the strength of your exhalation begins to weaken, reduce the amount of breaths in a cycle.

Kapalabhati (pronounced KAH-pah-lah-BAH-tee), or skull shining, is the same as the bellows breath, with two exceptions: Inhale slowly and exhale strongly; hold the breath for a few seconds after each exhalation. Skull shining is often done as a preliminary exercise to the bellows breath and has similar benefits. Since the skull consists of sinus passages, this technique is called skull shining because it shines or clears the sinuses. It is also said to make your nose prettier!

Shitali: Cooling Breath

Shitali (pronounced shee-TAH-lee) is great for summer! This technique is healing to the body and cools it from excessive heat. It clears the eyes and ears, satisfies hunger and thirst, activates the liver, and improves digestion. *Shitali* involves rolling the tongue, then inhaling through it like a straw.

➤ Roll your tongue into a tube and keep the tip of it slightly outside the mouth. (If you can't roll your tongue, just try to raise the sides as well as you can, or just stick it out!)

➤ Draw in the breath through the curled tongue as if you're sipping through a straw. Fill your lungs.

➤ When your lungs are full, bring your tongue into your mouth and close your mouth.

➤ Lower your chin slightly and retain the breath for a few seconds.

A Yoga Minute
Although tongue rolling has always been considered a simple, inherited genetic trait, recent evidence suggests otherwise. Identical twins' abilities to roll their tongues have been demonstrated to be discordant in a significant number of cases, and a few people who couldn't roll their tongues have actually been able to learn how. In general, however, tongue rolling is easy for some and virtually impossible for others.

Bhramari: Bee Breath

Bhramari (pronounced brah-MAH-ree) is good for insomnia. It imitates the sound of a bee and literally means "she who roams" (as a bee roams). Energetically, it helps awaken *kundalini* energy.

➤ You'll hear the soft, humming sound of a bee with this technique. Close off your right nostril with your right thumb. Inhale through your left nostril.

➤ Fill your lungs, close your nostrils, and retain the breath for a few seconds.

➤ Slowly exhale through the left nostril using your throat to make a soft "eeee" sound through your exhalation.

A Yoga Minute
Adults breathe an average of 16,000 quarts of air each day. According to yogic thought, your life is measured by breaths, so lengthening each breath lengthens your life.

➤ Keep the exhalation going as long as possible. Alternate nostrils. Gradually intensify the breath and increase the sound of the "eeee" (the bee is getting closer!).

Nadi Shodhana: Alternate Nostril Breathing

Nadi shodhana (pronounced NAH-dee shoh-DAH-nah) balances the male/female or *ha/tha* within. This means it balances the emotional and physical natures. For example, when your emotions become overwhelming, this technique brings you back to a balanced state. Gradually, the amount of time when both nostrils are closed should increase comfortably. Keep your finger movement to a minimum.

Finger position for nadi shodhana.

(1) Cover your right nostril with your right thumb.

(2) Inhale through your left nostril.

(3) Close your left nostril with the ring finger of your right hand. Your two middle fingers should be turned in toward your palm.

(4) Hold both nostrils closed for as long as you can, comfortably. Then, exhale through your right nostril.

(5) Inhale through your right nostril, then close it.

(6) Hold both nostrils closed for as long as you can, comfortably. Then, exhale through your left nostril.

(7) Inhale through your left nostril, close, exhale through your right nostril, and so on.

Breathing Postures

You can practice breathing exercises just about anywhere, but they'll be more productive if you practice them in certain positions. The bellows breath will work better when your spine is aligned and your lungs are able to expand to their maximum, not when you're slumped over in a chair watching television. Luckily, you have your choice of meditative postures to choose from in Chapter 17.

The Least You Need to Know

> ➤ *Prana* is the universal life force that permeates and animates everything, including you.

> ➤ *Prana* flows into the body via the breath, so controlling the breath controls the flow of *prana*.

> ➤ *Pranayama* are breathing techniques that, when practiced, result in better control of the mind and body.

> ➤ Breathing exercises can be practiced anywhere.

Ouch!
Just as you shouldn't push your body to achieve a difficult posture before it's ready, you also need to be aware of your breath capacity. Don't practice one-minute inhalations and two-minute exhalations your first time out! You may faint or hyperventilate. As always, listen to your body. It will tell you when you're going too far. Remember to go slowly.

Hatha Yoga: May the Force Be with You

Hatha Yoga is a yoga system that emphasizes the physical as a means to self-actualization, but the physical is more than strength and flexibility—it's control and purification, too. In fact, purification is key in *Hatha Yoga,* which develops the physical body in three ways: through cleansing rituals, *shodhana;* postures, *asanas;* and breathing techniques, *pranayama.* All three aspects of *Hatha Yoga* involve purification to some degree.

Know Thyself

Self-awareness means different things to different people, but here are some ways to look at self-awareness. Self-awareness is:

➤ Finding out that the alignment of your large toe is responsible for your headache.

➤ Pausing before your emotions take over your actions.

➤ Feeling truly connected to another living thing.

➤ Breathing deeply and slowly.

➤ Looking in the mirror and seeing beyond your reflection.

➤ Having vision and direction in your life.

➤ Recognizing that the sun salutation (see Chapter 16) is reflective of the ebb and flow of life.

➤ Finding the clear steadiness of the eyes in an externally changing face.

➤ Experiencing pure joy simply by looking at something beautiful.

➤ Finding inner peace.

When the body is strong, controlled, and purified, *kundalini* energy can move freely up the spine and through the *chakras* without getting blocked anywhere along the way. If *kundalini* energy gets blocked, both physical and mental problems could result. The body that's physically prepared for the rise of *kundalini* energy will derive the ultimate benefit from its power. *Hatha Yoga* is that physical preparation.

Joining the Sun and the Moon

Hatha Yoga is about balancing the opposing forces of the body, just as opposing forces are balanced outside of the body. Sun and moon, male and female, day and night, cold and hot—the universe is filled with opposites. Our bodies, too, are filled with opposites, and if these forces become unbalanced, our bodies and minds won't work as efficiently. *Hatha Yoga* balances us in many ways. Forward-bending postures are followed by back-bending postures, contractions are followed by extensions, upright positions are followed by inversions, and so on.

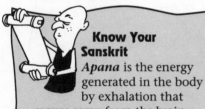

Know Your Sanskrit

Apana is the energy generated in the body by exhalation that moves away from the brain and carries impurities out of the body. *Bandha* means "to bind" or "to lock," and *bandhas* are muscular locks used during postures and breathing exercises to intensify the energy of *prana* and *apana* so it can eliminate impurities from the body. The three primary *bandhas* are anal (*mula bandha*), stomach (*uddiyani bandha*), and chin (*jalandhara bandha*).

Even the movement of *prana* is balanced through muscular exercises or *bandhas*. As *prana* is drawn into the body through the inhalation of breath, *apana* is the energy generated in the body by exhalation that moves away from the brain and carries impurities out of the body. *Bandhas* are exercises designed to lock the flow of energy in the body at the chin, to arrest *prana's* upward movement, and, in the pelvis, to arrest *apana's* downward movement.

The result is that *prana* and *apana* are retained within the body, joining together within *sushumna*, that hollow passageway through your spinal cord. Their mingling generates an intense energy that can help awaken the *kundalini* serpent power. This joining of opposites, of *prana* and *apana*, of sun and moon, of *ha* and *tha*, is at the heart of *Hatha Yoga's* power.

Most Westerners don't practice *Hatha Yoga* to the extent that they're even aware of the importance of *kundalini* energy, but traditionally, this awakening of the "serpent power" is the purpose of *Hatha Yoga.* Physical fitness—making the body beautiful—has traditionally been a peripheral benefit, but it has shifted to the primary focus for Westerners. Fitness is important in *Hatha Yoga,* but it means more than cut shoulders and washboard abs. Total fitness—of the mind, body, and spirit—is a far cry from body obsession.

If fitness is your goal, it doesn't hurt (and may even be ultimately helpful) to be aware of the power of balanced opposites inherent in your practice. It may steer you away from the path of body glorification—a possible side effect of heightened body awareness—and toward the more advanced paths of mental control (*Raja Yoga*) and spiritual awakening.

A Yoga Minute
In Hindu culture, cobras are considered reincarnations of important people. The Aztecs worshipped a snake god who symbolized light, luck, and wisdom. In Africa, some cultures worship pythons, and killing snakes is a crime. Egyptian kings wore snake representations on their crowns, and the crosier of Asklepios, the Greek god of medicine, is still a symbol of the medical profession.

Hatha Yoga *joins the opposites of sun and moon within the body. Here, the energies are drawn into the centered position of respect and thanks,* namaste, *or prayer pose.*

77

Training the Body to Free the Mind

Think how much time you spend worrying about your body! Check all the following statements that have ever crossed your mind:

- ❏ I'm too fat.
- ❏ I'm too thin.
- ❏ I'm having a bad hair day.
- ❏ My skin looks terrible.
- ❏ My body is unattractive.
- ❏ I have the best body in the room.

Our bodies are so much a part of us and so emphasized by our culture that it's extremely difficult not to put too much emphasis on physical appearance. Remember, though, that your body isn't all of you. In fact, your body is just one tiny part of you. You are the entire universe. You have the potential for perfection, contentment, and pure joy. Your body is just a convenient container for the glowing, spinning, luminous being that is you. In comparison to who you really are, even the most "perfect" body is a little, well...crude?

Wise Yogi Tells Us

Once you're comfortable in some of the postures, try adding a new dimension to your workout. Visualization is the process of picturing something beautiful—the ocean, a sparkling lake, a magnificent canyon, a spectacular sunset—whatever image makes you feel peaceful. Practice visualization while holding postures that are easy for you. Try holding onto this image for as long as you can before other thoughts take over.

You have one body, or do you? Actually, according to yoga, you have three bodies—the physical body, the astral body, and the causal body. These three bodies can function separately, but they are intimately interrelated, too. Maintaining an awareness of all three of your bodies will help you see more clearly who you really are. Self-actualization means knowing your *whole* self.

➤ The physical body is the crudest of the bodies, yet even though it's crude, it's our best tool for growth. We can't deny we have physical bodies, so yoga helps us make the most of them. The first three aspects of Patanjali's Eightfold Path strengthen and train the physical body: abstinences (*yamas*), observances (*niyamas*), and postures (*asanas*). (See Chapter 6.)

➤ The astral body is the vehicle of the spirit and corresponds with the mind. The astral body is strengthened through the next three steps of the Eightfold Path: breathing exercises (*pranayama*), sense withdrawal (*pratyahara*), and concentration (*dharana*). (See Chapter 6.)

➤ The causal body transcends the other bodies. It's the subtlest body and consists of the spirit. Individuality exists to a minimal degree in the causal body, which allows the spirit to shine and truth to be evident. The causal body is reached or experienced through the final two limbs of the Eightfold Path: meditation (*dhyana*) and superconsciousness or bliss (*samadhi*). (See Chapter 6.)

Hatha Yoga works under the assumption that the inner "you" is the "you" worth working on, but to get to the inner "you", the outer "you"—in all its crudity—must first be controlled. *Hatha Yoga* works to get the body under control so it doesn't block *you* from emerging in your full glory. It accomplishes this Herculean task by building strength and toning the organs and joints through exercises, by training the breath, and by keeping the body clean.

But the body isn't everything, remember. Control of the body and breath are *Hatha Yoga's* priorities, but the mind is *Raja Yoga's* territory. In *Raja Yoga,* mental control is the focus. Just as *Hatha Yoga* keeps the body from holding you back from your potential, *Raja Yoga* does the same for the mind, getting it fit and under control so it doesn't get in the way.

Hatha Yoga and *Raja Yoga* exist in a sort of symbiotic relationship. If you've mastered your body and your breath so that *prana* is able to flow freely and un-encumbered through your *chakras,* meditation is the next natural progression. The body is prepared to make meditation easy rather than an encumbrance. Then, successful meditation prepares the mind to stand back and let the spirit shine through.

> **Know Your Sanskrit**
> *Koshas* (pronounced KOH-shahs) are the five sheaths of existence that make up the body: the physical body, the vital body, the mind sheath, the intellect sheath, and the sheath of bliss.

Speaking of the body, don't believe for a minute that you see all of you when you look in the mirror. To put your physical appearance into perspective, consider that what you see is only one of five "envelopes" or sheaths of existence, *koshas,* that surround the embodied being.

The Physical

➤ The physical body, *anna-maya-kosha* (pronounced AH-nah MAI-ah KOH-shah) or "food envelope," consists of your material body.

➤ The vital body, *prana-maya-kosha* (pronounced PRAH-nah), is where *prana* lives and moves.

The Emotional or Astral

➤ The mind sheath, *mano-maya-kosha* (pronounced MAH-noh), is the seat of the part of your mind that interprets all sensory input. "I have an awareness of an emotion."

➤ The intellect sheath, *vijnana-maya-kosha* (pronounced vizh-NAH-nah), houses your intelligence and wisdom. "I am aware that I am more than my emotions."

The Causal (Where Everything Starts)

➤ The bliss sheath, *ananda-maya-kosha* (pronounced ah-NAHN-dah), contains the field of energy that links you with the universe and in which all is bliss.

Did you have any idea you were walking around with all those layers?

Physical Cleansing

But what's all this about keeping the body clean? You take showers. You wash your hair. You use deodorant. You don't smell bad. Isn't that enough? Not to the yogi! Of course, nothing should become an obsession, but to Hindu culture, where yoga has its roots, the body is impure and needs some serious hygienic uptake to keep it from becoming a hindrance to the spirit.

> **Know Your Sanskrit**
>
> *Shat kriyas* (pronounced SHOT-Kree-yahs) are the purification rituals of *Hatha Yoga*. *Shodhana* (pronounced sho-DAH-nah) is purification of the body.

This cleanliness is called *shodhana* and consists of cleansing rituals, *shat kriyas,* for the body. *Hatha Yoga* also concerns strict observance of dental hygiene. Yogis not only brush their teeth, but rinse their mouths, massage their gums, and scrape their tongues to keep them clean. And don't forget to visit your dentist every six months!

Read on and you'll find out about some of the *shat kriyas.*

Sthala Basti (Ground Colon Cleansing): Elimination Illumination!

Let's start at the bottom. This ritual helps relieve gas and keeps the bowels moving smoothly. It also improves the digestion and gives your body a lighter feel.

Sit with your legs stretched out in front of you. Grab your toes, right toe with your right hand, left toe with your left hand. Bend forward, bringing your head toward your knees just a little, so that it feels comfortable. Relax the abdominal muscles, then churn them up and down. While churning your muscles, "lock" your anus (called *mula bandha*). Be very careful not to push yourself too hard. This ritual should feel comfortable. Practice this ritual on an empty stomach, or drink a glass of pure water first.

Agnisara Dhauti (Fire Stomach Cleansing): Tummy Toner

This ritual is called fire stomach cleansing because it stokes the gastric fire and improves digestion. It helps keep the bowels healthy, cures constipation, and reduces belly fat. If you have abdominal problems or circulatory problems, you should avoid this cleansing ritual.

Perform this ritual by squatting just slightly from a standing position with your legs about one foot apart or slightly more. Exhale fully, then hold your breath. Next, perform the muscle churning described in the above ritual, but with the stomach muscles, moving them in more of a circular motion than an up-and-down motion. Rotate the muscles in this way as quickly as you can for as long as you can without discomfort. Work up to 100 or so churning rotations of the stomach muscles, but don't push to the point where you become exhausted. After the muscle churning, relax and let the breath flow in and out. This makes one round. Work up to several rounds, but not more than five.

If all these cleansing rituals seem like a little much to you, keep in mind that they are ancient Hindu practices based in a culture that considers the body ultimately earthy. Practice good hygiene to the degree that makes you comfortable.

Kapalabhati: Blow Off Some Steam

Kapalabhati (pronounced KAH-pah-lah-BAH-tee) is both a cleansing ritual and a breathing exercise (see a more detailed description in the previous chapter) meant to cleanse the respiratory passages and lungs. It is often included as a part of *pranayama* practice. This cleansing breath clears the sinuses, improves circulation, and charges your bloodstream with oxygen. It's said to increase longevity and prepare the body for the practice of *pranayama*.

Neti: Bless You!

Neti (pronounced NAY-tee) involves various methods for cleansing the nasal passages. One method is to sniff water into the nostrils and spit it out of the mouth, called *vuyt-krama* (pronounced VOOT KRAY-mah) (but please don't drown yourself!). The water should be neither hot nor cold. You can also buy *neti* bottles, specially made to pour water into one nostril, which will then come out the other nostril. We prefer to simply blow our noses when necessary, and suggest this might be the best course for you, too.

Trataka: Seeing the Light

Trataka (pronounced trah-TAH-kah) cleanses the eyes by focusing them on a candle flame until they water. Don't bring your eyes too close to the candle. A distance of two feet or more works well. The eyes are then washed with cold water. *Trataka* is said to strengthen the eyes and, in some cases, induce *clairvoyance*.

Stabilizing the Body's Energies

You may be anxious to hear a little more about that aspect of *Hatha Yoga* many Westerners consider the most interesting. Yes, the *asanas* are also important to the practice of *Hatha Yoga,* but not because yoga's purpose is to make you look great in a bathing suit or allow you to flaunt your flexibility.

✳ Ouch!
Perform each cleansing ritual in the spirit of loving devotion, always keeping non-violence (*ahimsa*) in mind.

In fact, even as we say that *Hatha Yoga's* emphasis is on the physical, we really mean *Hatha Yoga* emphasizes the physical in order to, eventually, *de*-emphasize the physical. Once you've mastered control of your body—once you're strong, flexible, and "master of your domain"—then you can forget about your body!

Because yoga's goal is to attain oneness with the universe—*samadhi*—and because in this state, the self, including the body, virtually disappears, all that body work is really just a way to learn how to transcend your body! And that will make your yoga journey easier. Think of it this way: All your life, you've wanted to live in Florida, or Alaska, or California, or wherever. But you live on the opposite side of the country. Finally, you're ready to start your big move, so you purchase a really nice car for your journey. As you drive across the country, you do everything you can to keep your car in top condition so you won't have any breakdowns or mechanical failures. Sure enough, you get there without a hitch!

Hatha Yoga is the same way. The idea is not the car, or the body, but the destination, and finding joy along the way. You want to get to Florida, and you know the best way to get there is to have a vehicle in great condition. Keep your body in great condition and your yoga journey won't be plagued with obstacles. And you'll be less likely to wind up in the shop for repairs! (In other words, at the doctor's office.)

Achieving Vitality

Pranayama is the final, crucial aspect of *Hatha Yoga* all yogis will do well to practice. We've spent the last chapter talking about *pranayama* in detail, so we'll just say a few more words here about *prana* and vitality.

Prana is vitality. Mastering *prana,* both physical and mental, is probably the single most important aspect of *Hatha Yoga. Prana* powers the universe with its energy, and it's the profound connection between you and everything else. Amazingly, something so simple as a breathing technique is the first step to becoming aware of the movement of *prana* through your body and throughout the universe. Even though *prana* can't be measured or observed, it can certainly be sensed by the yogi tuned in to its power. Wise yogis and others throughout history perceive *prana* on an intuitive level; those who use it will be astonished at its power. Try a little *prana* today, and you, too, will be on your way to greater awareness. *Prana* happens!

The Least You Need to Know

➤ *Hatha Yoga* is a balance of opposing forces.

➤ A trained body won't get in the way of spiritual enlightenment and can even encourage it.

➤ Cleanliness is next to enlightenment.

➤ *Prana* is in you, animates you, and flows through the universe.

Part 3
Starting Your Yoga Practice

Here's your comprehensive guide to getting started. You'll learn how to find a yoga class and a good teacher, how to practice on your own at home, what to wear, when to practice, and how to fit yoga into your busy schedule. You'll also find tips for changing the way you think about exercise, from banishing the "no pain, no gain" adage from your mentality to learning how your breath can enhance your workout.

You'll also have a chance to examine your own motives and reasons for considering yoga. An "Essay Test You Can't Fail" will help to direct your thinking inward and allow you to better analyze your own strengths and tendencies. Knowing your own body and mind will help you to craft a yoga routine that will work best for you.

Chapter 9

Where Do You Practice Yoga?

In This Chapter

➤ Choosing a yoga class

➤ Finding the right teacher

➤ Doing yoga on your own

➤ Yoga from books, tapes, and the Internet

➤ Visiting India

So you've decided to give yoga a try. Great! Now what? Now is the time to make a game plan. Decide how you would like to proceed with your yoga. Do you want to take a class and reap the benefits of a qualified instructor? Do you want to try yoga on your own for awhile, then consider a class later if you like what you experience? Maybe you want to go all out and book passage to Calcutta! Whatever course you choose to take, make sure you have the necessary preparation so you can get the most from your yoga experience. Your personality, your schedule, and your general inclinations will all have an effect on the type of yoga that will serve you most effectively.

Choosing a Yoga Class

Probably the best way to start out with yoga is to take a class. You can learn a lot from books and videos, but a real live teacher can address your personal challenges and direct you in ways a book can't. (But don't stop reading this book yet! We still have a lot left to tell you.) Consider the following reasons to take a yoga class:

➤ A teacher can see you from all angles, making minor adjustments in your postures to help you get the most from each position.

➤ A teacher can advise you on the best postures for your particular physical challenges, such as a stiff neck, lower back pain, or tennis elbow.

➤ If you have a class to attend at a pre-scheduled time, you may be less likely to put off or skip your practice. And regular exercise is the most beneficial for anyone.

➤ Other students learning yoga along with you can offer peer support and camaraderie, in addition to your teacher's encouragement.

➤ A class and a qualified teacher in conjunction with personal practice and lots of books on the subject will teach you more about yoga than any one of these methods alone.

Yoga classes vary greatly in their format and approach, so if you do decide to take a class, you'll first want to do a bit of shopping. The right yoga class is highly personal—what *you* love, your friends may not benefit from at all, and vice versa. If you are used to a high-energy, aerobic workout, you may initially be impatient with yoga's slower pace, although it will serve as an excellent balance for your life. If you're generally inactive, you may benefit more from a yoga class where steady, flowing yoga movements get the heart pumping.

You also might be confused about the wide array of yoga methods. The difference is largely due to who has most directly influenced the teacher or under which method the teacher was trained. Before signing up for a class, ask the teacher which school of yoga he or she practices, and then ask him or her to explain the basic philosophy of that particular school or method.

Make sure any yoga class you consider meets the following criteria:

➤ The yoga teacher is a qualified instructor. Anyone can teach yoga—not everyone can teach it well. Don't be fooled by health clubs touting "yoga" classes taught by club employees who might have read a book on yoga or who think all fitness is basically the same. Some health clubs offer excellent yoga classes, but you'll want to ask about the teacher's training.

➤ The class is small enough that the teacher can give you individual attention. You'll want help adjusting postures and creating a routine suited to your ability so you don't get injured or frustrated or bored silly.

➤ The class is conveniently scheduled and easy to get to. Otherwise, you know what will happen. Eventually, going to class will be too much trouble and it won't last.

If you don't like your first class, your first teacher, or the way you felt after your first yoga workout, don't give up. Some people overdo it their first time out and vow never to practice yoga again. If you can't relate to your teacher, if you pull a muscle, or if the class environment is high-pressure, competitive, or unpleasant in any way, you just haven't found the right class or the right teacher. Or maybe you weren't completely open to the experience—could your competitive nature have overshadowed the benefits you were receiving? Was the teacher encouraging a competitive attitude, or was the teacher inattentive to your needs? Maybe you couldn't understand what the teacher wanted you to do. (Teachers are human, too.) Many teachers are grounded in the non-competitive philosophy, but some still see yoga simply as physical fitness, with all its competitive aspects. Many are excellent at doling out individual help and counsel, but others may have classes that are too large for a really personal approach.

The most important thing you can do for your yoga practice is to find a teacher you feel comfortable with, so keep looking until you find him or her. And remember what you have learned so far: Yoga is about fitness for and knowledge of your whole self, not just your body.

The bottom line? Be patient in your search. It may take awhile to find the right class and the right teacher for you, but many yogis believe that when the student is ready, the right teacher will appear. Keep your mind and heart open.

Reflective Pose.

Wise Yogi Tells Us

Having trouble finding a yoga class? Try the following sources:

➤ A natural foods/health store

➤ A health club or fitness center

➤ Your local hospital

➤ Your local university, college, or community college

➤ Local holistic health practitioners

Finding Your Personal Guru

You've heard the word, we're sure, but you may be confused as to what a *guru* actually is. Literally, the word means "dispeller of darkness," and that is the *guru's* role: to help you dispel your own spiritual darkness. A *guru*-disciple relationship between mature individuals is really a journey of spiritual revelations and discoveries for both disciple and *guru*. The *guru's* "job" is to give you spiritual guidance and insight, and to insist that you think for yourself. In fact, it is essential that a disciple have the freedom to follow or not follow that guidance. A good disciple will travel toward spiritual independence, but a *guru* makes a great travelling companion with an excellent road map, to get you well on your way.

The concept of the *guru* is a little hard for us Westerners to swallow. After all, we like to be self-sufficient. We aren't a submissive, follow-the-leader type of culture and the idea that we should surrender to a superior, putting our physical, mental, and spiritual development in his or her hands, makes us uncomfortable. This isn't a difficult concept for many Easterners, whose culture has taught them, over the course of centuries, that the best way to truly learn anything—a craft, a posture, a philosophy, enlightenment—is by loyal devotion to a wise individual who has sage advice and knowledge to impart.

Know Your Sanskrit

Acarya (pronounced ah-CAHR-yah) means "teacher." *Buddhi* (pronounced BOO-dee) means "intellect."

We Westerners like to question, and our doubting natures are only encouraged when we hear story after story about spiritual teachers and leaders who have gone astray. Our modern world is full of temptations, and sometimes *gurus*, priests, evangelists, healers, and others whose purpose is to lead others to a higher spiritual plane cave in to temptation. A true, enlightened *guru* will remain your spiritual guide for a lifetime, but these days, good *gurus* are hard to find! (And many a *guru* will counter that good students are equally hard to find!)

But you may not need a *guru*—at least not in the traditional sense. For some, a *guru* is a crucial part of the yoga journey, but for others, a teacher is the perfect guide. A qualified yoga teacher with whom you truly connect can be your most valuable resource. A great yoga teacher can change your life and improve your practice of yoga far beyond what you could figure out on your own.

Most importantly, don't be discouraged if you haven't found the *acarya* or *guru* who is right for you. Be patient, keep your eyes open, keep practicing, don't be afraid to be picky, don't put up with mediocre instruction or a teacher who doesn't understand you, and eventually, you'll find the perfect fit.

Going Solo at Home

If you aren't quite ready for the commitment of a class, or if for any other reasons you don't want to or aren't able to take a class, do-it-yourself yoga can be very rewarding. Design your own workout from the poses in this book (see Chapter 12), find a comfortable practice area, dress in comfortable clothing (see Chapter 10), designate a regular practice time—whether once a week or twice a day—and get ready for your very first *asana!*

Setting Up Your Practice Area

One of the great things about yoga is that you can do it almost anywhere—in the bedroom, in the living room, even outside! Your environment should consistently include several things, however:

➤ A soft surface. Non-skid carpets are good surfaces for practicing yoga, but if your floor isn't carpeted or is slippery, use a small rug, a blanket, or a yoga mat, which is a thin rubber mat that can be placed on any surface for a comfortable, non-skid surface. You need the firmness of the ground, but the surface on which you work should be soft enough to be comfortable, too. If you practice outside, bring along a blanket or mat that can get a little dirty.

➤ A source of warmth. In summer, you probably won't have to worry about keeping warm, but in the winter or in a drafty room, warmth can be an issue. Keep a blanket nearby to drape around yourself during still poses, breathing exercises, and meditation. Your muscles need to be warm to stay flexible, and you also need to be comfortable to get the most from your practice. Practicing outside in the sun on a warm day is ideal. If you practice inside in the winter, consider a small electric heater for your practice area.

➤ Fresh air. If you practice inside and weather permits, open a window and take a few deep breaths of fresh air before you start. Practicing outside will, of course, immerse you in fresh air (unless you live in a polluted environment, in which case you are probably better off practicing inside). If the weather doesn't permit—if it's too cold or too hot outside—don't worry about the fresh air. You'll get some when the temperature is milder.

> **✳ Ouch!**
> Keeping warm while practicing yoga is extremely important. If your muscles are cold, they can stiffen and lose flexibility, increasing your chance of injury. Warm muscles and joints are most conducive to a yoga workout. Also, in quieter poses and during meditation, you'll become colder more easily because you aren't moving.

Practice in an area free of obstacles and distractions. Practicing yoga amidst clutter and confusion is difficult and even counter-productive. As we've mentioned before, cleanliness is important to yoga, and that includes an uncluttered and clean environment. Although a seasoned yogi can find a sense of serenity in any setting—even your family room where your teenager is playing video games and your twin toddlers are practicing for a career in large-building demolition—you may not be able to focus quite as well as you would in a quiet room, all by yourself.

Even if the rest of your house is a perpetual disaster area, try to keep one special "yoga spot" clear, clean, pet-free, kid-free, and relatively quiet. Before you know it, the rest of your house will "magically" become less cluttered and more simply furnished. It's yet another positive influence yoga can have on your lifestyle.

> **Wise Yogi Tells Us**
> When practicing postures at home on your own, it may help to keep in mind the following five steps to every pose:
>
> ➤ Visualize your body holding the pose.
> ➤ Gracefully flow into the pose.
> ➤ Become one with the pose—find the peace and balance.
> ➤ Gracefully flow out of the pose.
> ➤ Reflect and release. Let go. Feel the silence.

Yoga from Tapes and Videos

Another great way to learn yoga—the next best thing to a real, live teacher—is a yoga videotape or audiotape. With a tape, you can see (or at least hear) a teacher. You can watch the postures performed or hear them described, which can be easier to follow than a static picture in a book. The teacher on the tape can offer advice and wisdom vocally. Some people comprehend information better if they see or hear it than if they read it, while others benefit much more from the written word.

If your teacher has made tapes or videos, you can use them to extend your in-person yoga practice by taking your teacher home with you via electronic media. Taking advantage of all possible levels of study will result in more learning opportunities.

Wise Yogi Tells Us

No matter how different we are from each other, we all have one very important and illustrious quality in common: We're all human! Keep in mind the following six universal laws for being human.

➤ You will be given a body.

➤ You will be taught lessons.

➤ There are no mistakes in life, only lessons.

➤ If a lesson is not learned, it gets repeated.

➤ The more often a lesson is repeated, the harder it gets.

➤ You know you've learned your lesson when your actions change.

One advantage of the audiotape over the videotape is that your focus won't be glued on the television, but can be directed inward instead. Only your hearing will guide you, so although figuring out how to do a posture may be more difficult, many simpler postures, and especially breathing and meditation work, are perfect for the audiotape medium.

Whichever method is most helpful to you is the one you should pursue. Don't worry about what anyone else does. This is *your* yoga. A visit to your local library, video store, or bookstore will probably reveal a wealth of available videos and audiotapes you can borrow, rent, or buy. Try the library and the video store first. This way, you can sample a variety of yoga teachers and programs without committing. Once you've found a few you like, consider buying the tapes for your personal collection. Then, whenever the desire strikes—2:00 a.m. on a Tuesday, 11:00 p.m. on a Friday—you can do yoga!

Yoga from Books

We hope you don't have the impression that you *can't* learn yoga from a book. For some, it's the only way! Remember *svadhyaya,* the *niyama* that encourages self-inquiry? Reading books on yoga and practicing from a book are all part of this observance, which helps you to understand yourself. Many excellent books on yoga exist, illustrating thousands of postures, breathing techniques, and meditation techniques. Books allow you to learn a broader spectrum of information than a teacher alone will probably be able to convey. Plus, you can go to the library and come home with 10 or 12 different books on yoga— much easier than sampling 10 or 12 different teachers!

Books cover yoga in a variety of ways, from an array of suggested workouts to the history of yoga to essays on spirituality to suggestions for daily yoga-friendly living. It's impor- tant to spend time reading, studying, and filling your mind with the types of ideas and concepts that inspire you. If you study a posture on the written level, your mind will understand it in a different way, and the body may even find it easier to follow. We can't always be movin' and shakin'!

A Yoga Minute
The world is full of wise yogis—even celebrities! The following celebrities have all practiced yoga: Jane Fonda, Helen Hunt, Karen Allen, Sting, Quincy Jones, Ali McGraw, Woody Harrelson, Ruth Buzzi, Tom Smothers, Carol Lynley, Justine Bateman, Jeff Bridges, John Saxon, Maud Adams, Herbie Hancock, Sarah Miles, and Dixie Carter.

If you thrive on reading, read to your heart's content—but don't *just* read. You also need to *act.* Get up and try what the book suggests. Following the postures from a picture and some text might be challenging at first, but once you find the posture, it will feel right, and pretty soon, you'll have your sequence of poses memorized.

But don't stop there! The more you learn about yoga, the wiser you'll be. Find books with more *asanas* you haven't tried yet. Check out the Bhagavad Gita. Find a teacher whose views make sense to you, and read everything you can by her and about him/her. You may find that as your life changes, your yoga goals and interests change and grow. Just go back to the library or the bookstore and find another book more in keeping with your developing state of mind. And always maintain a balance between reading and doing, doing and reading. Mind, body. Body, mind.

What better first book than the one you have in your hands! We hope this book is piquing your interest and that you have begun your yoga journey with us. After you've mastered this book, you won't feel like a "complete idiot" about yoga (even though you never *were,* as we explained in Chapter 1). You'll be able to progress in your yoga practice with confidence and aplomb.

Yoga on the Net

For all you computer-heads and Internet lovers out there, despair not! The Internet is brimming with great yoga resources, from class information to "postures of the week" to peer support to spiritual guidance and inspiration. Of course, you always want to be careful whom you are talking to and where you are sending your money—use your common sense, then start surfing for yoga sites! Keep in mind that these sites do frequently change, as do their addresses. Here are a few to check out:

➤ "YOYOGA! With Joan" is Joan's (yes, the Joan co-authoring these very words!) marvelous yoga site with *asanas* of the week, yoga tips, and other wonderful wisdom, including the ever-popular "Yo Joan!" forum for all your yoga questions. Look up Joan at http://www.yoyoga.com.

➤ The Yoga Research Center homepage is a great site with information on the center and its activities, lots of great yoga-related articles, and links to other yoga-relevant sites. Find it at http://www.members.aol.com/yogaresrch/index.htm.

➤ Yoga Internet Resources is a great guide to yoga on the Net with tons of fantastic links. Check it out and start surfin': http://www.tiac.net/users/mgold/www/yoga.html.

➤ Yoga Community Newsletter is a printed monthly newsletter's on-line version, self-described as "dedicated to co-creating a healing community aligned with spirit, aligned with the resonation of unity and unconditional acceptance of all paths and all voices." Includes an *asana* of the month and even poetry. Look it up at http://www.members.tripod.com/~evarose/YogaCommunity_index.html.

➤ The *Yoga Journal* is probably the most famous yoga magazine, and well worth the read. Browse through it at http://www.yogajournal.com.

➤ *Yoga International* is another excellent and popular yoga magazine. Check out highlights of current issues and back issues at http://www.earthchannel.com/yogaintl/index.htm.

➤ The Spirituality/Yoga/Hinduism homepage has beauty and brains—beautiful art, great graphics, and lots of information. Check it out at http://www.geocities.com/RodeoDrive/1415/index.html.

➤ The entire Bhagavad Gita is on-line for your reading pleasure at http://www.theion.com/articles/gita/gita-contents.htm.

Passage to India

Maybe you're serious about yoga—and we mean *really* serious. If you have the time, the resources, and the desire, you might consider actually venturing across the ocean and visiting yoga's homeland, India. After all, if you want to learn from the masters, shouldn't you go where the masters live?

Well, not necessarily. So many wonderful yoga masters have come to the United States to live and teach that you needn't traverse the ocean to meet or study with them. A trip to India may be more valuable for you if you are interested in exploring yoga's historical context, or if you are simply fascinated with the culture. Of course, India today is far more Westernized than it used to be, and it may not be what you expect. On the other hand, maybe it will meet your every expectation. If you're a traveler at heart and feel your own personal journey would be richly enhanced by the trip, go ahead!

But hold on, hang up the phone, don't call your travel agent just yet. If a trip to India interests you, you'll get the most from it if you spend a good deal of time and effort learning everything possible about yoga right where you are. Once you've learned what your own country can teach you, then you'll have the knowledge, skill, and connections to reap the benefits of a trip to yoga's homeland.

And if the idea of a trip to India doesn't appeal to you? Of course that's fine! You can learn all you need to know right where you are. Wonderful, competent, and qualified yoga teachers exist in virtually every city, and you can practice yoga just as well in your own living room as you can on another continent (probably better!).

The Least You Need to Know

➤ Yoga is best learned from a good teacher in a class environment.

➤ Finding a teacher who is right for your personality is important for successful yoga practice.

➤ Yoga can also be learned at home through books, video and audio cassettes, and the Internet.

➤ Going to India can be a rich, rewarding cultural experience, but you don't need to go there to do yoga.

THAT'S A LITTLE FORMAL.

Y'THINK?

Chapter 10

How to Practice Yoga

In This Chapter

➤ How to dress for yoga

➤ How to wear the right attitude

➤ How to be kind to your body

➤ Gently exploring your limits

➤ Using your breath to boost your workout

Knowing how to practice yoga involves more than knowing how to do the postures. You won't be able to relax very easily in scratchy, stiff clothing that doesn't allow you to move freely. Likewise, the attitude you "wear" can hinder your practice. Learning to suspend your doubts, worries, and fears during your yoga practice is important for progress in your yoga journey. So is understanding when you are pushing yourself too hard, listening to your body to determine what it needs and what it doesn't need, and being prepared for deep breathing by knowing a few basic principles.

Loose Clothing and an Open Mind

You can't practice yoga well unless you're comfortable. The right clothing is important because if you can't move easily, if your clothes are in the way, or if you are in any way unnecessarily distracted—say by a tight waist or stiff fabric—you won't be able to concentrate fully on your yoga postures. There isn't any set yoga "uniform," but consider the following points when deciding what to wear for your workout:

➤ Your clothes should be loose and flexible, but not baggy. Tight clothes are restricting, and baggy clothes can get in the way of your movements. T-shirts and shorts or leggings, tank tops and biking shorts, or a not-too-baggy sweat suit are all ideal.

➤ Dress for the temperature. If the weather is cold, choose long sleeves and comfortable pants that don't restrict your movement (sweatpants or leggings are both good choices). Remember to keep a blanket nearby in case you get chilly.

➤ Your clothing shouldn't bind anywhere. If you can feel your clothes around your waist or at your ankles or wrists, they are probably too tight. Also, binding clothes will restrict the flow of energy through your body.

➤ You should be able to distinguish the basic shape of your body. Your teacher will need to see how you are holding the postures so he or she can make sure you are doing them correctly. If you are doing yoga on your own, relatively form-fitting clothing will allow you to check your form and alignment in a mirror without trying to imagine how your body looks under that over-sized T-shirt and those baggy pants.

➤ Yoga is best performed in bare feet. The more you practice yoga, the more sensitive and in-tune with your environment you'll become, and that includes your feet! Bare feet learn to hold the floor, balance the body, and participate fully in the alignment and movement of the postures.

➤ Don't forget to remove all metal jewelry before your practice, especially necklaces and bracelets. Yoga is about freeing the flow of energy in your body, and that energy could be disrupted by metal.

➤ Avoid wearing perfume, strongly scented deodorant, or cologne during your yoga practice. It can be unpleasant to others in your yoga class, especially during *pranayama* (breathwork).

➤ And what's the most important thing to wear? An open mind! The most perfect yoga outfit won't do you any good if you aren't mentally prepared. Before every yoga practice, take a few moments of quiet to prepare for your workout. Think about what you are about to do and what you want to accomplish. If you're just getting started, even if you aren't completely convinced yoga can do everything people say it can, willingly suspend your disbelief, just for a little while. An open mind means a body open to new movements and achievements. You may surprise yourself at what you can accomplish when you aren't wasting your energy doubting yourself and your workout.

Wise Yogi Tells Us

If you have long hair, don't forget to tie it back before your yoga practice. There's nothing more distracting than finally achieving a headstand after months of practice, only to get hopelessly tangled in your long and unruly hair!

Are You Kidding? My Body Won't Do That...

Now that you're properly attired, you *look* like a yogi—but do you *feel* like a yogi? Maybe you're reluctant to begin that very first practice because you know you aren't flexible or you're convinced you won't be able to achieve any of the postures you've heard about or seen.

The problem with an attitude of doubt is that it not only undermines your self-confidence, but it implies that you see yoga as a competition. We've said it before, but we can't emphasize enough how important this concept is, especially for competitive and goal-oriented people: Yoga is not a competitive sport! If you can't do the lotus position today, that doesn't matter one iota. Eventually, with regular practice, it will come. And even if it doesn't, it's still not a reflection on your ability as a yogi. You are much more than your body.

If you have a hard time relinquishing your competitive nature, try addressing your inner thoughts with these responses:

➤ Your thought: "I'm much more flexible than that poor guy next to me!"

Your response to yourself: "My body is responding well today."

➤ Your thought: "I'll never be able to do a headstand!"

Your response to yourself: "I'll master this shoulderstand any day now, as long as I keep practicing. Maybe then I'll think about trying to learn the headstand."

➤ Your thought: "I think the teacher likes me best."

Your response to yourself: "I've really found a teacher who understands me and my yoga needs."

➤ Your thought: "At this rate, I'll never be as flexible as that girl in the front."

Your response to yourself: "That girl in front does that posture extremely well. I'll try to visualize how it would feel to hold the posture that way, and maybe my body will understand the posture better."

➤ Your thought: "I look really hot in this new workout gear," or "I look really hot in this muscle shirt and bicycle shorts," followed by, "I wonder if there will be any cute guys/girls in the class."

Your response to yourself: "I feel really good in these clothes. I think they will be great for yoga." (What do you think your yoga class is, anyway—a singles' bar?)

Each posture you try should be a movement you're able to perform. Accept your current level of fitness, and respect it. Also, accept how you feel from day to day. You may be able to do postures one week that you suddenly are unable to achieve the next week. So many factors besides how "in shape" you are determine your ability to achieve a pose. Your mood, your stress level, the time of day, how well you have warmed up, your current feelings about yourself—all these conditions will affect your workout. Each day, find your own movement and level.

Then start at that level, progressing as your body allows. Some days you may move ahead noticeably in your flexibility or strength. On other days, you may feel as if you have regressed. That's natural and the regression will soon correct itself, so don't let it worry you. A good teacher can help you determine how fast you can advance, but you can also listen to your body because it will tell you, too—as long as it isn't being overruled by your ego.

Remember that yoga is about toning down the ego. Your ego is what tells you to try to out-do the girl next to you or to match the picture in the book precisely. Your ego encourages you to try postures that are beyond your current fitness level or to hold postures too long or to try the most difficult version of a posture first. Your ego lets seemingly nonchalant comments slip out of your mouth such as "I could do the lotus pose the first time I tried," or "You found the plow position difficult? That's strange," or even, "I can't believe you could stand on one foot for so much longer than I could!" Let all that go. It doesn't help you. It only holds you back. When your ego acts up ("How come I don't look like that when I do the shoulderstand?"), gently steer your mind in another direction. Remind yourself that this is your journey, and your progress is all that matters. The yoga road has no maximum or minimum speed limit!

No Pain, Supreme Gain

If you've ever participated in any team athletics, whether elementary school kick-ball or professional basketball, you've probably been told by some coach or teacher somewhere along the line that if it doesn't hurt—or isn't, at the very least, mildly unpleasant—then you just aren't working hard enough.

The interesting thing about yoga, and one of its distinctly non-Western qualities, is that it allows you to work incredibly hard without ever feeling pain, discomfort, or even displeasure of any kind. Yoga should be innately enjoyable because:

➤ It doesn't hurt. Causing yourself pain would be to ignore the observance of *ahimsa* (non-violence).

➤ It boosts *all* of you. A successful yoga workout increases self-esteem, along with fitness and awareness.

➤ Yoga purifies your body, mind, and soul. Being clean feels good!

➤ Even at its most serious, yoga is just plain fun!

Yoga should never cause you pain. Pain means violence and injury. Violence and injury mean a setback. Better to move slowly and steadily forward than to jump ahead in leaps and bounds, then fall back bedridden for a month. You'll gain so much more strength, flexibility, sensitivity, and awareness if you are so attuned to your body that you push it to its limit and perhaps just slightly beyond, but never far enough to hurt anything. Respect your body, don't abuse it—it's an integral part of you, after all.

> **Ouch!**
> If you happen to overdo it during your yoga work-out and find yourself in serious pain, do yourself a favor and *go to your health-care provider immediately*! Ignoring the pain won't make it go away, and in some cases, could result in a serious or chronic health problem. Just do it.

Of course, none of us is perfect and in any physical activity, occasionally we all overdo it, especially when we're trying to outdo someone (or even ourselves!). We know you're trying to listen to your body and not be competitive. But just in case, watch out for the following signs you may have injured yourself:

➤ Severe back pain and muscle spasms could be a sign of a back sprain, often caused by a sudden bending of the spine that tears ligaments.

➤ Immediate, acute shoulder pain which gets worse over the course of a few hours may be caused by a tear in the tendons and/or muscles around the shoulder joint. A severe tear may inhibit movement and can be caused by a minor fall on an outstretched hand.

> **A Yoga Minute**
> Surveys of industrialized nations show that over 75% of the population over 45 years of age suffers from lower back pain.

➤ Pain in the knee and an inability to straighten the knee followed by swelling that lasts for two weeks or more may be due to torn cartilage. This can happen when a bent knee is twisted.

➤ Foot pain from standing for excessive amounts of time or over-using the foot can result in a *strain* or *sprain*.

➤ Dizziness can be a sign of low or high blood pressure or blood sugar levels. If you become dizzy, sit down immediately. Check this condition with your doctor.

➤ Headaches can have numerous sources. One reason people get headaches is from insufficient oxygen. *Pranayama!* Breathing exercises may help your headaches, and the stress-reducing aspects of yoga can also be helpful for this common problem.

Of course, the best way to handle an injury is to prevent it. Stay alert to your body. Communicate with your muscles and joints. Be kind to them. Remember *ahimsa* (non-violence)!

Finding the Edge vs. Feeling the Burn

"But if yoga is so easy on your body, how are you supposed to get anywhere?" you may wonder. Well, let's modify that "easy" part. Yoga isn't always easy. Just because you aren't committing violence to your body doesn't mean a yoga workout is akin to a day sunbathing at the beach. On the contrary, yoga can be tough and intensely challenging.

The difference between yoga and other types of exercise is that the challenge and the progression are deeply internal and subtle. Perhaps you've been trying to accomplish a pose in which you bend forward and touch your head to your knees. The first time you try it, you don't even come close. You can barely bend forward without your back causing you pain, so bend your knees and slowly work bringing the head and upper body down. Slowly build so that your back strengthens and you can straighten your knees. Lean into your farthest point in the stretch and hold it. Remember to keep breathing, letting your breath travel through your body and into the pose. Holding the pose won't hurt—not exactly—but you'll definitely feel something. Your muscles may shake a bit and that's okay, as long as you aren't forcing the issue. You may even break a sweat. You're feeling the "edge" of your flexibility, and also, an edge of your awareness. Your muscles are waking up and saying, "Hey! What is it you want us to do? This is weird, but, okay, we'll give it a try." Your mind is waking up, too, and taking notice.

The next time you try this pose, you get a little closer, maybe three or four inches from your knees. The farthest point of the stretch is now a little farther than it was before. You stretch to this point and hold it. Now your muscles have become accustomed to a new "normal" level of flexibility. You find the new edge and test it, not to the point of pain, but just to see where it now lies. Your muscles feel it and so does your mind.

A few weeks, or months, or maybe a lifetime later (how long it takes isn't important because it's not a competition), you lean into the stretch and wow! There it is! Suddenly, your head is resting quite easily on your knees. You've stretched your boundaries and pushed your edge to a new level. At this point, you may simply feel triumphant, but you may also feel an awakening to a new level of awareness. No longer simply proud of yourself, you're now aware of yourself in a new way. Therein lies yoga's power—the physical process breaking into the mental process and lifting the whole of you to higher and higher states of awareness.

Keep in mind that every posture contains an "edge," or a point past which, for today, at least, you can't quite go. This is the point around which you want to linger because it's the source of yoga's power. You'll soon see how productive it is to recognize an edge but not let it define you.

Wise Yogi Tells Us

Your breath has four modes:

➤ Inhalation

➤ Exhalation

➤ Retained breath after inhalation

➤ Retained breath after exhalation

Learning how to use each mode when it is most beneficial will greatly enhance your practice.

Don't Forget to Breathe

And once again, we remind you of your ever-present breath. Although breathing exercises are performed separately from the postures, breathing is also important during the postures. Of course you have to breathe while exercising, but becoming aware of your breath, even breathing in a specific way according to the posture you are holding, will enhance your practice and help your body to work better.

A few breath-savvy concepts to keep in mind while practicing your *asanas:*

➤ Inhalation most often occurs when your chest opens, your limbs extend outward or upward, and your head is up.

➤ Exhalation most often occurs when your chest contracts inward, your limbs move close to your body, your head is down, and your body curls into itself.

➤ Retaining the breath after an inhalation helps stabilize and energize the chest area.

➤ Retaining the breath after an exhalation helps stabilize and energize the abdominal area, and releases toxins from the body.

➤ Forward-bending poses are conducive to exhalation, then retention.

➤ Back-bending poses are conducive to inhalation, then retention.

Ouch!

If, during your workout, you become out-of-breath or fatigued, *stop!* Yoga isn't circuit-training, marathon running, or nonstop anything. Rest is encouraged within a workout—as a transition from one type of posture to another, as a chance to feel the after-effects of a posture, and to maintain awareness. Bodies aren't meant to be exhausted, but to be gently and lovingly improved and maintained.

Breathing deeply and well during exercise keeps a steady supply of oxygen in the blood so muscles can work at their peak. Breathing keeps the mind calm and focused, which will further enhance your workout. And since the breath is the vehicle by which *prana*, the universal life force, enters the body, you'll certainly want to breathe deeply during your workout. *Prana* is the energy that keeps you vibrant and animated. It's the key to a great workout, so get as much into you as possible! Breathe! Breathe! Breathe!

The Least You Need to Know

➤ Wear comfortable clothing during yoga.

➤ Don't be competitive.

➤ Don't force any posture until it hurts, but keep exploring your limits.

➤ If you have any lingering pain, consult a doctor immediately; don't wait for it to become chronic.

➤ Breathe deeply and often!

Chapter 11

When to Practice Yoga

In This Chapter

➤ Making a schedule

➤ How to stick with it

➤ Squeezing yoga into your busy day

➤ How yoga revitalizes you in different ways depending on the time of day

Time, time, time—never enough of it, and it just keeps on passing us by. During the course of our busy lives, it's easy to become overwhelmed by the demands on our time. Family, friends, work, school, home—all require their share. The furnace needs to be repaired, the dishes are dirty, the kids need to be picked up from soccer practice or ballet or the baby-sitter's. You can't neglect time with your spouse, you have to finish the inventory at work, the baby needs some serious cuddling—and has anyone walked the dog, lately?

Or maybe you're a student. You have five papers due in the next month. Calculus has completely eluded you. Seven chemistry problems are due tomorrow, and you're also supposed to have finished *War and Peace* by last week. Your roommate won't turn down the music, the library is closed because of a flood, and it's just starting to thunder, so studying outside isn't an option. You hear a rumor that your history teacher is planning a pop quiz for tomorrow.

And we're suggesting you add some time for yoga?

Yep. And you'll be glad we suggested it, too. You do have time for yoga, even if it doesn't seem like you could possibly track down one spare second. All it takes is a little organization and some creative thinking.

Ouch!
Always practice yoga on an empty stomach. Just before breakfast or dinner is ideal. Digestion will interfere with what yoga is trying to accomplish in your body and a full stomach will make exercise uncomfortable. Your whole body, including your internal organs, should be focused on your practice, not on processing that spaghetti dinner!

Time to get organized! All great accomplishments start with some type of plan. An effective yoga practice has a plan involving two important aspects:

➤ How often will you practice each week?

➤ What will you do during the course of each practice?

The first question depends a lot on your schedule, your motivation, and your desire. Ideally, yoga should be practiced three to six times per week. If you take a class once a week, that counts as a practice. Then, practice on your own using the routine you and your teacher have crafted for you. Or, if you are on your own, set up a specific schedule of yoga days. A regular schedule is the best way to reap yoga's benefits. Yes, even just once a week counts as a regular schedule (but you may soon find that once a week won't be enough, and you'll find more time, and more...).

When planning your weekly yoga schedule, remember that even though yoga isn't harsh on your body, you should still give yourself at least one day every week to rest. Rest is crucial for yoga. The time spent in *asanas* (postures) is balanced by the time spent resting, and it is this rest time when the body heals and replenishes its resources. Or, rest every other day. Survey the following list of suggested yoga schedules, and choose one that fits your life, or modify one to suit you:

➤ Monday, Wednesday, and Friday: Yoga 20 minutes before work.

Tuesday, Thursday, and the weekend: Rest.

➤ Monday through Friday: Yoga for 30 minutes right after work.

Weekend: Rest.

➤ Tuesday and Thursday: Yoga for 15 minutes first thing in the morning (energizing poses) and 15 minutes before bed (relaxing poses).

Weekend: 30 minutes of yoga in the afternoon.

Monday, Wednesday, and Friday: Rest.

➤ Saturday and Sunday: 60 minutes of yoga.

Monday through Friday: Rest.

➤ Saturday: 60 minutes of yoga.

Sunday through Friday: Rest.

Once you've got a schedule, keep it in your head, write it down, post it on the refrigerator—whatever it takes. Then follow your schedule! Remember *tapas*, the *niyama* about self-discipline? Here's a great chance to use it. You'll feel great about yourself if you faithfully stick to your yoga schedule.

Now, what about the schedule for your routine itself? Your teacher can help you to craft the perfect yoga practice for you, taking into consideration any special needs you have or problems you'd like yoga to address (bad knees, allergies, back pain, frazzled nerves). Or, refer to the appendixes of this book for various suggested routines after reading Chapter 12 to more clearly define your own purpose. Don't forget that every yoga practice should include the following:

➤ A warm-up. It's important to get your muscles warm and activated before you start stretching them. Warm-ups help prevent injury and make a wonderful transition from daily life to yoga-mode. A short walk in the fresh air makes a great warm-up because it sends blood to all your muscles and gets those joints moving. (The quality of your walk is more important than the length—use the time to prepare your body and mind.) You can get a similar effect simply by massaging your legs, feet, arms and hands. Work those muscles and joints to get them ready for action. If you're lucky enough to know a massage therapist, a professional massage before (or after!) yoga practice can be most therapeutic. You might also try a warm shower or bath, or a heating pad on stiff areas, to warm your muscles before your workout.

➤ A balanced set of poses. Postures that bend or twist to one side should be balanced with postures that bend or twist to the other side. Forward bends balance back-bends. Right-side-up poses balance inverted poses. Poses that stretch and expand are balanced by poses that curl and contract. Energizing poses balance relaxing poses. You get the idea.

➤ Every yoga workout should conclude with the final relaxation or corpse posture. In this pose, mighty healing takes place—for your body and mind. Don't neglect this pose because you think you don't have time to just lie there. It's probably the most important of all the postures. (See Chapter 19.)

➤ *Pranayama*, or breathing exercises. Remember those breathing techniques from Chapter 7? After you practice your *asanas*, set aside a short time for the practice of a breathing technique or two. Replenish your body's *prana*, or life force!

Wise Yogi Tells Us

The most spiritual time of day and the most ideal for practicing yoga is just before sunrise (about 5:30 a.m.). If you make it a habit to practice yoga before sunrise, then relax with a cup of herbal tea to watch the dawn, you'll find a new sense of peace pervading your days. And to think you've been sleeping through all that beauty!

➤ *Dhyana,* or meditation. You might not be ready to include meditation in your workout. If that's the case, that's fine. Diligently practice your *asanas* and *pranayama,* and you may find that meditation soon becomes a more compelling prospect. Or, if you would like to try it but are short on time, you might consider meditating at a different time of day. Whenever you meditate—after your *asanas* and *pranayama* or during separate sessions—remember that meditation is part of yoga, too, and will have a direct benefit on your workout. (Your workout will have a direct benefit on your meditation efforts, as well.)

Wise Yogi Tells Us

If you're feeling depressed or even just a little blue, which should you do: meditation or postures? If you guessed postures, you're right! The action of the postures is designed to move impurities and negativity out of the body. Meditation, on the other hand, involves stillness and concentration. If you are filled with negative feelings, meditation could actually concentrate them and make you feel worse. Meditation is best practiced in a positive frame of mind. Here's a rhyme to help you remember:

If you're down, move around.

Feeling great? Meditate!

How to Stick with It

To really get the most out of yoga, a commitment is in order. Although occasional yoga is better than no yoga, the life changes and dramatic benefits will come more quickly and easily if you practice yoga regularly, whether that means a few times a week or a few times a day. Commitment-phobic, are you? Don't be! This is a relationship with yourself, so even though you might discover some surprises (what relationship doesn't have a few of those?), this commitment is well worth the effort you put into it.

Still, even for the most well intentioned, cultivating a new habit can be difficult at first. If you're having trouble sticking to your yoga schedule, try the following strategies. One of them may be just the inspiration you need.

➤ Let's make a deal. First yoga, *then* breakfast—no yoga, no food. Or, first yoga, then a long, hot bubble bath. No yoga, no bath. Whatever deal you make with yourself, be firm. At first, breakfast, a bubble bath, or whatever your deal involves will seem like a reward, but before long, yoga will become its own reward and you won't need to make any more deals—unless they involve using your yoga practice as the reward! (If I clean the whole kitchen, then I get to practice yoga for 30 whole minutes!)

➤ It's a family affair. Get your partner or kids involved! When you don't feel like practicing, someone else in the family probably will, and that can be enough of a motivation. (Who could deny a preschooler begging to "play" yoga?) Conversely, when your partner or kids are feeling less than motivated, you may be the one to encourage them. (See Chapter 25.)

➤ Associate yoga with another pleasurable activity, then always link them. To use a previous example, every time you get up early to do yoga, you also get to relax with a cup of tea and watch the sunrise. Or, whenever you do yoga, your family knows they can't bother you for an entire 30 minutes, or however long you can convince them to do without you. Maybe you can even work up to a whole, glorious hour! Yoga will mean peace, relaxation—time for you, and you alone.

➤ Keep a yoga journal. Every day that you practice yoga, take a few moments in the morning or evening (or whenever you have time) to write down how long you practiced, what time of day it was, what exactly you did, and then, most importantly, how you feel about it. Did you make progress today? Did you feel like you experienced a setback? How do you feel now? Are you still carrying the feeling of your practice, or is it gone? How is your stress level? Don't feel you have to address all or even any of these questions—they are just suggestions. Whatever questions or issues seem personally relevant or important to you should be the subject of your journal entries. Keeping written track of your practice in this way will not only encourage you to practice regularly, but will also serve as a valuable and interesting record to the more advanced yogi you will be in the future. Someday it may be fun and enlightening to see how far you've come and what path you took.

➤ Put yoga on your to-do list right alongside all your other important daily duties, then check it off when you have finished. Subconsciously, you may not be giving yoga a high priority and that's why it's so easy to forget or put off. Consciously placing yoga high on your list, equal to (if not higher than) such important tasks as getting the car fixed, turning in that report to your boss, or buying the groceries for your big dinner party, may be the motivation you need to accomplish your yoga practice every time it's scheduled.

Maybe another strategy will work better for you, but have a strategy! Commitments require a plan, but ideas without a plan rarely amount to anything. Take your yoga seriously, commit, exercise a little self-discipline, or simply allow yoga to be so fun and refreshing that you wouldn't possibly skip a workout! Soon you'll have no trouble making yoga a natural part of your life.

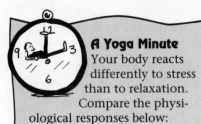

A Yoga Minute
Your body reacts differently to stress than to relaxation. Compare the physiological responses below:

STRESS

heart rate increases
muscle tension increases
breathing rate increases
blood pressure increases
blood clotting time decreases

RELAXATION

heart rate decreases
muscle tension decreases
breathing rate decreases
blood pressure decreases
blood clotting time increases

Yoga-Bytes at Home, School, and Work

If you're an extremely busy person, as most of us seem to be these days, you may find it difficult to find time for yoga. Perhaps you think your day is so densely packed with activity that yoga will never fit. Don't despair! The great thing about yoga is that you get big results even when you spend just a little time each day.

Three 10-minute (or even 5-minute or 3-minute) slots for postures, the first for warm-ups, the second for more strenuous postures, and the third for relaxation postures, are all you need to start practicing yoga, and you can spread them throughout the day if necessary. You may find that the increased energy you gain magically adds time to your day for even more practice!

You can even slip tiny little "yoga-bytes" into your day to keep you focused and feeling great. Try squeezing in yoga during the following "free times" at home, at school, and at the office.

Yoga on the Home Front

Here are some yoga-bytes to try at home:

➤ Get up 10 minutes before the rest of the family to practice. Morning is a great time to practice the cat pose. Get down on your hands and knees, then arch your back up as high as you can while lowering your head. Imagine you are a cat stretching after a long nap. Then, relax your back and bring your head up. Do this a few times, breathing with the movements. This exercise keeps your spine limber and gets you ready to pounce on the new day!

➤ Practice right after your shower, before getting dressed. Try the lightning bolt pose (see Chapter 13) to get your energy soaring.

➤ Practice the mountain pose while waiting for the pasta to boil. Watch the bubbles slowly building and rising to the surface. What powerful forces are heat and energy! Reflect on how to choose to use the "bubbles" that inevitably build up inside you.

➤ Practice while waiting for the laundry to dry. Stand behind a chair. Place your hands on the chair's back. Take a large step back. While continuing to hold onto the chair, straighten your arms out and bend forward. Now lift one leg straight out behind you. Balance. This pose strengthens the legs and stretches the spine.

➤ Practice deep breathing while running your bath water. (See Chapter 7.)

➤ Practice your regular yoga routine while the rest of the family is watching television. (Eventually, they may decide what you are doing is more interesting, and join you!)

➤ Practice with the kids for a family-bonding yoga session. Kids usually love yoga, especially moving like different animals. Try the cat pose (described above). Everyone purrrr like a cat! Then try the tree pose (see Chapter 13). Ask your kids what it's like to be a tree. Be a family of trees in different kinds of weather—a gentle breeze, a thrashing thunderstorm, a perfectly still day. Are your trees sturdy and strong, or young and flexible? Does the wind barely stir them, lash them all around, or knock them right down?

➤ Practice just before you go to sleep, but stick to relaxation postures such as the child's pose and lotus pose (see Chapter 17) or *shavasana,* the corpse pose (see Chapter 19). Otherwise, you may be too energized for slumber.

Know Your Sanskrit

Shavasana, also known as the corpse pose (*shava* means "corpse"), is perhaps the most important of all the yoga *asanas* and involves total relaxation while lying, "corpse-like," on the ground. *Shavasana* is a surprisingly challenging pose.

School Days

Yoga-bytes for the stressed-out student:

➤ Are you nervous about a test you are taking? Breathe! Increase your exhalation so it's longer than your inhalation. Do this a few times. Come back to the test. This type of breathwork releases toxins from your body and centers your mind.

➤ Feeling a lot of tension in your back? Sit up straight. Keep both knees and feet together and facing forward. Twist the upper body. Bring one arm around the back of your chair. Do not overtwist the neck. Look behind you. This movement improves circulation to the spine and brain. It also improves flexibility and eyesight.

➤ As you walk across campus from class to class in the fresh air, take a moment to focus on your surroundings. Breathe the fresh air. Feel the sun on your face, the wind in your hair. Instead of

Ouch!

Eyestrain can result from staring at a computer all day. Try a yoga fix: Keeping your head still, look up as far as you can, focus on something, and count to three. Look down, focus, and count to three. Repeat six or seven times, focusing in different directions, then close your eyes and rest. When you open your eyes, they'll feel remarkably refreshed.

worrying about the test you just took or the quiz you are about to take or the paper due tomorrow, let all your worries go—just for a minute!—and live wholly in the moment.

Yoga Makes Work Less Work!

There are also a few yoga-bytes you might like to try at the office, if your situation permits.

➤ Practice on your coffee break, instead of drinking coffee. (Yoga is far more energizing, once you break that caffeine addiction!) Sit with your fingers wide apart on top of your knees. Inhale deeply. Open your mouth wide and stick out your tongue. Look up and exhale strongly. Repeat the process a few times (not in front of your boss!). This releases emotions, tensions in the face, and self-consciousness. It also helps to break a depression cycle.

➤ Practice right before your lunch hour. While sitting, as you take a long inhale, stretch one leg straight out in front of you and hold it up parallel to the floor. Pull your toes back towards your head. Hold for three counts. Lower your leg as you slowly exhale. Do each leg a few times. This improves your hip joints and strengthens your legs so your knees won't be as stiff when you stand.

➤ At the end of a long work day, pause for a moment, to get centered and re-focus before you head home. Stand up and stretch your arms up over your head. Look up. Bend forward and touch the ground. Bend your knees if you need to. You have just connected the sun to the earth. After an accomplishment like that, you're ready to head home.

Yoga Renewal

Depending on what time of day you practice yoga, you can experience different kinds of renewal. We humans are deeply affected by the time of day. We all have a *circadian* (daily) *rhythm,* or physiological rhythms associated with the 24-hour clock. Have you noticed you have more energy in the morning or in the late afternoon or at night? Are you a "morning person" or a "night person"? Are you usually hungrier at a certain time of day, or sleepier, or happier, or more depressed? Probably, if you take the time to notice, you'll be able to determine how your feelings, emotions, and energies change throughout the day. So it only makes sense that morning yoga, afternoon yoga, and evening yoga will all be a little different. And remember, yoga is *about* rhythm and balance, of body, mind, and spirit. Our very lives move to the rhythm of our heartbeat and our breath.

Although each person's rhythms are different, people have a few similar tendencies. Keep the following in mind when deciding what time of day to practice yoga:

➤ Early-morning yoga tends to be slower. Do not rush into postures. Gently and steadily move through your workout.

➤ Late-morning to midday yoga will probably be more intense. The body is awake now and ready to rock and roll (literally!). This is a perfect time for *vinyasa,* a way to practice yoga that involves a steady flow of yoga postures.

➤ Afternoon yoga is centering. The body naturally takes a siesta in the mid-afternoon, so a more intense workout may help you get through this time. If you end your workout with *shavasana* (the corpse pose), you'll be ready for the rest of your day.

➤ Evening or late-night yoga is unwinding. Let the strain of a busy day float away. If your day was unusually stressful, an intense *Hatha Yoga* workout will help to release tensions before you go into a nice, long *shavasana.*

Know Your Sanskrit
Vinyasa is a steady flow of connected yoga *asanas* linked with breathwork in a continuous movement. It is a dynamic form of yoga.

No matter when you practice, yoga will renew you. Yoga has many purposes: to energize, heal, relax, re-align, and inspire you, among others. But all paths and purposes lead to renewal, or a new you, free from stress and preoccupation with the self.

The Least You Need to Know

➤ Establish a plan that works for you—how often you will practice yoga, and what you will do within each practice.

➤ When starting out, you may need to use a few strategies to help you stick with your practice.

➤ You can easily fit in short yoga practices throughout your day.

➤ Yoga can help relieve tension from home, school, and work.

➤ Your yoga workout will be different depending on when you practice.

Chapter 12

Crafting Your Personalized Yoga Practice

In This Chapter

➤ Defining your yoga purpose

➤ Why knowing your own style will improve your yoga practice

➤ A yoga essay test

➤ How to learn from your answers

Just as it's important to have a plan for your yoga practice, it's also important to have a purpose. If you don't really know *why* you want to practice yoga, you won't really know *how* to practice yoga. You're an individual and you bring a unique mix of motivations, emotions, tendencies, biases, needs, wants, and traits to your practice. Being familiar with all of these will not only help you determine which postures will be best for you, but will also be a great help to your yoga commitment.

Define Your Purpose

What are you looking to gain from your yoga practice?

➤ Are you primarily looking for a good fitness program?

➤ Are you in need of stress reduction?

➤ Do you suffer from a physical condition that you believe yoga could alleviate?

➤ Does Eastern philosophy fascinate you?

➤ Do you want to increase your mind power?

➤ Do you like the idea of a holistic fitness program?

➤ Are you interested in yoga because you've seen how it's benefited others?

If you really aren't sure, take some time to relax and really dig deep into your mind. Think about why you want to be a yogi. You'll get some ideas if you just give yourself time to ponder the question.

> ### Wise Yogi Tells Us
>
> When you start to analyze yourself, your motives, your intentions, and your personality, try to be as objective as possible. Don't judge yourself, just see yourself. Try to be like a mirror. A mirror doesn't say, "Hey, you look great today!" or "Whoa, you better not go out looking like that!" Your ego says those things. Be the mirror. Just reflect.

Sense Your Style

You'll also want to get in touch with who you are before you begin your yoga practice. What is it about you, the individual, that will make your yoga experience unique?

➤ Are you naturally energetic?

➤ Are you resistant to exercise?

➤ Are you an optimist? A pessimist?

➤ Are you most concerned with the physical you? The intellectual you? The emotional you?

➤ Are you easily excited?

➤ Are you the calm, relaxed type?

➤ Do you consider yourself self-confident?

A Yoga Minute
Spell the word "guru" out loud: G-U-R-U. Yes you are! Good for you!

Even if you aren't sure about the answers to these questions, give them some thought, too. Take the time to get to know yourself. The point of this entire chapter, and especially of the following "test," is to get you in touch with who you are so yoga can *do* its job.

A Yoga Essay Test You Can't Fail

If you break out in a cold sweat at the thought of a test, think of this as a self-evaluation. No one else will read your answers (unless you show them to someone), so be as honest as you possibly can. Don't try to fool yourself. Your yoga journey will be better and more fulfilling if you really understand your goals, motivations, and desires.

For each question, write what first comes into your mind, and here's a new twist—keep on writing for a minute or two. Even if you feel you've answered the question in one sentence, continue on and write anything that occurs to you, but try to keep closely focused on the question. This exercise is called "freewriting," and you might be surprised at what leaps out of your subconscious mind and onto the page. We suggest that you use these self-evaluation exercises to begin your yoga journal. After you've been practicing yoga for a period of time, say six months, return to the self-evaluation and see if you'd still answer all the questions the same way....

Wise Yogi Tells Us

If you have a hard time analyzing your own personality, imagine you're someone else who's just met you. Try to look at yourself through the eyes of another person. What's your first impression of this new friend (you)?

Don't feel you have to hurry through this test. You don't even have to complete it in one session. But try to complete it before you dive into your yoga practice. Just as a doctor needs to understand all of a patient's symptoms before he or she can make a diagnosis, so you should fully understand your own physical, emotional, mental, and spiritual states before you start to improve them.

The most important thing to remember when completing this test: Don't censor yourself! Write what you really feel about each question. Really think about who you are and what you—not anyone else—think about the question. Don't even consider what you "should" think (whatever that means!). Just feel whatever it is you *do* think. Let it all hang out, and then we'll take a look at who we're dealing with: you!

Ouch!
Thinking negatively about yourself—negative self-talk—can become a habit. Breaking this nasty habit can be difficult, but it's possible. First, make an effort to notice when you feel negative. Second, consciously try to rephrase your negative thoughts into positive ones. Eventually, you'll retrain your mind to accentuate the positive!

1. If I had to describe myself to someone who doesn't know me, I would say:

   _____

   _____

   _____

2. I've got an "outer me" I show to the world, and an "inner me" that's more private. Here's how I'd describe the "inner me"—the qualities I have that people might not notice at first, or that I consider mine alone and not necessarily for sharing:

   _____

   _____

   _____

3. If you have anything even slightly negative in your answers to the last two questions, underline it. Now: I could argue that the above negative qualities are also positive qualities when I look at them this way:

   _____

   _____

   _____

4. My best friends would describe me as:

   _____

   _____

   _____

5. When I'm confronted with someone who has different beliefs than mine, I feel:

   _____

   _____

   _____

6. If I could give one of my personal qualities to everyone in the entire world in order to make it a better place, I'd give everyone my:

   _____

   _____

   _____

7. The qualities in someone else that spark my admiration are:

   _____

   _____

   _____

8. This is the way I feel about my chosen profession, especially in terms of how it reflects my personality and satisfies my needs and ambitions:

   _____

   _____

   _____

9. If someone stole my parking space, would I be more likely to react physically (for example, jump out of the car and deck them), verbally (for example, shout at them, swear profusely, or say something nasty about their appearance or intelligence), or emotionally (think to myself that the person is a jerk, or imagine elaborate scenarios of revenge, or brood on the incident all day)? This is how I would be likely to act:

   _____

   _____

   _____

10. I think the greatest thing about the world today is:

    _____

    _____

    _____

11. I think some of the problems with the world today are:

    _____

    _____

    _____

12. I think the greatest thing about me is:

    _____

    _____

    _____

13. Here are my thoughts on the existence of a divine power:

    _____

    _____

    _____

14. If I could change one thing about the world, it would be:

    _____

    _____

    _____

15. If I could change one thing about myself, it would be:

   _____

   _____

   _____

16. I bought this book because:

   _____

   _____

   _____

17. I think it will be important for my yoga teacher to have certain qualities, such as:

   _____

   _____

   _____

18. I hope to accomplish the following from my yoga practice (ranked in order of importance):

   1. _____
   2. _____
   3. _____
   4. _____
   5. _____

19. Since yoga is about more than touching your toes, if someone is in a difficult yoga pose, are they necessarily doing yoga? Explain some reasons why or why not.

   _____

   _____

   _____

20. Considering all of the above, I can think of 5 reasons why yoga might benefit me, personally:

   1. _____
   2. _____
   3. _____
   4. _____
   5. _____

Let's Get Personal

See, that wasn't so bad! We hope you even thought it was kind of fun! And now that you're finished, it's time to see the answers. Here they are: You get an A+. It's true! You answered every single question correctly.

If you find that, when evaluating yourself, most of your answers are negative ones ("I'm selfish," "I have low self-esteem," "I don't have very many friends," etc.), nip that negative self-talk in the bud! Whenever you catch yourself forming a negative thought, restate it in the positive ("I am aware of my needs," "I often put others first," "I have a few really good friends").

This test has no wrong answers, but that doesn't diminish your accomplishment. You have undertaken a fairly intense self-evaluation, and what you have learned will only make your yoga practice more fulfilling and effective. Continue to think about your answers to these test questions as you go through your day. Consider it the beginning of a beautiful friendship with your higher self.

Wise Yogi Tells Us

If you find yourself reluctant to complete this test because you don't like to write, try speaking the answers into a tape recorder, or even discussing the questions with a close friend. The point is to get yourself thinking about who you are, what you think, and what your personal journey is all about.

The first step is getting to know all of you, even the parts of you that you aren't so proud of. The next step is learning to be proud of the whole package. We hope you have a better idea of your own self-concept after taking this quiz, but even if you aren't completely pleased with what you discover, the most important thing you can do now is accept yourself. You are a unique individual, and you are human. Of course you aren't perfect. Nobody is perfect. But we are all moving through life, exploring who we are, where we are, and why we are. We're all working towards self-discovery at our own pace. Take it easy on yourself. You're working at your own speed and learning as you go, like the rest of us. You are an amazing person, worthy of self-respect and self-love. In fact, you are miraculous. Feel good about who you are and where you are, and yoga will be a natural avenue of self-care.

The Least You Need to Know

➤ Getting to know yourself better will make yoga better!

➤ Know thyself.

➤ Know thyself.

➤ Know thyself.

➤ (...and then it will truly be) Nice to Know You, Too!

Part 4
Energize: Postures to Build Strength and Endurance

On to the workout! Part 4 consists of energizing postures you can try, master, and incorporate into your workout. Standing poses build strength, endurance, and steadiness. Balance poses improve poise and self-possession. Backbends release the flow of energy through your body. Twists and inversions rejuvenate and revitalize you.

Vinyasa is a method of yoga in which postures are strung together in a sequence with deep breathing to create an active, flowing routine full of movement and energy. Depending on which postures you include in your vinyasa, you'll experience a mild to strenuous cardiovascular workout. We'll show you a few examples, then set you free to create your own vinyasa routines. Have fun!

Chapter 13

What Do You Stand For?

In This Chapter

➤ The importance of standing poses

➤ The importance of posture for yoga and for life

➤ Lots of fun standing postures to try: mountain, triangle, side angle stretch, warrior, and lightning bolt

➤ Balance poses, too: tree, eagle, plank, and arm balance

So, are you ready to start moving? Great! You may be eager to jump right in and try the headstand or the full lotus position, but learning the basics first is important. You wouldn't be able to play an advanced piano concerto competently without first mastering the scales. In yoga, those "scales" can be likened to the most basic of poses, the mountain pose, from which many standing poses begin.

Moving Mountains

But even before we tackle the mountain, let's consider the importance of standing poses. Standing poses develop and strengthen your legs, those all-important limbs and vehicles of motion. Standing poses also improve your balance, align your hips and spine, and maintain an equilibrium throughout your body. Try to master the standing poses before you attempt to master the more complicated ones. You'll notice an almost immediate improvement in your leg and hip flexibility, as well as increased strength and general stability throughout your entire body. Your balance and posture will improve, too.

Before you start posturing, remember a few important yoga tips:

➤ Hold each pose for three breaths (both inhalation and exhalation) to start, and gradually increase the time you hold each pose as you are able.

➤ Don't feel you have to look just like the picture! More importantly, find peace within each pose, and progress as your body allows.

➤ For each pose, make sure you have a counter-pose, to keep your body balanced. For example, bends to the right should be balanced with bends to the left, forward bends with backbends, contractions with expansions, etc.

➤ Generally speaking, exhale as you go into forward bends and inhale as you go into backbends.

Posture Makes Perfect

You spend a lot of your life standing—but do you stand well? Notice how you're standing the next time it occurs to you, whether you're in line at the grocery store, filling up at the gas station, or stir-frying vegetables at the stove. Chances are, you'll notice that your posture is less than straight, tall, aligned, and balanced. Maybe you carry one shoulder higher or lower than the other. Maybe you shift your weight to one hip, stoop forward, or lean your head to the left or right. Even if you're fairly balanced, you may not be standing as tall as you could be, and your muscles may not be in command over gravity or bad habits.

Posture is more important to your health than many people realize. Ask any chiropractor—if the body isn't aligned, the energy gets "clogged" in certain areas and doesn't flow freely. If part of you is energy-deprived, you're out-of-balance, and the more out-of-balance you become, the greater your chances of succumbing to stress, depression, and disease. Good posture helps a body to heal itself, so help your body to be its best. The first step in learning how to stand? Be a mountain.

Wise Yogi Tells Us

Here's an easy way to maintain good posture while standing: Pretend that you have a loop attached to the crown of your head, and a string tied to the loop. Imagine someone above you is pulling on the string. Feel how your entire spine and neck shift and stretch as the string pulls upward. That's what good posture feels like!

Tadasana: Mountain Pose

The mountain pose is an important basic pose to learn well. It is deceptively simple in that it appears as easy as standing, but actually requires great concentration because the entire body must be equally balanced. *Tada* means "mountain," and *sana* means "straight," so *tadasana* (pronounced tah-DAH-sah-nah) means standing straight like a mountain. As you stand in *tadasana,* try to feel the firmness and stability of a mountain.

The mountain pose benefits your body in many ways. It helps to maintain balance and posture, which leads to internal balance, which leads to good health. You must have a clear understanding of this pose and be able to hold it well before you can hold any of the other standing poses well—including the headstand, which is really just an upside-down version of *tadasana!*

Ouch!
When holding the mountain pose, be careful to stay balanced. If you stand off-balance, your spine's elasticity and alignment will be compromised. Also, tilt your hips slightly in, which will naturally tilt your stomach back towards your spine. The heels on our shoes (even on our gym shoes!) constantly push our hips back and our stomachs out. Realign them with *tadasana.*

When holding *tadasana,* it's important to breathe. Let your lower ribs expand on the inhalation. Imagine your diaphragm lowering to make room in your lower chest. You are a soldier of peace in *tadasana,* so there's no need to put up your armor or feel any tension. Try to notice the difference between tension and simple awareness.

As you complete the pose, distribute your weight evenly between your heels and toes, between each leg, over each hip. Think *balance.* Soften your belly with each breath.

(1) Put your feet together with your toes pointed forward. Your arms should hang by your sides with the palms facing towards your body.

(2) Feel your spine and the back of your neck lengthening (remember that string pulling up the crown of your head?). Pull up the thigh muscles and lift the front of your body. Relax your hands and face.

Trikonasana: Triangle, the Happy Pose

Forming triangles with your body will teach it a sense of direction. The basic triangle, or *trikonasana* (pronounced trih-koh-NAH-sah-nah), is known as the happy pose because it opens your Venus *chakra* (the energy center located behind your heart) and allows joy to fill your body and radiate within you and from you. *Trikonasana* tones your spine and waist. It stimulates your bowels and intestines, strengthens your legs and ankles, improves your circulation, and develops your chest. It also strengthens the breath.

As you come back into *tadasana,* feel your chest opening. Breathe freely and deeply.

(1) Stand with your feet about three feet apart, right foot pointed forward, left foot turned out comfortably about 90 degrees.

(2) Bend to the left, reaching your left arm towards your left foot, and stretching your right arm straight up over your head. If you can, rest your left hand on your left ankle or calf.

(3) Look straight ahead or towards the sky and stretch your neck. Feel the triangle formed by your legs and the ground, as well as the rough triangle shape formed by your entire body. Breathe deeply.

(4) Slowly come back to a standing position, then repeat on the other side.

The revolved triangle pose may, upon first glance, look like the regular triangle pose, but look closer. The body is twisted around so the left hand is by the right foot. This is considered a more difficult pose that incorporates a full spinal twist into the triangle.

Wise Yogi Tells Us

In *trikonasana*, don't worry if you can't reach your ankle at first. The length of your stretch doesn't equal the quality of your yoga. Don't be so eager to touch your ankle that you tilt your body forward, cutting off your body's energy flow. Pretend your shoulders must stay pressed against an invisible wall behind you. You'll stay straight and your energy will soar!

✷ Ouch!

In the side angle stretch, be careful not to overextend your bent knee. It should be at or nearly at a right angle to the floor. Also, don't let your back leg flop. Keep it active by pushing down on your back heel. If you don't like the smell of your armpit as you look up against your arm, well… change deodorants!

Parshvakonasana: Side Angle Stretch

Parshva means "flank" or "side" and *kona* means "angle"—hence, *parshvakonasana* (pronounced par-shvah-KOH-nah-sah-nah) means side angle stretch! This pose tones your legs, strengthens your knees, and lengthens your spine. It relieves back pain and sciatica problems, and stretches and strengthens the hips and stomach.

Exhale as you go into this pose and inhale as you come out, as well as breathing while you hold the pose.

(1) Stand with your feet three to four feet apart. Point your left foot forward and turn your right foot out.

(2) Bend your right knee into a right angle with the floor and lean into the stretch so that the right side of your body moves towards the top of your right thigh and your right hand reaches toward the ground beside your right foot. Don't worry about touching the floor with your hand. Concentrate on the side stretch of your body.

(3) Stretch your left arm over your head so that it forms a relatively straight line with your left leg and torso. Your left palm should face downward. Look up towards your arm and feel the stretch from your toes into your fingertips. Breathe deeply.

(4) Return to the mountain pose, then repeat on the other side.

Virabhadrasana: Warrior Pose

It takes the tremendous strength of a warrior to "conquer" inner peace. The warrior pose, or *virabhadrasana* (pronounced vee-rab-hah-DRAH-sah-nah), fills the body with nobility and strength, calling upon the power and nourishment of the sun while firmly planting the feet upon the earth. *Vira* means "hero" and *bhadra* means "auspicious," so *virabhadrasana* means "heroic auspicious posture." Wow! Didn't you always want to be part yogi and part Conan? We'll demonstrate three different versions of *virabhadrasana* here: warrior 1, warrior 2, and warrior 3.

Warrior 1

The first warrior pose aids in deep breathing, relieves a stiff neck and shoulders, strengthens the legs, and trims the hips.

Be sure to exhale as you go into the warrior pose, and inhale as you go out of the pose. Think "strength" instead of "tense." Be careful to relax your muscles while in the warrior pose. Keep your face and neck relaxed. Breathe normally. Feel the warrior strength gathering inside you.

(1) Stand with your feet three to four feet apart. Turn your right foot out, and turn your left foot so that it is facing slightly toward the right foot.

(2) Bend your left leg into or close to a right angle and rotate your body to the right, directly in line with the left leg.

(3) Raise both arms over your head with your palms facing each other. Look straight ahead or upward.

(4) Keep your back foot firmly planted and your back leg straight. Push down on your back heel. Take three rich, full breaths.

(5) Return to the starting position and repeat on the other side.

131

Warrior 2

The second warrior pose has the same benefits as the first, but also strengthens and shapes the legs, relieves leg cramps, brings flexibility to the legs and back, tones the abdomen, and strengthens the ankles and arms.

(1) Begin as for the warrior 1 pose but keep the upper body facing forward as you bend the left leg into or close to a right angle with the floor.

(2) Lift both arms straight out to form a "T" shape with your body. Look toward the left arm. Keep your shoulders down.

(3) Hold the pose for at least a few breaths, return to the starting position, then repeat on the other side.

Warrior 3

The warrior 3 position develops the strength and shape of your legs and abdomen as well as giving you agility, poise, better concentration, and improved balance. It is considered a more difficult pose. Be sure to exhale going in to all the warrior poses, and inhale coming out.

(1) Assume the warrior 2 pose, then lean forward slightly and lift your back leg.

(2) Extend your arms in front of you with the palms together and look towards your hands.

(3) Return to a neutral position, then repeat on the opposite side.

Utkatasana: Lightning Bolt Pose

The lightning bolt pose, or *utkatasana* (pronounced yoot-kah-TAH-sah-nah), is a powerful pose. *Utkatasana* means "raised posture." As you form the shape of a lightning bolt, you are filled with the dynamic energy of lightning. *Utkatasana* removes shoulder stiffness, strengthens your legs and ankles, lifts your diaphragm, massages your heart, tones your back and stomach, and develops your chest.

(1) Begin in *tadasana,* the mountain pose.

(2) Bend your knees and lift your arms over your head with palms together or slightly apart. Be careful to keep your knees from buckling inward; keep your feet together, or slightly apart.

(3) Extend your arms so they are in line with your torso. Feel the shape of the lightning and breathe deeply. ZAP!

(4) Return to *tadasana.*

(5) Exhale as you bend your knees, then inhale as you return to the mountain pose.

A variation of the lightning bolt pose is called "squat on heels and toes." This pose consists of standing with your feet hip-distance apart, then squatting first on your toes, then on your heels. This variation develops the ankles, knees, and arches. Be careful to keep your knees over your ankles. Don't let them droop in or out as you bend. This further strengthens the quadriceps and ankles.

Moving into the "squat on heels and toes" pose.

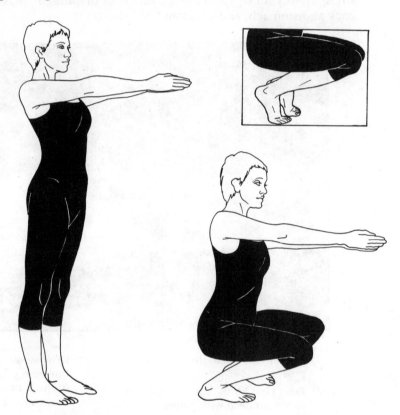

Balance Poses

We've emphasized before that balance is extremely important in the practice of yoga. When your body is balanced, a connection is formed between the two sides of the body (*ha* and *tha,* as in *Hatha Yoga*).

Vrikshasana: Tree Pose

Vrikshasana (pronounced vrik-SHAH-sah-nah) is one of the most basic balance poses. *Vriksha* means "tree," and a tree is soundly rooted in the earth but grows upward with branches reaching out to the sun. Wind may move the branches, but the tree stands firm. *Vrikshasana* tones the legs, opens the hips, and promotes physical balance. It also develops concentration and mindfulness.

Throughout *vrikshasana*, keep your breathing steady and regular so it doesn't interfere with your balance.

Ouch!
In *vrikshasana*, be careful not to raise one hip higher than the other. Keep your hips even by lowering the position of your foot on your inner thigh. Don't bend your straight knee or elbows. Keep your hands firmly pressed together so they don't slip. And breathe! Holding your breath won't help you to balance—it will only cut off your oxygen.

(1) Begin in *tadasana*, the mountain pose.

(2) Bring your left leg up and balance the sole of the left foot on the inner thigh of your right leg, as high as you are able.

(3) Bring your hands together in front of your chest with palms together (as if you were praying), then raise the arms over your head, keeping the palms together.

(4) Return to *tadasana*, then repeat with the right leg.

Ardha Baddha Padmottanasana: Half Bound Lotus Pose

The purpose of this more advanced variation of the tree pose is to keep the trunk steady with the help of your arm. It has the same benefits as the tree pose but allows you to open your hips more fully, which in turn opens the Jupiter *chakra* (the energy center located on your spine behind your pelvis). It also allows a fuller chest expansion.

Don't be frustrated if you have trouble getting into the half bound lotus pose. If your hips are not open enough yet and your knee isn't pointing towards the floor, it'll be difficult to connect your hand with your foot and could also overstrain your knee. Give yourself time and keep practicing the regular tree pose. Eventually your body will accommodate you.

(1) The half bound lotus is similar to the tree pose, except your bent right ankle rests on the front of your straight left thigh.

(2) Bring your right arm behind your back and connect it to your right foot in front.

(3) Lower your knee slightly towards the floor and raise your left arm over your head. Take three breaths.

(4) Return to the starting position, then repeat on the other side.

Garudasana: Eagle

The eagle is a god in Indian mythology, and so is considered sacred and important. As with the tree pose, *garudasana* (pronounced gah-roo-DAH-sah-nah) improves balance and concentration as well as develops the ankles and removes stiffness in the shoulders. Symbolically, the eagle represents the life force/*prana*.

(1) Begin in *tadasana*, but with the knees slightly bent.

(2) Bend one leg over the other like you are crossing your thighs, then hook your ankle around the back of your other ankle. Try to stay balanced between your heel and toe.

(3) Bend your elbows and bring one arm under the other arm, connecting your palms in front of your face. Even though your body is twisting every which way, imagine your torso lifting and straightening. Breathe!

(4) Return to *tadasana*, and repeat on the other side. This pose is usually easier going one way than it is going the other way, but try it both ways and eventually you'll balance.

Plank Pose

The plank pose develops strength in your arms and legs. It helps to create a balanced and strong body. It is often used as a transition pose, leading or connecting one pose to another.

(1) Lie on your stomach with your fingertips in line with your shoulders and your elbows bent in toward the body, toes curled under.

(2) Push yourself up into a push-up position and hold.

(3) Try to keep your body in line. You will discover where the weakest sections of your body are, the longer you hold. Breathe. Push your heels out to keep your lower back from caving in.

(4) Use this pose as a transition into the following arm balance pose.

Vashishthasana: Arm Balance

Vashishthasana (pronounced VAH-shish-THAH-sah-nah) is a pose named after the Indian sage Vashishtha. *Vashishthasana* strengthens the wrists and arms and tones the lumbar and coccyx regions of the spine. It also develops concentration, non-attachment to either achievement or failure, and an undisturbed, steady mind.

Ouch!
Keep breathing steadily throughout *vashishthasana*. Don't let your hips droop down because this will cause strain to your back and put undue force on your arms. Keep your elbows straight and keep your foot balanced on your leg. Don't let anything droop!

(1) Begin in the plank pose.

(2) Turn your entire body to the right and balance your right arm and foot on the side of your body. Your torso should be in a straight line, held in a diagonal to the floor by your right arm.

(3) Lift your left arm up straight in the air with the palm facing forward.

139

Learning the basic standing postures is a great way to start, and balance poses will increase your stability. Practicing these basics will improve all aspects of your yoga practice and give you an inner peace and strength, too.

The Least You Need to Know

➤ Standing poses like the mountain, triangle, side angle stretch, warrior, and lightning bolt, are an important basis for strength and balance.

➤ Posture has a profound effect on our health and well-being!

➤ Practice the basic standing postures before you progress to more complicated poses.

➤ Balance poses like the tree, eagle, plank, and arm balance create stability and a centered sense of being.

➤ *Hatha* is finding balance. (If you can't find the balance, let out a good "HA!" and try again.)

Bending Over Backbends

A few people have naturally flexible spines and find backbends easy, but for most people, backbends are a challenge. We tend to spend more of our lives bent slightly forward and our spines just aren't used to bending the other way. All the more reason to practice backbends, however—for the sake of balance.

Open Up and Laugh More

Whether you are naturally flexible or not, bending poses are extremely beneficial for improving your spine and toning your internal organs. This releases your *chakras* so energy and joy can flow through you unimpeded. After a few good backbends, you may just laugh out loud.

Start by performing a simple stretch to open your neck, shoulders, and chest. Just like the figure in the drawing on the next page, sit up straight in a chair and begin to arch your neck back. Inhale as you do it. Focus your gaze upward. Feel that openness in the center of your chest? It's as if you're lifting your heart—and your spirits as well! It's important to arch your neck only as far as you can support it; just like the first window in the drawing. Try forcing your lower lip over your upper lip, as you see in the second window. It's hard to frown in a back-bending posture! Again, in backbends, you always want to be supported—avoid the impulse to crunch your neck back as the figure is doing in the third window of the drawing. A crunched neck is very anti-yoga and can lead to discomfort and injury. Now, *smile.* Doesn't it feel good?

Let's get bent!

Opening stretch before bending. Avoid crunching your neck as the figure in the third box is doing!

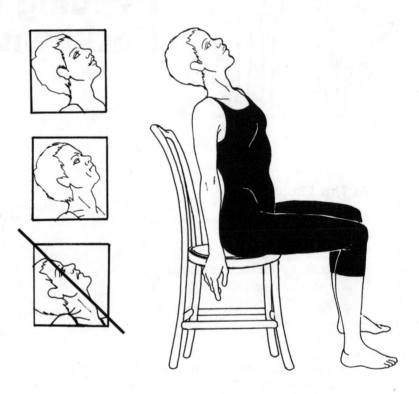

Bhujangasana: Cobra Pose

Bhujanga means "serpent," and the cobra is a sacred and revered serpent in India. But what is a serpent? Basically, one big spine! In the cobra pose, *bhujangasana* (pronounced BOO-jhan-GAH-sah-nah), concentrate on allowing the strength of your spine to move you. The cobra pose helps to align your spinal disks, open up your heart *chakra*, and strengthen your back. It also strengthens your nervous system and your eyes.

When practicing the cobra pose, keep your elbows in toward the body. As your shoulders rise off the floor, don't scrunch them up around your neck. Keep your eyes open and peering up to tone your peripheral vision (typically the first part of the eyesight to degenerate!).

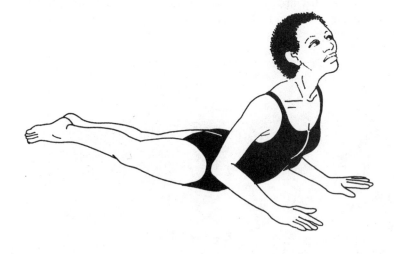

(1) Lie on your stomach, flat on the floor, with your heels and toes together. Place your hands on the floor on either side of your chest. Your face should be resting against the floor.

(2) Inhale and lift your forehead, then chin, then shoulders, then chest off the floor. Keep your hips pressed against the floor.

(3) Look upward and breathe. Try sticking out your tongue and opening your mouth wide, to help release your face. Then return to the starting position.

(4) To test the strength of your spine, lift your palms off the floor, as you see in the second figure in the drawing. See how much of your body comes down—if it's a lot, your arms are doing a good portion of the work. Keep focusing on the spine instead.

Dhanurasana: Bow Pose

Dhanurasana (pronounced DAH-noo-RAH-sah-nah), a.k.a. the bow pose, is a high-energy pose. Imagine your body is like an archer's bow held taut and ready to launch an arrow.

> **A Yoga Minute**
> Some doctors believe many cases of back pain are psychologically caused. Deep stress or emotional problems may manifest themselves as a backache.

This pose keeps your spine supple, tones your abdomen, massages your back muscles, strengthens your concentration, and decreases laziness.

When in the bow pose, be sure to grab your ankles, not your toes or feet. If you can't grab your ankles, simply bring your hands back as far as you can alongside your body. Remember to move your hands towards your ankles, *not* your ankles towards your hands. Keep your elbows straight, not bent, and don't lift your shoulders up to your ears—keep them pressed down.

(1) Lie on your stomach. Bring both arms behind you and bend both knees.

(2) Grasp your ankles with your hands. Pull your body so it feels tightly drawn like a bow, and look up. Hold for two or three breaths.

Half Bow

In the half bow, the bow is strung one string at a time. When in the half bow, be careful not to lean over to the side that is held straight. Balance both sides of your body. Be sure to breathe. You'll be able to tell how much caffeine you've had lately by how much your straight hand shakes!

(1) Begin on your stomach as with the bow pose, but extend your left arm straight over your head, palm down.

(2) Bend your right knee and bring your right arm back toward your right ankle.

(3) Push your stomach into the floor with your tailbone tipped toward the floor. Lift your head and chest. Keep your focus on the out-stretched arm.

Rocking Bow

The rocking bow is the full bow plus! It aids digestion, relieves constipation, and tones the intestines. The fuller the bow, the easier it is to rock and roll!

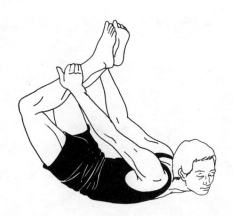

(1) Get into the bow pose.

(2) Using your breath, rock your body back and forth. Inhale as the body rocks back, exhale forward. Keep your arms straight.

Wise Yogi Tells Us

Swami Vishnu Devananda says, "OM is a bow, the arrow is the Soul, Brahman is the arrow's goal." Backbends are so good at making it easier to breathe deeply—by opening up the chest and abdomen—that many people crave backbends! The deep breathing gets more oxygen to the brain. As a result you feel stimulated, refreshed, and energized. Get the double benefit by completing your yoga backbends with a few balancing forward bends to relax the spine and a few moments of meditation on the swami's words.

✳ Ouch!

Be careful not to let your legs roll in while in upward facing dog. Lift your inner legs. If you feel off-balance, concentrate on centering your balance on your feet. Weak legs will cause your back to curve in and hurt. Keep them strong! Don't bend your elbows or knees.

Urdhvamukha Shvanasana: Upward Facing Dog

Urdhva means "upward" and *mukha* means "mouth" or "face." *Shvan* means "dog." *Urdhvamukha Shvanasana* (pronounced OORD-vah MOOK-hah shvah-NAH-sahn-ah) looks like a dog stretching upward. (Yoga shows great respect for dog poses—after all, what is "dog" spelled backwards?) Upward facing dog is great for a stiff back. It strengthens the spine, alleviates back aches, increases respiration and circulation (especially to the pelvic area), and strengthens the eyes.

(1) Go into the cobra pose, then inhale further and straighten your arms, keeping your back legs strong, which takes the pressure off the back.

(2) Lift the front of your body off the floor and look up.

(3) Inhale going into the pose, exhale going out.

Matsyasana: Go Fish

A fish must open its gills to breathe; *matsyasana* (pronounced mahtz-YAH-sah-nah) fills the lungs with air, improving the yogi's ability to float in water (try it!). The fish pose energizes the calcium-regulating parathyroid gland (located in your neck), strengthens the abdomen, improves the voice by opening the Mercury *chakra* (located in the throat), and relieves mental tension.

Half Fish Pose

The half fish pose is a simpler version of the full fish pose (see next page).

In the half fish pose, don't let your feet fall to the side. Keep your knees straight. Make sure the top of your head, not the back of your head, rests on the floor. Keep your elbows in, breathe regularly, and don't put your weight on your head. Let your elbows and arms support your weight.

(1) Lie flat on your back with your feet together and your knees straight.

(2) Place your palms facing down under your tailbone with thumbs touching.

(3) Inhale, then lift your upper chest and arch your back. Allow your head to tilt back.

(4) Rest the top of your head lightly on the floor. Feel the strength of the lift in your arms and chest. Hold for three breaths, then exhale as you come down.

Full Fish Pose

This pose is the same as the half fish pose, except your legs and feet are in the full lotus position (see Chapter 17) and your hands hold your feet. If you cannot do the full lotus, simply cross your legs. Your hands do not need to hold your feet if you aren't in full the lotus position. This variation further opens the pelvis and promotes energy flow through all your *chakras*.

> ### Wise Yogi Tells Us
>
> Whenever a particular pose opens a *chakra*, concentrate on that area while holding the pose. Feel the energy flowing through and from the target *chakra*. Your mind can help open your *chakras* even further.

Ustrasana: Camel

Ustra means "camel," and *ustrasana* (pronounced oohs-TRAH-sah-nah) imitates the hump of a camel. Your shoulders and chest become more open and mobile through the camel pose. Your abdomen is stretched, digestion is improved, rib muscles are strengthened, and the pose can also help sciatica. Sciatica is a painful condition felt in the hip or thigh, resulting from inflammation of the sciatic nerve, a long nerve that starts in the hip and runs down the back of the leg.

When practicing the camel pose, pretend there is a wall in front of you and you are pressing your thighs towards it. Bend only as far backwards as you can while keeping your neck properly supported.

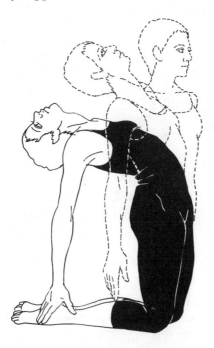

(1) Legs and feet together or slightly apart.

(2) Hips and thighs stretch forward as arms and top of body reach back.

(3) Eventually hands will touch heels, but take it gradually.

Cakrasana: Doin' Wheelies!

Cakrasana (pronounced tshah-KRAH-sah-nah) makes your body strong and mobile, like a wheel. It stretches and strengthens the stomach, improves the concentration by bringing blood to the head, and gives greater control over the body. It also prevents bad posture, tones the extremities, improves the memory, heightens energy and vitality, brings a feeling of lightness to the body, and improves circulation to the trachea and larynx. The trachea—also known as the windpipe—is the passageway between the larynx and the lungs.

Know Your Sanskrit

The wheel pose is the most dynamic of backbends. It's the one that effectively stimulates all of the *chakras*. Hence, the name of the pose: *Cakrasana*.

The larynx is the area of the throat containing the vocal cords.

➤ Lie flat on your back with your knees bent.

➤ Bend your elbows towards the sky and bring your palms next to your ears, fingers facing your feet.

➤ Lift your naval (think of lifting your Mars *chakra*, located behind your naval) so your body forms an arch.

In the half wheel variation, the stomach remains flat and the elbows are bent. In full wheel, the head is completely off the floor, and the arms and legs are straight.

In the wheel pose, your hips may feel too tight to lengthen sufficiently. If your shoulders are tight or your arms are weak, you may be unable to push yourself up into position. Just keep working at it and one day, POW! There it is.

The Least You Need to Know

➤ Back-bending poses are important for increasing flexibility, as well as keeping various internal organs open and free.

➤ Open, toned organs result in open *chakras* and a free flow of energy throughout the body.

➤ Backbends are great for people who work at computers all day—correcting that hunched-over posture.

➤ Backbends make it easier to breathe deeply and fully—stimulating the body and getting more oxygen to the brain.

Twistin' and Standin' on Your Head

Twists are wonderful ways to clear out your system. They free and re-align your spine so that every part of your body works better. Twists massage the internal organs and help the body force toxins out to be carried away for elimination. *Prana* is allowed to enter the spine and energize it. For balance, always remember to do *both* sides of a spinal twist.

And talk about a fountain of youth—inversions are amazing postures that balance all that standing and walking around right-side-up. Blood flows to the brain, gravity works the other way on every part of your body—in fact, after a good headstand, you'll feel almost like you've spent the day at a spa. So get ready to break out of the old habit of existing upright!

Maricyasana: Spinal Twist

Maricyasana (pronounced MAH-rih-si-AH-sah-nah) gives the spine a nice, lateral stretch, increasing spinal elasticity. The spinal twist also improves side-to-side mobility; decreases backaches and hip pain; contracts and tones the liver, spleen, and intestines; reduces abdominal size; improves the nervous system; prevents calcification at the base of the spine; frees the joints; and rouses your *kundalini* energy (see Chapter 5). Whew! It's energizing just saying all that!

(1) Sit on the floor with both legs out in front of you.

(2) Bend your left leg over the outside of your right leg, then turn to the left.

(3) Bend your right arm and place your right elbow on the outside of your left knee. Keep your shoulders down.

(4) Twist your spine and push your chest forward to lengthen the spine.

(5) Return to starting position and repeat on the other side.

Bound Knee Spinal Twist

This variation opens your hips, too, but be sure to keep your back straight and shoulders down. And remember to enjoy this pose. If you aren't enjoying this pose, continue with one of the other spinal twists instead.

(1) From a sitting position with your legs straight out in front of you, bend your left knee and bring your heel to your hip bone.

(2) Turn to your right, bringing the left shoulder around the left knee.

(3) Bring your right arm behind your back and connect your hands.

153

Lying Down Spinal Twist

This variation tones the spine and strengthens the legs. It can also be quite relaxing as gravity helps you out.

(1) Begin lying down with your knees bent and your palms together in front of your chest in prayer (*namaste*).

(2) Straighten your arms toward the sky and let your whole body fall to the right.

(3) Lift your left arm and bring it up and over to the ground behind you. Gaze toward your left hand.

(4) Breathe. Enjoy. Relax.

(5) Bring your left hand back to your right hand. Roll over and do the other side for balance.

Setu Bandha Sarvangasana: Bridge Pose

Yes, *setu bandha sarvangasana* (pronounced SAY-too BAHN-dah SAHR-vahn-GAH-sah-nah) looks like a bridge. *Setu* means "bridge" and *sarvangasana* is composed of *sarva* (all), *anga* (limb), and of course, *asana* (posture). *Setu bandha sarvangasana* also strengthens the neck and back; tones the entire spine; and bathes in blood and nutrients the pituitary, thyroid, and adrenal glands. The bridge pose also helps intestinal function. This pose is a good preliminary to the shoulderstand.

(1) Lie flat on the floor with your knees bent and your feet hip-distance apart. Keep your hands to your sides.

(2) Bring your heels toward your buttock and lift your hips. Place your hands under the lower back for support, point the hands toward your spine. Bridge builds supple wrists. Keep your elbows next to your body. Your head, neck, and shoulders should stay on the floor.

(3) Tighten the buttocks muscles to support your lifted torso. Make sure your knees are aligned with your ankles, that they face forward, and that they don't fall in or out as you hold the pose.

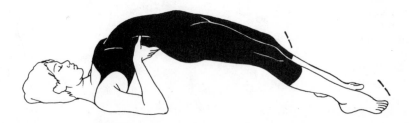

(4) To try the extended bridge, walk your feet out until your legs are straight. Keep those abdominals lifted and buttocks muscles working— you don't want your bridge to sag! Extended bridge is a very difficult pose. Be kind to your back. Few can do this pose without pain. Why not try a half bridge to start (see the following)?

- For the half bridge: clasp your hands under your body, drawing your elbows in, and lifting your body higher.

Sarvangasana: Shoulderstand

Sarvangasana (pronounced SAHR-vahn-GAH-sah-nah) is a great inversion that stimulates the thyroid gland and the Mercury *chakra* (located in the throat). It reverses the pull of gravity on your internal organs and reduces the strain on your heart because your heart doesn't have to work as hard to pump to the extremities when inverted. Shoulderstand helps with varicose veins; purifies the blood; nourishes the brain, lungs, and heart; strengthens the eyesight; and is a great headache remedy.

(1) Lie flat on the floor, then bring both legs and hips up in the air. Lift up by contracting your abdominal and buttocks muscles; don't just swing your legs up.

(2) Support your lower back with your hands. Face your fingers inward, toward your spine.

(3) Bring your shoulders away from your ears and push your feet toward the ceiling. Breathe fully.

The shoulderstand requires the supervision of a qualified teacher. Practice it by bringing your legs back, as in the first drawing, then holding there. To protect your neck, it is best to go up into a full shoulderstand, especially the first time, under the guidance of an instructor. Typical problems during shoulderstand are the tendency to crunch the neck, hold the breath, and twist the neck. Think of your neck lengthening as you hold the pose. Put a folded towel or blanket under your neck, right at the tip of the shoulders. Breathe! Don't allow your elbows to slide outward, and keep your neck lengthened and your feet together.

Halasana: Plough Pose

Halasana (pronounced hah-LAH-sah-nah) looks like a plough, and *hala* means "plough." Plough pose stimulates the spine; strengthens the nervous system; improves the circulation; releases neck tension; relieves constipation; decreases insomnia; promotes mental relaxation; activates the Mercury *chakra* (in the throat); improves communication; and stimulates the stomach, spleen, small intestine, heart, liver, gall bladder, and kidneys.

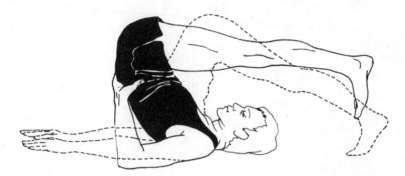

(1) Lie on your back with your knees bent and your hands at your waist.

(2) Inhale and raise your legs, hips, and buttocks off the ground. Curl backward, keeping the legs straight.

(3) Exhale as you let your feet lower to the floor behind your head. Touch your legs to the ground only when they are straight and you feel no strain in your neck.

(4) Clasp your hands under your body, facing away from your feet.

157

In plough pose, be sure to keep your knees straight. Don't twist the head or neck. It helps to learn from a teacher or experienced yogi before you try it. Don't force your toes to the ground. Let gravity do this slowly.

Plough Variation: Hands to Feet

This variation is identical to the first plough, except that the arms are stretched on the ground overhead and touching the feet. This pose further opens and stretches the shoulders.

Photo of hands to feet, a plough variation.

Shirshasana: Headstand

Shirshasana (pronounced sher-SHAH-sahn-ah) is probably one of the most famous yoga poses and is considered the King or Queen of the *Hatha Yoga* poses. It stimulates the whole system, improving circulation and strengthening the nervous system, emotions, and brain. Plus, when your body is ready for it, it's fun!

But be sure your body is ready. You must have sufficient arm, shoulder, neck, and stomach strength, plus be well versed at *tadasana* (remember back in Chapter 13?), the mountain pose, so you can balance your weight evenly while upside-down. Otherwise, your neck will hurt. Too much pressure on your head is not good! Your weight should be supported by your arms, shoulders, and the strength of your abdomen. The strength of these areas is developed in standing poses. Develop yourself on your feet before standing on your head.

Ouch!
As wonderful a pose as the head-stand is, it shouldn't be practiced under certain circumstances. If you have high blood pressure, heart problems, or are pregnant, don't attempt the headstand or any of the inverted poses. You may still be able to do inversions with no problem, but talk to your yoga-friendly doctor first.

(1) Get down on your hands and knees. Grab your left elbow with your right hand and your right elbow with your left hand.

(2) Bring your elbows to the ground and release the hold of your hands. Keep your elbows this distance apart for best support.

(3) Interlace your fingers so your arms form a point, then cup the top of your head in your hands at the top of the point.

(4) Slowly walk your feet in toward your body, straightening your back, then slowly raise your feet into the air.

(5) Breathe! Then come back down slowly. Remain with your head down for a few minutes before sitting up.

Wise Yogi Tells Us

When first attempting the headstand, use a wall for support. The more comfortable and stronger you become, the less you'll need the wall, until soon you'll be doing headstands anytime, anywhere!

Padma Shirshasana: Lotus Headstand

In *padma shirshasana* (pronounced PAHD-mah sher-SHAH-sah-nah), while in the headstand, bring your feet into the full lotus position. (Don't worry, we'll get to that in Chapter 17.) This opens the hips. This is definitely an advanced posture. Find a qualified teacher for personal guidance on this one, okay?

Photo of lotus headstand, a headstand variation.

Adho Mukha Vrksasana: Handstand

In *adho mukha vrksasana* (pronounced AHD-hoh MOOK-hah vrik-SHAH-sah-nah), *adho mukha* means "face down" and *vrksa* means "tree." To properly perform this "face-down tree" pose or handstand, your arms must be strong. Practice the downward facing dog pose (*adho mukha svanasana*, described in Chapter 18) to develop your arms and prepare your body for the handstand.

The handstand gives you tremendous energy. It strengthens your arms and shoulders, plus gives you all the blood-cleansing effects of inversions. If trying this pose scares you, work with a partner who can spot you. The handstand, however, requires a lot of combined abdominal and upper-body strength—if you're not strong enough, concentrate on perfecting headstand poses and the downward facing dog pose.

Inversions can be incredibly refreshing and invigorating. Twists also keep the spine flexible and youthful, so dive into this yoga fountain of youth!

(1) Perform downward facing dog in front of a wall, as the yogi is doing in the drawing. Place your hands on the floor, shoulder-width apart, and about three to five inches from the wall. Slowly walk your legs in toward the wall.

(2) Exhale and lift one leg straight up. Follow quickly with the other. Keep your arms and legs straight and firm. Push your shoulders away from the floor.

(3) Hold the pose for as long as is comfortable. Breathe! Exhale as you come down.

161

The Least You Need to Know

➤ Spinal twists gently massage internal organs, strengthen the spine, and purify your system.

➤ Inversions—the bridge, shoulderstand, plough, headstand, and handstand—are yoga's fountain of youth: They keep you young!

➤ Inversions send blood to the brain—that's brain power!

➤ Avoid inversions if you have high blood pressure, heart problems, or are pregnant.

Chapter 16

A Continuous Flow

In This Chapter

➤ Yoga's sun salutation

➤ Yoga's moon salutation

➤ Combining postures in a sequence of motion

➤ How to create your own flow—move and groove!

You're probably convinced by now that yoga can be tough and challenging to your strength and flexibility. But what about working up a *real* sweat? That's where *vinyasa* (pronounced vin-YAH-sah) comes in! *Vinyasa* is a set of yoga postures, all strung together into a flow of movement. Rather than just choosing a posture, holding it, releasing it, then moving on to the next posture, *vinyasa* combines the series into a long, fluid, unified movement. Poses are held within a *vinyasa,* but the difference is that when you come out of one posture, you flow immediately into another posture. The right flow will give you a great workout, in addition to improving your balance, grace, speed, strength, and agility.

Sweat with the Rhythm

Continuous flow sequences of yoga postures can be an invigorating cardiovascular workout. For example, repeating a flow of postures requiring a good deal of strength in quick succession takes stamina and good lung capacity. Or, you can choose a slower repetition of postures and really enter each one fully and deliberately, meditating on the sequence as you perform it. However you choose to practice yoga postures in a continuous flow, let the rhythm of your body and your breath move you to new levels of mind/body awareness. Breath is extremely important in *vinyasa*: connecting posture to posture and movement to movement. A good general guideline is to exhale when going into forward bends and inhale when going into backbends. So let's go with the flow!

Uttanatavasan: Leg Lifts

Uttanatavasan (pronounced ooh-TAHN-ah-tah-VAH-sahn), leg lifts, are considered *vinyasas* because of the steady movement within each pose. Leg lifts strengthen your stomach, which in turn supports your lower back. The deeper your breath during this *vinyasa*, the easier and smoother your movements will become. Leg lifts also help prepare your body for the headstand. (Remember back in Chapter 15?)

The single leg lift:

(1) Lie on your back. Bend your left leg slightly; avoid lower back strain.

(2) Straighten your right leg up toward the sky. Push your heel out and slowly lower your leg straight down.

(3) Keep repeating this movement on the same side, connecting each repetition with breath: Inhale as your leg goes up, exhale as your leg goes down.

(4) After a satisfying number of repetitions (three or four), switch to your left leg.

And now for the double:

(1) Begin the double leg lift with your palms facing down and tucked under your tailbone, to keep your lower back from rising off the floor.

(2) Slowly inhale as you bring both legs straight up.

(3) Exhale as you bring both legs straight down.

(4) Do as many lifts as you can, then rest.

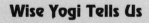

Wise Yogi Tells Us

While flowing through a leg lift *vinyasa*, cup your hands over your ears and listen intently to your breath as it connects movement to movement. Is it smooth? Rocky? Does it sound like the ocean? The wind in the trees? The space between the stars? Link the rhythm of your breath to the movements of your muscles. Notice everything. Look inward.

Be careful not to let momentum swing your legs up during leg lifts. Keep your movements slow and complete to build your strength, touching the ground and pausing before each lift. Don't separate your feet or bend your knees when you come down. If your back hurts, keep one knee bent, foot on the floor, but keep the other leg straight.

If you have a sensitive back, bend the knee you are not lifting and keep this foot firmly on the ground. This will protect your lower back as you continue to strengthen it with leg lifts. Leg lifts build stomach and back muscles. Continuous practice of leg lifts can help alleviate lower back pain (which a majority of persons in America suffer from).

Surya Namaskara: Sun Salutation

The sun is the center of our solar system, and without its energy and warmth, we wouldn't be able to exist on this planet. This *vinyasa* is a devotional (not to mention great exercise). *Surya namaskara* (pronounced SOOR-yah nah-mahs-KAH-rah) offers thanks and greetings to the sun, and although it can be performed any time, it is particularly appropriate and wonderful when performed at sunrise, out-of-doors, facing east. *Surya* means "sun," and *namaskara* literally means "taking a bow."

The sun salutation energizes, strengthens, and tones all the major muscles and organs in the body.

Ouch!

When performing the sun salutation, keep your awareness focused. If you go too fast, your mind may stray from attending to the body, breath, and devotion to the sun. You should go fast enough to keep the movements flowing and get your body warm, but not so fast that you don't feel in control of your movements or breath.

(1) Begin in the mountain pose with your hands in *namaste,* or prayer position. Center yourself and concentrate on a devotional attitude.

(2) Inhale. Raise your arms up over your head and tilt them slightly back, as if you are encompassing the sun with love.

(3) Exhale. Bring your hands straight down to the floor. Bend your knees to protect your lower back. Eventually, you may straighten your legs. Bring your palms alongside your feet. This position is a symbol of thanking the earth, where our feet are firmly planted.

(4) Keeping your hands down, inhale and step your right foot back behind you. Stay low to the ground and look up. This represents that we are on the earth through the strength of the sun.

(5) Exhale. Bring both legs back behind you and balance in the plank pose, as if you were about to lower yourself into a push-up. Push out at the heels for strength. This represents finding a balance between the sun and the earth. Pause.

(6) Exhale further. Bring your knees, chest, and chin to the floor. Keep your tailbone up off the ground. You are thanking the earth.

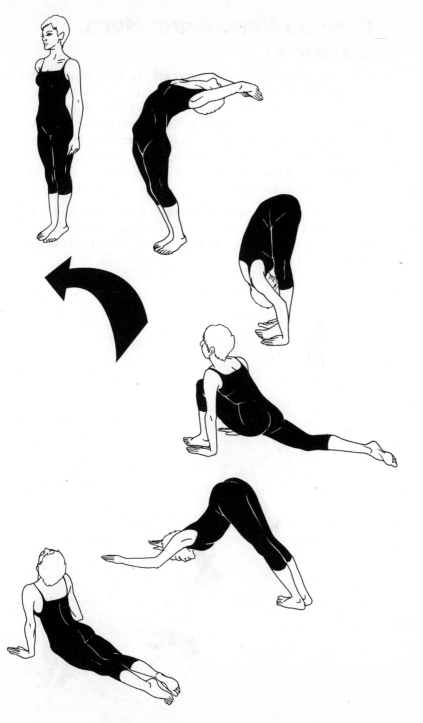

(7) Inhale into the cobra pose and look up. Let the sun's warmth strengthen you.

(8) Exhale and push up into the downward facing dog pose. Take the strength of the cobra's spine and lengthen it.

(9) Inhale as you bring your right foot forward. Look up and thank the sun as you proceed on your journey.

(10) Exhale and bring both legs together. With your palms alongside your feet, humbly devote yourself to the sun. Open your moon *chakra* (located at the back of your head) to the sun's kind and steady energy.

(11) Inhale as you bring your arms and body up, tilting into a slight backbend, again embracing the sun with love.

(12) Exhale as you bring your hands back into the prayer position, standing in *tadasana*, the mountain pose.

(13) Repeat the entire sequence again for a complete round. For the second half-round, bring the left leg back, then forward, to create a balance.

167

Know Your Sanskrit

Namaste (pronounced nah-MAHS-tay) is a *mudra* in which the palms and fingers come together in the prayer position. Hands are held with your thumbs against the chest in an attitude of focused devotion. *Namaste* can also be held loosely behind the back with the fingers pointed up. *Namaste* means "Obeisance to you" or "I salute the divine light within you."

Chandra-Namaskara: Moon Salutation

This *vinyasa* restores vitality, strength, and flexibility to the entire body. It also improves digestion through the continual compression of the intestinal tract. *Chandra* means "moon," and just as the sun salutation greets and honors the sun, so *chandra-namaskara* (pronounced SHAHN-drah-nah-MAHS-kah-rah) greets and honors the moon. Try practicing this *vinyasa* outside on a clear evening when the moon is in full view. Serenity!

Quite an energetic sequence of poses! The moon is a lunar/ emotional symbol. The strong physical movements in a moon salutation help to balance our emotional side with our physical side.

(1) Stand in the mountain pose with hands in *namaste,* or prayer position. Inhale and bring yours arms over your head in a slight backbend, keeping your palms together. You are greeting the moon.

(2) Exhale and bring your palms to the floor. You are thanking the earth for allowing you to stand on it.

(3) Inhale and step your left foot back. Touch the side of your ankle to the floor. Your right leg is lunged forward with the weight of your body on your toes.

(4) Exhale and switch the position of your feet. Keep your left knee at a right angle to the floor with your right knee touching the floor. Your weight is now supported by your left foot and right knee.

(5) Inhale and lift your arms straight up overhead toward the moon, then exhale into the child's pose, a symbol of turning inward.

(6) Now inhale and step your right foot back with the side of your ankle touching the floor. Your left leg is lunged forward with the weight of your body on your toes.

(7) Exhale and switch the position of your feet as before. Your right knee is at a right angle to the floor and your left knee is touching the floor. Your weight is now supported by your right foot and left knee.

(8) Inhale and lift your arms straight up overhead. Thank you, moon! Then exhale and bring your hands back to the floor. Inhale into the upward facing dog pose. Strong and steady, the moon circles us.

(9) Exhale into the child's pose again, the moon *chakra* at the back of your head will open for healing energy. Inhale, bring your hands straight up overhead, and look up.

(10) Exhale and bring your hands back to the floor. Inhale, push your hands against the floor, and stand up into *tadasana* (the mountain pose).

169

Create Your Own Flow

The sun and moon salutations are popular *vinyasas* because they combine a series of poses that so nicely balance each other (a backbend then a forward bend, and so on). But you, too, can create your own series of postures. Just keep them balanced—forward with backward, upright with inverted, one side with the other side, a stretch with a contraction, and so on. This will become easier as you familiarize yourself with the postures in this book.

Here are a few suggestions to get you started. All poses mentioned here are described elsewhere in this book or are explained below.

Warm Wonder Vinyasa

Starting in downward facing dog (Chapter 18), flow into the plank pose (Chapter 13) (like a push-up pose with the arms straight), exhale, bend the elbows and lower the body straight to the floor. Inhale, push yourself up into upward facing dog (Chapter 14), exhale, push back into downward facing dog, inhale, push one leg forward, turn to the side and straighten up into the triangle pose (Chapter 13). Do both sides in triangle, then exhale as you bend your other knee and bring your hands alongside your foot. Push back into downward facing dog. Hold for as long as comfortable, exhale into the child's pose (Chapter 18), then rest.

Solar Flare Vinyasa

Start in the mountain pose (Chapter 13), then jump your feet three to four feet apart and assume the warrior 2 pose (Chapter 13). Hold for a few breaths, then change your body position to face forward with your arms overhead in the warrior 1 pose (Chapter 13). Hold for a few breaths. Switch to the other side, doing warrior 1 and 2 in the other direction. Now, keeping your feet separated, turn your entire body to face forward and bend straight over with your knees straight. Bring your hands toward the floor and hold for a few breaths. Come back up, jump your feet together, bend your knees, place your palms flat on the floor. Bend down into the child's pose (Chapter 18). Rest.

Mild and Mindful Vinyasa

Start in *shavasana* (Chapter 19). Inhale and bring your hands under your tailbone, lifting up into the fish pose (Chapter 14). Hold for a few breaths, then come out of the pose, exhaling, and rolling over into the child's pose (Chapter 18). Stay in child's pose for a few breaths, inhale, sit up, exhale, and move into the hero pose (Chapter 17). Inhale as you move up, then exhale into the staff pose (Chapter 17). Inhale into any meditation pose (take your pick—see Chapter 17), and—you guessed it! Meditate for a while.

The Least You Need to Know

➤ A *vinyasa,* such as the sun or moon salutation, is a sequence of postures strung together and performed in a series of flowing movements.

➤ A *vinyasa* is coordinated with the breath.

➤ *Vinyasas* are great exercise for body and soul!

Part 5
Calming Down: Postures to Quiet the Body and Mind

These postures balance those in Part 4, calming and quieting the body and mind. First are the sitting poses in Chapter 17, including poses excellent for meditation. Sitting poses center the body and are conducive to a calm and tranquil mind.

Forward bending poses are internalizing. As the body bends forward, folding in on itself, the mind can focus more easily inward. Chapter 18 describes forward bends, both sitting and standing, for you to try.

Chapter 19 is devoted to the most important of all the postures, shavasana. *Also known as the corpse pose,* shavasana *is both the easiest and most difficult, because it involves simply lying on the floor in an attitude of complete and total relaxation. Sound easy? Just wait until you try to clear that active mind! Ideally, you'll be able to release your body completely. The corpse pose is ultimately relaxing—10 minutes of* shavasana *every day is a great way to manage the stresses in your life.*

Chapter 17

Are You Sitting Down?

In This Chapter

➤ The sitting postures: staff, butterfly, hero, and cow

➤ Special poses for meditation: easy and kneeling

➤ Finally, the lotus pose!

It's time to take a load off! Lots of great and challenging yoga postures, as well as the meditative postures, are accomplished while sitting. Sitting poses keep your hips and legs flexible. You may even want to adapt some of the following poses for when you happen to be sitting on the floor outside of your regular yoga practice—just one more way to fit yoga into your day!

Flooring It

Everybody turf it! Yes, sit down on the floor. (Perhaps a welcome relief after a strenuous round of sun salutations.) You should feel comfortable in sitting poses, especially the meditative poses, because your body shouldn't distract you from your meditation. If you have a hard floor, a yoga mat or rug (one that won't slide around) will keep you comfortable. A carpeted floor is also fine. Don't use your bed—your practice surface should be comfortable but firm. You'll need the resistance of the floor for many of the postures and a bed has too much "give." Ready? Set? Sit!

Dandasana: Staff Pose

A staff is a big stick used for support, like a walking stick. It is also a symbol of authority—he or she who holds the staff looks in charge! The staff pose increases your concentration and clarity of focus. *Dandasana* (pronounced dahn-DAH-sah-nah) is also great for your alignment. Concentrate on your upper body becoming straight and powerful as a staff.

(1) Sit on the floor with your feet straight out in front of you. Keep your palms flat alongside your hips with your fingers pointing toward your feet. Keep your knees and toes together, your heels pushed out, your toes relaxed. Your shoulders should be down, your chest open.

(2) Push your palms lightly down against the ground to create space in your spine. Lengthen the top and bottom of your body. Center your weight over your hips. Breathe.

If the staff pose is uncomfortable, sit on a folded blanket until you become more flexible. Don't puff out your chest. Imagine, instead, that your head is being pulled upward, which will also keep your back from sinking down and your chin from coming up. Your chin should be in line with the floor.

Baddha Konasana: Butterfly Pose

Literally translated as "bound angle pose," this pose imitates a butterfly resting its wings on a lotus blossom. When holding *baddha konasana* (pronounced BAH-dah koh-NAH-sah-nah), imagine the delicate beauty of this image of the butterfly. The butterfly pose opens your hips and Jupiter *chakra* (the *chakra* located in your pelvic area). It also loosens your knees and ankles.

(1) Sit on the floor and bring the soles of your feet together, drawing them towards your body.

(2) Open your chest and press your knees towards the ground as far as they will go. Don't bounce your legs up and down. Instead, allow gravity to gently release your hip joints.

(3) Tilt your lower back inward to align the spine. Don't let your lower back sway out.

(4) As your hips loosen, you will eventually be able to bow forward.

Wise Yogi Tells Us

While practicing the butterfly, keep your entire back straight. If your upper back becomes rounded as you pull your feet in, leave your feet further from your body—hold onto your shins or thighs if you can't reach your feet. Concentrate on the image of the butterfly. If you catch yourself frowning with unpleasant effort, loosen the pose a bit, think about beauty, and smile!

Virasana: Be a Hero!

A hero stands tall and proud, even when sitting on the floor! The hero pose refreshes your legs, stretches your knees, and balances your Saturn *chakra* (located at the base of your spine). *Virasana* is pronounced vir-AH-sah-nah.

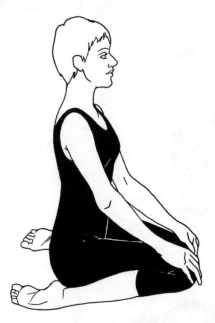

(1) Breathe deeply—heroes *always* breathe deeply! Feel your diaphragm lowering as your body fills with air.

(2) Sit back on your heels, gradually separating your feet until you are sitting on the floor between your legs.

(3) Keep your knees from buckling in and move your lower back forward without inflating your upper chest.

The hero pose can be hard on delicate knees if performed too quickly or attempted before your flexibility allows it. Go very gradually into this pose so you can feel at what point your knees are telling you to stop. If this is hard to do, place a telephone book under your buttocks. Every time you practice, tear out one page. In other words, go slow. You'll get a little further each time.

Gomukhasana: Holy Cow!

To us Westerners, the cow may be less than glamorous. Sure, it may adorn the pot holders, aprons, and cookie jars in our country kitchens, and we may think cows are awfully cute, but we don't take them too seriously. In India, however, the cow is the most sacred of animals, worshipped for its giving nature—cream, butter, and dung, which is used as fuel for fire. Appropriately, the cow pose is meant to lead to a feeling of openness and giving. It also stimulates the nerves at the base of your spine, aids in longevity as it keeps your lower vertebrae from calcifying, opens your shoulders and chest, and activates your Saturn and Jupiter *chakras* (located at the base of your spine and your pelvic area, respectively), helping to raise *kundalini* energy. *Gomukhasana* (pronounced goh-moo-KHA-sah-nah) is composed of *go,* which means "cow," *mukha,* which means "mouth" or "face," and of course, *asana,* which means "posture."

> **Ouch!**
> Don't be frustrated if your hands can't grasp each other. You don't want to pull a muscle! Have the patience of a cow. You'll get there eventually. Cows take their sweet time, and so should you!

(1) Sit with your legs in front of you, then bring one knee on top of the other. Draw your heels towards your body in this cross-legged position.

(2) Point one elbow toward the sky with your palm facing back behind you. Point the other elbow toward the ground with your palm facing out behind you. Bring your hands towards each other, clasping them if you can.

Meditative Poses

Technically, you can meditate just about anywhere and in any position, but ideally, you should try to meditate in one of several meditative poses. Why? There's nothing magical about the meditative poses, except that they arrange your body in a way ideal for meditation. Your spine is aligned so energy can flow freely. Your body is relaxed and comfortable. Meditative poses should feel so wonderful that you barely notice your body. If a meditative pose is uncomfortable or painful, you aren't quite ready for it yet. Try others instead.

A Yoga Minute
People who meditate are less sensitive to carbon dioxide.

Mudras are special hand positions that you can use while meditating to channel energy back through the fingers into the spinal column's *chakras*, directing and rebalancing *prana* in the body. Choose from the *mudras* in the illustration; mix and match *mudras* to enhance your yoga practice of meditation.

Wise Yogi Tells Us

Hands placed with the palms down on the knees give you a sense of grounding and centering energy. Hands placed with the palms up on the knees give you a sense of releasing energy, opening, and liberation.

Mudras *for Meditation*

Namaste

OM

Jnana

Buddhi

Sukhasana: Easy Pose

Sukhasana (pronounced soo-KAH-sah-nah) is a great meditation pose for beginners. *Sukha* means "joy," and this pose should feel so good that it fills you with joy! *Sukhasana* facilitates *pranayama,* quiets the mind, and stills the body.

(1) Sit in a simple crossed-leg position, with either leg on top. Try to sit more often with the leg that is least comfortable on top, to balance your body. Rest your hands on your knees and breathe.

(2) If your back starts to arch, put a pillow under your tailbone to align the spine. Think about happiness and joy!

Vajrasana: Kneeling Pose

Vajrasana (pronounced vahj-RAH-sah-nah) is also called the *Zen* pose, as this is the meditation pose used by *Zen Buddhist* monks. *Vajra* means "thunderbolt" or "diamond," and *vajrasana* aids circulation to the feet, lifts the spinal column, and relieves pressure on the diaphragm.

A Yoga Minute
Zen is a sect of Buddhism in which enlightenment is sought through introspection and contemplation rather than formal study of religious texts. *Buddhism* is a religion that teaches right living, right thinking, and meditation as a means to enlightenment.

(1) Again, breathe! Sit back on your heels, keeping your heels and knees together.

(2) Keeping your spine straight, place your hands on your knees. If your knees hurt, go back to the easy pose, and smile!

Padmasana: Lotus Pose

At last, the venerable lotus pose! You've heard about it, maybe you've seen it, perhaps you've even tried it. *Padmasana* (pronounced pahd-MAH-sah-nah) represents a lotus flower open to the light (*padma* means lotus). It keeps the spine from sagging and keeps you comfortable in meditation for longer periods of time than other positions. It also keeps the body from toppling over if you fall asleep during meditation (many wise souls have!). The lotus position also keeps your chest open, gives your diaphragm lots of room, and opens your Venus *chakra* (located behind your heart).

(1) Sit on the floor and begin to breathe deeply.

(2) Bring your left ankle on top of your right thigh, then your right ankle on top of your left thigh (or the other way around—and next time, try to switch which foot is on top).

(3) If your ankles hurt, practice non-violence by returning to the easy pose. The lotus pose requires strong ankles and open hips. Practice yoga's standing postures to build ankle and hip strength.

It's easy to be so concerned with trying to achieve the lotus pose that you forget the point of being in the pose: to be comfortable in your body. Because yoga is such an internal process, even if you're sitting in a perfect lotus pose in what appears to be quiet meditation, inside you may not be practicing yoga at all. You may be distracted, worried, or suffering. True meditation is effortless and joyful. If your ankles or any other part of you (including your feelings) are in agony or pain, meditation will be much more difficult to achieve. Find an easier pose, or postpone meditation in favor of more active postures. (Exercise is great when you're feeling low.) Come back to meditation when your mind is ready, and only then in a position your body loves.

Baddha Padmasana: Bound Lotus Pose

The bound lotus is the same as the lotus, except that your right arm goes behind your back and holds your right foot, while your left arm goes behind your back and holds your left foot. Whichever arm crosses on top, go the opposite way next time. *Baddha padmasana* (pronounced BAH-dah pahd-MAH-sah-nah) deepens all the benefits of the lotus pose, and you'll be able to breathe more deeply.

The bound lotus

The Least You Need to Know

➤ Sitting postures strengthen and increase flexibility in your hips and legs.

➤ *Mudras* are hand positions that enhance meditation by rechanneling energy that emanates from the fingers back into the body where it can stimulate your *chakras*.

➤ Meditate only in a posture that is perfectly comfortable. Some suggestions: easy, kneeling, and lotus.

➤ If you're down, move around. Feeling great? Meditate!

Chapter 18

Take the Forward Path

In This Chapter

➤ Why bend forward?

➤ Forward bends: child's pose, standing head to knees, feet apart side angle, sitting one leg, bound half lotus, *yoga mudra,* boat, tortoise, and downward facing dog

➤ Modifications, challenges, and other tips to improve your yoga practice

Forward bends are important for several reasons. They're wonderful for helping you to focus inward and quiet your mind. As your body bends forward, it folds your heart into its center. Forward bends are also important to balance backbends, so include a few of each in your yoga practice.

Forward bends are great for stretching out and loosening up the lower back muscles and also for lengthening the hamstrings. Believe it or not, the leg muscles often hold more stress than any other muscle group in the body! Forward bends help you reach that inner place where you can allow the lower back and hamstrings to relax and become fluid. Okay, one, two, three, reach!

Mudhasana: Child's Pose

The child's pose makes you feel safe and nurtured, as if you were still in the womb. *Mudhasana* (pronounced moo-DAH-sah-nah) activates your Venus and moon *chakras* (located behind your heart and at the base of your skull, respectively), relieves lower back pain, and improves your complexion. It also stimulates respiration because it compresses your diaphragm.

When practicing the child's pose, put some pillows or a blanket under your head to help lengthen your back if you find it hard to bend forward, or place a pillow or blanket between your knees and calves if your knees feel strained.

(1) Sit back on your heels, then bring your forehead to the floor.

(2) Rest your arms alongside your body with your palms facing up. The pose should feel completely relaxing.

(3) Breathe deeply. Feel your diaphragm rising and sinking with each breath, like a baby's tummy. A baby hasn't yet learned shallow chest-breathing, so breathe like a baby.

Uttanasana: Standing Head to Knees Pose

Uttanasana (pronounced OOH-tah-NAH-sah-nah) stretches the entire back side of your body. It also tones your abdomen, decreases bloating, refreshes your mind, and clears your head. To accomplish this, you may have to bend your knees. As you become more flexible, you'll be able to grasp your big toes with your index fingers. For those who can fold in half, give yourself a hug!

(1) Stand with your feet together. Raise your arms overhead.

(2) Exhale and bend forward at your hips. Work towards touching your nose to your knees. Keep your knees straight unless your back hurts, in which case you can bend your knees.

(3) Be careful not to rock your weight back to your heels. Keep your weight evenly distributed over your feet. Don't round your back or turn your feet out; instead, bend forward from the hips, lengthening through the lower back. Don't force your head toward your knees—let gravity do the work as your head and neck stay relaxed. Don't be concerned with how far you bend. Focus on how open you can become as you "lift" forward.

Parshvottanasana: Feet Apart Side Angle Pose

In *parshvottanasana* (pronounced PARSH-voh-tah-NAH-sah-nah), you will tone your abdomen; straighten drooping shoulders; and make your hips, spine, and wrists more flexible.

(1) Stand with your feet three to four feet apart. Turn one foot out and face that foot.

(2) Bring your hands into the *namaste* or prayer position, but behind your back with your fingers pointing up. If this is too difficult, simply clasp your hands behind your back, or keep your hands at your sides as you move forward.

(3) Inhale, lengthen the spine upward, then exhale, bringing your head toward your front knee.

(4) Imagine your chest, rather than your head, moving toward your knees to help lengthen the spine and prevent rounding of the back. Keep breathing throughout this pose.

Janu Shirshasana: Sitting One Leg Pose

In *janu shirshasana* (pronounced JAH-noo shur-SHAH-sah-nah), *janu* means "knee" and *shirsha* means "head." You may guess that this pose, then, involves bringing the head and knee together. The sitting one leg pose tones your abdomen, liver, spleen, and kidneys. It quiets your mind and aids digestion, as well as stretches and strengthens your lower back and chest. Men suffering from an enlarged prostate will benefit from this pose.

Wise Yogi Tells Us

If you feel stress on your back doing the sitting one leg pose, bend the knee you are reaching toward. Angle your body directly over this knee. Release any competitive thoughts. Forget your goals and open your heart. Bend at the hips, not at the waist. Don't hurry, smile, and be patient with yourself. Slowly your leg and hip will open. Have fun with the process.

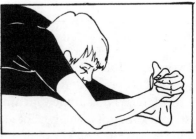

(1) Sit on the floor with your left leg straight in front of you, toes pointed up. Your right leg should be bent in toward the straight leg.

(2) Raise your hands over your head, exhale, and slowly bend forward over your straight leg.

(3) Hold the stretch, then inhale as you rise back up. Repeat on the other side.

Ardha Baddha Padma Pashchimottanasana: Bound Half Lotus Pose

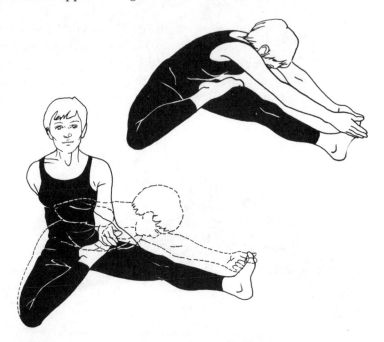

Ardha baddha padma pashchimottanasana (pronounced AHR-dah BAH-dah PAHD-mah PAH-shih-moh-tah-NAH-sah-nah) is identical to the sitting one leg pose, except the foot of your bent leg is in a half lotus position, with the foot placed on the opposite thigh.

> ✷ **Ouch!**
>
> Not every pose is for every body. Be patient and kind with your body and your body will respond accordingly. You will be amazed at the power of TLC (tender loving care!).

(1) Bring your arm around your back and connect your hand to this foot.

(2) Open your chest, exhale, and slowly bend forward. Repeat on the other side. If you can't achieve this pose, be patient and don't push your body. The pose will come.

> **Wise Yogi Tells Us**
>
> Just a friendly reminder to your ego: Take a hike! When performing any yoga pose, especially more difficult poses, don't allow your ego to take over. If you find yourself thinking, "Look at me touching the floor!" or "Wow, I'm so good at this!," re-adjust your thoughts. The goal of yoga is to eliminate ego, not to encourage it. Feel how the posture you're holding helps your mind to become clear and see the truth: that you are one with the true world.

190

Yoga Mudra: Ego-Be-Gone!

Yoga mudra (pronounced YOH-gah MOO-drah) is a symbol of unity. This important pose inspires feelings of devotion and humility. It also stretches your legs and hips, opens your shoulders, and aids the gastrointestinal tract.

(1) Sit cross-legged or in the kneeling pose.

(2) Bring your hands together behind your back and lower your head to the floor.

(3) Lift your clasped hands up over your head.

Naukasana: Boat Pose

A yogi holding *naukasana* (pronounced now-KAH-sah-nah) looks like a boat bobbing on the waves, and *nauka* literally means "ship." This pose tones your stomach and intestines, strengthens your back, and activates your Mars *chakra* (located behind your naval).

(1) In the full boat, sit on the floor with your knees bent in front of you and your arms holding your knees.

(2) Lean back, bring your feet off the floor, and balance on your tailbone.

(3) Raise your feet straight up in the air. Imagine you are bobbing on top of the water like a little rowboat.

The half boat: Keep the knees bent, and feet in a right angle to the floor. Bring your hands alongside your feet with your palms facing in.

In both boat poses, don't hold your breath, even as you are concentrating on balancing. Your feet may fall to the floor at first. Work to keep them either straight up or at a right angle. Keep your knees together.

Kurmasana: Tortoise Pose

Another self-explanatory pose, but quite a difficult one, too: You'll look like a tortoise when you practice *kurmasana* (pronounced koohr-MAH-sah-nah). This pose keeps your lumbar limber! (In other words, it makes your spine more flexible.) It also strengthens your neck, massages your thyroid, aids digestion, and rejuvenates your nervous system. Take it slow—just like a tortoise!

Does the tortoise pose seem impossible? Simply lower yourself as far as you can, smile, and enjoy the journey to the floor, even if it takes many, many yoga practices. Tortoises are not in a hurry. They live loooong lives!

A Yoga Minute
Hypothyroidism, the underproduction of the thyroid hormone, is a common condition and may underlie many different recurring illnesses and chronic fatigue. Symptoms of an underactive thyroid include fatigue, weight gain, weakness, dry skin, hair loss, recurrent infections, depression, and intolerance to cold.

(1) Start in the legs apart version of the sitting one leg pose. Then, bend your knees and place your arms under your knees with your palms facing down.

(2) Slowly straighten your legs and bring your chest forward. Your chin will eventually reach the floor. This position massages your thyroid.

Adho Mukha Shvanasana: Downward Facing Dog Pose

Another pose named after the esteemed canine. Downward facing dog, *adho mukha shvanasana* (pronounced AH-doh MOO-kah shvah-NAH-sah-nah), brings heat to your body, strengthens and stretches your spine, and gives your heart a rest.

(1) Get down on your hands and knees. Lift your tailbone up, bringing your knees off the floor.

(2) Bring your shoulders and head down. Keep your knees bent at first, then slowly bring your heels to the floor and straighten your legs.

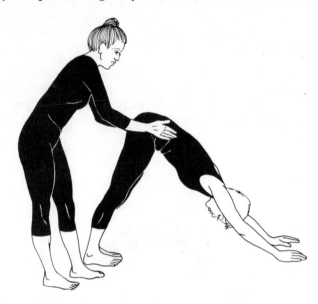

If downward facing dog hurts your wrists, you may not be balancing your weight evenly. Try to shift weight back into your heels. Hold the pose only as long as you are comfortable. Little by little, your balance will shift and this pose will eventually become quite soothing. Stretch out your lower back: Instead of rounding it, lengthen it. Remember the way your back is stretched out in child's pose? Think about lifting your tailbone to the sky. If necessary, keep your knees slightly bent to return a natural curve to your lower back. When you are flexible and strong enough to perform downward facing dog fully and peacefully, you will place as much weight in your heels as you do in your hands. To get this feeling of the full pose, have a partner lift your hips up and shift your weight back to center, just as we've shown in the illustration.

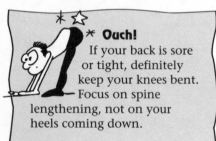

Ouch!
If your back is sore or tight, definitely keep your knees bent. Focus on spine lengthening, not on your heels coming down.

The Least You Need to Know

➤ Forward bending postures such as standing head to knees, feet apart side angle, sitting one leg, bound half lotus, *yoga mudra,* boat, half boat, tortoise, and downward facing dog, help you to internalize and quiet your mind.

➤ Forward bends are great for loosening the lower back and stretching out the hamstrings.

➤ Forward bends and backbends balance each other and should be practiced together.

Dead to the World

Of all the yoga poses, *shavasana* (pronounced shah-VAH-sah-nah), also known as the corpse pose, is the most important. *Shava* means "corpse," and just as it sounds, the corpse pose consists of lying on the floor in complete relaxation, still, peaceful, and corpse-like. "How can lying on the floor be important?" you might ask. Or better yet, "How can imitating a corpse be important?" Both good questions! Here's a good answer: The essence of peace comes from within, not from without. *Shavasana's* goal is to relax the body so completely that the body becomes irrelevant, as if it were deceased. With the body "gone," the mind is set free to blossom.

"But a corpse is dead!" you might continue to argue. "Isn't yoga about life?" Yes! But life and death are inseparable—they are all part of a bigger reality. By learning the corpse pose, you learn to live. By focusing inward, which means focusing beyond the body, the ego, and the superficial trappings of the "you" who walks around every day—clothes, habits, personality—you'll ultimately connect with the beauty of the universe. The surface "you" can finally fall away, and the inner "you," the Real You, can emerge. Imagine the resounding cosmic question: Will the Real You please stand up? If you've mastered *shavasana,* you'll know just who the Real You is! As your body lies corpse-like, the Real You can stand.

How to Be a Corpse

Shavasana involves more than collapsing onto the floor in a crumpled heap after a long, hard day and *wishing* you were dead. Let's practice the corpse pose with a little more focus!

(1) Lie comfortably on your back on the floor, and separate your legs so your feet are two to three feet apart. Let your toes fall out to the sides. Close your eyes.

(2) Separate your arms so that each hand is two to three feet from your body with each palm facing up.

(3) Roll your head from side to side, releasing tension in your neck.

(4) Roll your shoulders down and away from your ears.

(5) Allow your attention to travel up and down your body, scanning for tight spots or contracted muscles. When you find a tight spot, gently tell the area to relax (out loud, if it helps). For example, "Chill out, right shoulder!" You may have to say it twice. Place a pillow under your knees or head if this helps you relax.

(6) Repeat your body scan until your body is completely relaxed.

(7) Now bring your attention to your breath. Listen to your breath. Don't try to control it. Simply observe it. Feel it flowing in and out of you. Make the sound and feel of your breath the sole focus of your attention.

(8) If part of your body starts to tense up, redirect your mind to the tense area and focus on relaxing it again, then return to the breath.

(9) As thoughts pop into your mind ("If my computer crashes again today I'm gonna throw it out the window." "That new guy at the office sure is cute!"), let them pass back out of your mind. Imagine they are soap bubbles—allow your breath to blow them away softly, up into the sky.

(10) Come back to the breath. Back to the breath. To the breath. The breath. Breath. OM.

One for All and All for OM!

Maybe lying on the floor is no problem for you, but everything after that is a real challenge. It isn't easy to relax, let alone clear the mind. OM to the rescue! We've mentioned the *mantra* OM a few times already in this book, but let's look at it again in terms of its power to center and relax you. OM is the sound frequently chanted by yogis because it is an all-encompassing sound. According to yogic thought, if all of life were translated into a single sound, the sound of the universe, that sound would be OM.

Try saying the sound now, right where you are sitting (or standing, or lying down, or wherever you happen to be at the moment). Take a deep breath, breathing from the diaphragm, and sing out the "O" sound as long as you can without your voice faltering. Don't be afraid to put some sound and strength behind it. If you're worried about keeping your volume down too much, you might not give the sound the breath support it requires. Stay strong and sing out the sound, which is pronounced like "OH," then slowly let the "O" sound come to a close in a resonating, vibrating "MMMMM" sound.

A Yoga Minute
Gandhi's last words to his assailant as he fell to the ground, January 30, 1948, from a violent gunshot wound, were "Rama, Rama," which means "Praise God." This is the essence of yoga: to have one's thoughts continuously uplifted, even (especially!) in the transition from one existence to another.

Now take a breath, close your eyes this time, and try it again. Let the sound stretch out for as long as you can with the support of a deep breath. Use up all your breath, but don't strain yourself. Doesn't that feel good? Do it again if you'd like to. Notice how, when your entire body is vibrating with that sound, it's easier to concentrate on the breath and the sound than whether or not to have dessert with dinner tonight or who you can convince to do the dishes.

Also, notice how much OM sounds like "Amen." If you've been to or go to church, you've probably heard the "Amen" sung at the end of every hymn. Have you ever noticed that when a chorus of voices sings "Amen," the voices often bloom from a single note into a harmony, like a multi-petaled flower opening in sound? Think how nicely this concept fits into the yoga way of thinking. Many voices harmonize to form a single, beautiful sound that is more complete than one voice alone, just as the universe is a beautiful blending of each soul into a single vibration of love.

In a nutshell, the point of chanting OM is to let the incredible power of sound and vibration work for you, pushing away worldly concerns and physical discomforts to bring your mind to a singular (yet universal) focus. Try it the next time you try the corpse pose. You'll be blissfully surprised!

When the Easiest Is the Hardest

Some of you may still be stuck on the idea that *shavasana* is the most important of all the postures. "How hard can it be?" you might wonder. "How hard can it be to lie on the floor and relax?" Actually, *shavasana* is also the most challenging pose, even though it seems, at first, to be the easiest. In a way, the corpse pose is both the easiest and the hardest pose. Unlike some poses, where you first need to spend a lot of time developing strong ankles or upper arms or balance, the corpse pose can be assumed by anyone who can lie on the floor.

On the other hand, not only is relaxation a true challenge for many, but *shavasana* has a strong mental component, without which you aren't truly practicing *shavasana*. Just as you can hold the lotus pose perfectly without truly practicing yoga, you can certainly lie in what appears to be a perfect *shavasana* without coming close to a yogic state of mind. Ideally, *shavasana* could be practiced in the midst of total chaos because the yogi in *shavasana* has utterly released him- or herself from the body. The body is merely a shell or a vessel, while the soul is directly connected with the universe. Certainly it takes a long while to reach this point, and the corpse pose can be practiced quite productively before this state is reached, but this is the ideal destination, and a challenging journey it is!

Let *shavasana* become a part of your workout and take it just as seriously as any other posture—even *more* seriously. Your body will learn how to release all its tensions and will benefit even more from the other postures because of its time spent in *shavasana*. Your spirit, too, will learn how to soar beyond the limits of its "container." Now *that's* a powerful skill!

Wise Yogi Tells Us

Even though *shavasana* isn't meant to put you to sleep, practicing it in bed at night—particularly the steps for relaxing the body—can help to lure even the most hard-core insomniac towards dreamland.

Open Up and Let Go: The Body

Your body is a complex organism with thousands of parts, all connected and related, yet separate, too. It's no easy task to relax the whole thing, let alone transcend it completely. When practicing *shavasana*, it can help to have a plan for releasing each part of your body a little at a time. Read over the following steps for releasing and relaxing the lower body, upper body, and face. Enough times through and you'll have the steps memorized.

The Lower Body: Going Nowhere

Once you are in the corpse pose and have followed all the steps mentioned above, but before you focus on your breath:

➤ Tighten one foot, curling the toes and contracting your foot muscles for a few seconds, then release and feel the tension flowing from your foot.

➤ Flex your ankle and tighten your calf, then relax both.

➤ Lift your entire leg two inches off the ground. Tense your leg, especially the large thigh muscle. Squeeze! Then let your leg fall to the ground. With the release, imagine all the tension falling away.

➤ Repeat the above three steps with your other foot and leg.

➤ Lift your hips two inches off the floor and squeeze your buttocks as tightly as you can for several seconds, then release the contraction and drop your hips back down. Feel all the tight areas releasing and relaxing. Your hip joints should feel loose and your buttocks muscles completely relaxed.

The Upper Body: Still Rhythms

Continuing upward:

➤ Contract your stomach muscles as tightly as you can, then release them.

➤ Lift one arm about two inches off the floor. Squeeze your hand into a fist and hold it tightly. Flex your arm muscles for several seconds, then relax your entire arm and let it fall. Feel stress and tightness flowing down your arm and out the ends of your fingers. Repeat with the other arm.

➤ Tighten your chest muscles, then release them. As you release them, try to feel your heartbeat. Tell your heart to relax, slow down, and rest.

➤ Bring your shoulders up to your ears, tensing them for several seconds. Release them and feel all the stress dropping away. Many people carry lots of tension in their shoulders. If you're one of them, you may want to do this one several times until your shoulders feel truly loose.

Ouch!
If lying flat on the floor is uncomfortable for your back, put pillows or blankets under your knees. This protects your lower back from undue strain. If your head or neck is uncomfortable, rest your head or neck on a small pillow, but make sure your throat feels open—too many pillows could block the flow of energy through your neck. Too few pillows could cause your neck to overstrain backwards. If you have low blood pressure and your feet get cold, wear socks. Strive for a feeling of openness in all parts of your body.

The Ultimate Facial: Losing Your Senses

And now for the rest of you:

➤ Lift your head two inches off the ground. Tense all your neck and facial muscles, scrunching up your face like a prune. Purse your lips and imagine you are trying to bring every part of your face to your nose. Release and lower your head.

➤ Raise your head again and open your eyes and mouth as wide as you possibly can. Stick your tongue out as far as you can. Really stretch that face for several seconds, then relax and lower your head to the ground.

➤ Roll your head slowly and gently from one side to the other.

➤ One at a time, scan your senses. First, notice what you can taste, then let it go. Take your mind away from your taste buds. Next, notice what you can smell, then release your sense of smell. Notice everything your body is touching, then imagine you are floating and can't feel anything. What can you hear? Let it go. Turn off your ears and focus inward. Last of all, let go of your sight (even though your eyes should already be closed) by releasing all tension around your eyes. If you see light through your eyelids, gently push away your awareness of it.

➤ Now, go back over each body part again, but this time, mentally tell each part to relax. Really focus on each area, one at a time, and coax it to release all pain and tension. Consider this the start of a wonderful relationship between your mind and your body. Why shouldn't they converse?

➤ After you've completed all the above steps, you should feel very, very relaxed and internalized. Mentally scan your body a few more times, seeking out pockets of stress and releasing them. If any sense sensations try to creep back in, gently ignore them. Now you're ready to leave your body behind and ride the breath.

Open Up and Let Go: The Mind

You've moved past your body, and are now immersed in your mind. But that has to go, too. Yes, the mind is as distracting as the body when it comes to true relaxation—maybe more so! Even as you lie in the corpse pose feeling proud that you've managed to transcend your body, at least to some extent, your mind is holding you back from true awareness. How? By making you feel proud, for one thing! Pride belongs to the ego, and in true awareness, there is no ego. So what's an active-minded person to do? Simple: Stop thinking.

Me, Stop Thinking? Forget About It!

To many, the prospect of not thinking seems far more of a Herculean effort than the most complicated yoga posture. We *are* our minds...aren't we? Not according to yogic philosophy. In fact, wise yogis tell us that we aren't our bodies or our minds at all. These are merely tools to help free our souls and bring them into fuller and more unifying consciousness.

As you rest in *shavasana* attempting to keep your mind at bay, think about your mind merely as a tool to help you in your task. When used at the wrong time or for the wrong job, a tool can be a hindrance, but when used correctly, it will make any job easier. During *shavasana,* it's time to put the tools down. Put away your thoughts. Let them go. You can always pick them up again later.

Dream a Little Dream

Imagine waking up one morning with the memory of a beautiful dream. In the dream, you are walking through your home and everything is familiar until you come upon a door you've never noticed before. You open the door and step through it into a new universe. Pure beauty surrounds you and you are filled with a feeling of bliss. You realize that you are perfect. You have no faults, no sins, no shortcomings, no guilt. You are a being of pure light and the whimsically lovely universe that encompasses you is also you. Love radiates from you and into you. You vaguely remember the comparatively ponderous and painful life of striving on the other side of the door through which you came, but as you look behind you, the door is gone and you realize that other life was just a dream.

And then you wake up. Which was real and which was the dream? Yogic philosophy says that this life we lead in these earthbound bodies and minds is the dream, and that pure bliss is the reality. Yoga helps us to wake from this dream. But even dreams exist for a reason, and we all move through this dream of our lives to learn about our souls. This dream is a lesson, but it's still only a dream (though an awfully vivid one!).

Of course, we don't mean that right now you are really asleep and dreaming all of this. Life isn't a dream in the sense that we are used to thinking of dreams. But according to wise yogis, our interpretation of life is an illusion. Anything that isn't eternal and isn't blissful is an illusion. Yoga, and especially *shavasana,* helps us to work past our bodies and dig through our thoughts until we unearth the jewel that is cosmic consciousness. How extraordinary to awake to such a reality!

Wise Yogi Tells Us

"Do not take life's experiences too seriously. Above all, do not let them hurt you, for in reality, they are nothing but dream experiences…If circumstances are bad and you have to bear them, do not make them a part of yourself. Play your part in life, but never forget that it is only a role."

—Paramahansa Yogananda

Give Your Mind a Breather

But let's get back to this "dream" we're all living and striving through called life. We have to live in the world and we can't lie in the corpse pose all day long. We have to eat, sleep, make money, do our daily chores, care for those who depend on us. What good is *shavasana* during the rest of the day?

Have you ever left all your worries behind and taken off for a vacation, even if just for the night? Maybe you found a last-minute baby-sitter and whisked your spouse off for a romantic evening alone. Maybe you took a personal day off work, got in your car, and drove somewhere you've never been before. If you've never done such a thing, you should try it. It's rejuvenating, giving you a new perspective on your everyday life. But even if you aren't at liberty to leave your regular life for a while, you can still practice *shavasana*—a mini-vacation for your mind.

If you had a job where you had to work the same hours your mind has to work, you'd probably collapse in less than a week. Of course, our brains are made to be busy, but even the most efficient brain needs a break now and then. *Shavasana* turns everything off: the senses, the emotions, the thoughts. Only breath exists, and pure consciousness. If you've ever uttered the words, "At last, I can just sit here and do nothing!" then you know how your brain feels when you practice *shavasana*.

Quest for Peace

Perhaps the most compelling reason for us Westerners to practice *shavasana* is that it simply brings more peace into our lives. Imagine yourself calmer and more clear-headed, able to take any situation in stride, handle any emergency with unruffled confidence. The regular practice of *shavasana* can give you this gift. We can all use more peace in our lives, and this needn't be a futile wish. Take an active role in bringing peace to your life through *shavasana,* because even the most hectic and chaotic external life is miraculous and wonderful when peace lives inside you.

The Least You Need to Know

➤ If you practice only one yoga pose, practice *shavasana*.

➤ Mastering *shavasana* can be more strenuous and requires more discipline than the most physically demanding of yoga postures!

➤ Learning to quiet the mind and remove scattered thinking will bring you peace.

Part 6
Living Your Yoga

This final section will help you incorporate yoga into your daily life in lots of ways. First, Chapter 20 talks about diet and how what you eat can affect who you are. Yoga divides foods into three categories: sattvic, rajasic, and tamasic. Find out which category your favorite foods belong to, and how they might be helping or hindering your physical and mental well-being.

Chapter 21 introduces you to the five sheaths of your body—yes, you have all five, and they can all be affected when you are sick, injured, or just in a rotten mood. Next, you'll read about how different postures and other yoga lifestyle changes can help you with various minor complaints, and even how you can help your body to help itself when you suffer from more serious health conditions.

Last of all, you'll read about fun yoga postures you can try with a partner, and how yoga can enhance the lives and unique challenges of women, men, children, and seniors, alike. We'll introduce you to yoga for PMS, yoga for pregnancy, and yoga for menopause. We'll explain why a lot of Western guys have trouble with yoga, but why yoga can be fantastically rewarding for them. Guys, trust us, you're gonna love it! We'll show you how to have great fun "playing yoga" with your kids, and we'll give you some great yoga tips for your golden years, too.

Chapter 20

You Are What You Eat

In This Chapter

➤ Three types of foods bring out three types of personal qualities

➤ Moderate eating is best

➤ The benefits of a lacto-vegetarian diet

Now that you've got a handle on yoga's basic principles and are happily posturing away, let's consider another extremely important, but often overlooked, aspect of yoga: diet. It only makes sense that if your body, mind, and spirit are one, how you feed your body will influence the whole package. Western scientists have long recognized that a healthy diet is crucial to good health, although through the decades the definition of "healthy" has certainly changed.

Gunas Gracious!

There exists a fundamental principle that is the yoga diet's primary influence. Yogis have traditionally divided food into three categories, called *gunas: sattvic* food, which promotes health, vitality, strength, and tranquillity; *rajasic* food, which promotes excessive energy, agitation, and discontentment; and *tamasic* food, which promotes lethargy, laziness, and inactivity.

Samyama is what yogis strive for. It means holding consciousness together through concentration, meditation, and contemplation in an attempt to understand everything about the object of one's investigation, whether that be poetry, the study of medicine, or the study of yoga postures. *Samyama* is the final state that results from the active process of learning.

On the other hand, *duhkha* is what often leads us astray. *Duhkha* is a feeling of discomfort or pain, suffering, sickness, or simply mental limitation. It is that deep-down feeling that something is wrong or out of place. *Duhkha* keeps you from achieving *samyama*. It makes you feel like you don't have the ability or are somehow inadequate—not healthy enough or strong enough or smart enough. *Duhkha* can arise out of excessive desire for something—even for enlightenment! It can be likened to a mental "virus" that infects your attitude and progress.

> **Know Your Sanskrit**
>
> *Samyama* (pronounced SAHM-YAH-mah) is a state that exists when concentration, meditation, and contemplation are all producing a perfectly balanced concentrated meditational state. *Sam* means together, and *yama* means discipline. *Duhkha* (pronounced DOO-kah) is pain, suffering, trouble, and discomfort. From *dur,* which means "bad," and *kha,* which means "axle hole" or "space" (hence, being in a bad space), *duhkha* is a mental state during which limitations and a profound sense of "wrongness" are perceived. *Duhkha* holds us back from self-actualization.

So how are *samyama* and *duhkha* related to the three *gunas*? Too many *rajasic* and/or *tamasic* foods produce *duhkha*, that's how! Balance is maintained with *sattvic* foods, and in fact, yoga itself can be seen as a process of "sattvification." It helps to keep you *duhkha*-free.

So we know we want to maintain a *sattvic* state of mind as often as possible. What better way than to eat a *sattvic* diet? Since feeding the body is akin to feeding the mind, *sattvic* food will encourage a *sattvic* mental state, once we are balanced. However, *sattvic* foods won't necessarily be able to balance someone who is very *rajasic* or *tamasic* (yes, people can be *sattvic, rajasic,* and *tamasic,* too). For instance, a very *rajasic* person may need to eat more *tamasic* food to find a balance. Then, *sattvic* food makes a great "maintenance diet." A swinging pendulum isn't easy to stop. The way it best comes to rest is by a slow change in the intensity of its swing.

> **Wise Yogi Tells Us**
>
> Feeling stressed out? Gently heat one cup of low-fat milk on the stove or in the microwave. Pour it into a mug and add one tablespoonful of honey and a pinch of dried ginger. Stir, find a comfy seat, and relax. Sip slowly. Ahhhhh! Don't drink milk? Cut a two-inch slice of fresh gingerroot, peel it, and slice it into disks. Put it into the bottom of a mug or cup and pour boiling water over it. Let it steep for about five minutes, then remove the ginger. Add a squeeze of fresh lemon juice and a tablespoonful of honey. Mmmm!

What's Your Nature?

As you can see, the *gunas* don't just apply to food. They are qualities that can be applied to the universe in general. The mind is made up of these three states. *Tamas* is dullness, lassitude, and constancy. *Rajas* is activity and agitation. *Sattva* is clarity, tranquillity, and compassion. These three states also represent the three states of personal evolution: first the mind is dull, then it becomes active, and then, ideally, it finds true compassion.

The wild activity of *rajas* is considered on a higher plane than the inert *tamas* because without activity, one cannot reach compassion (*sattva*). Most people swing around from quality to quality, experiencing each at different points in their lives, even throughout the day. However, one aspect is usually dominant in each person's personality.

Yes, one of these qualities is probably dominant in you. Knowing which is your type can help you to balance yourself. If you're a typical *rajas*-natured Westerner, for example, you can consciously minimize or eliminate *rajasic* food from your diet, replacing it with *sattvic* food. You'll probably notice a distinct difference in the way you feel—calmer, clearer, and less agitated.

Not sure which type you are? Take this mini-quiz to get a better picture of yourself.

1. If I'm feeling under a lot of stress, I'll be most likely to:
    A. Go take a nap. At least I'll be able to forget about it all for awhile.
    B. Pace back and forth, worrying and wasting time.
    C. Analyze why I'm under stress and make a plan to deal with it.
2. I would describe my diet as:
    A. Centered around my food addictions: caffeine, sugar, or salt. Meals are really important to me because I have to have my food! It would be very difficult for me to give up any food I love.
    B. Very irregular. I grab a bite of whatever is handiest when I have the time. Sometimes I forget to eat, or am so stressed out that I eat way too much without realizing it.
    C. Healthy, well-balanced, with lots of fruits and vegetables. Not a big fan of meat.
3. In my personal relationships, I tend to be:
    A. The passive one.
    B. The dominant one.
    C. Fairly equal with the others in my life.

If you answered mostly As, you're probably *tamas*-natured. You'd rather lie on the couch than go for a jog; you tend to get addicted to pleasurable things like sugar, cigarettes, or coffee; and you have a hard time getting things done. You may have difficulty getting yourself into a habit of practicing yoga postures, but yoga will be of great benefit to you.

If you answered mostly Bs, you're probably *rajas*-natured. You're typically overwrought, excited, anxious, or agitated. You get a lot done and fast, but you have a hard time relaxing and quieting your mind. For you, meditation is a real challenge, but you could really use the skill of being able to calm that over-active mind of yours.

If you answered mostly Cs, you tend to be *sattvic*-natured. You tend to practice moderation in many aspects of your life, and the yogic lifestyle will probably be relatively easy for you to adopt. You find a sense of peace in yoga postures, you find meditation enjoyable, and you already follow the yogic diet without even intending to! In fact, you may wonder why you haven't discovered yoga before now.

Yogi Food

So let's cut to the chase: What kind of food is *sattvic* food? *Sattvic* foods are pure foods. Most foods that are fresh, organically grown, additive- and preservative-free, unprocessed, and alkaline are considered *sattvic*. These include the following:

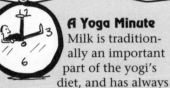

A Yoga Minute
Milk is traditionally an important part of the yogi's diet, and has always been considered *sattvic*. However, milk today is not what it used to be. Factory farms with their hormone- and antibiotic-laden cows packed in tiny stalls in sunless enclosures, pasteurization, and shipment to supermarkets in plastic packaging have all compromised milk's *sattvic* nature. In addition, many people are lactose intolerant, meaning that they lack the necessary enzyme needed in the body to digest milk.

➤ fresh fruits and juices

➤ most fresh vegetables

➤ whole-grain cereals

➤ nuts and seeds, especially almonds and sesame seeds

➤ pulses (dried peas, beans, and lentils)

➤ milk and milk products, including butter

➤ honey

Sattvic foods help you to think more clearly because your body is unclouded and unhindered by impurities, chemicals, and stimulants. *Sattvic* foods promote contemplative thought, vitality, energy, tranquillity, happiness, and overall health. Most serious yoga practitioners exist primarily on *sattvic* foods, although because food in and of itself is not an obsession for the healthy yogi, occasional tastes of other foods when these are offered aren't a problem. The wise yogi eats moderately, and moderation means *not* being obsessive about anything, even moderation!

If you're unable to drink milk or choose to avoid all dairy products (a truly non-violent approach to eating), simply update our list of *sattvic* foods by eliminating milk. Stick with organic produce and whole grains, the foods that remain *sattvic* even in our complicated world.

Pungent, Spicy Westerners

As we've mentioned, most Westerners tend to be *rajas*-natured because Western life is so *rajas*-oriented. Our culture rewards high energy, overachievement, even anxiety and agitation if they help to get the job done! *Rajasic* foods are generally the stimulating kind: spicy, sour, pungent, and bitter. The following are examples of *rajasic* food:

➤ all meat
➤ all fish
➤ eggs
➤ hot peppers
➤ most strong spices, especially black and red pepper
➤ coffee, tea, cola, and other stimulating, caffeine-laden beverages

Ancient cultures often fed their warriors meat before sending them off to battle because it was known that meat increased aggression and agitation. After a good meat-fest, warriors could fight and kill better. Assuming you don't have the need to fight and kill anyone, however, why not try cutting down or even eliminating most *rajasic* foods from your diet? You may find a new sense of calm and a clearer head.

Of course, a little *rajasic* food now and then won't hurt anyone. It's what you do most of the time that counts. But if you exist on steak and eggs, or spicy beef burritos, or sausage-and-pepper sandwiches, or coffee and diet cola, even a non-yogi can tell you that you aren't going to be at your healthiest.

Wise Yogi Tells Us

If you aren't ready for all-out vegetarianism, try it for a day. Tell yourself you can have a cheeseburger tomorrow, but today you'll stick with hearty split-pea soup over rice or a steaming plate of pasta with sautéed mushrooms. Tomorrow, before your cheeseburger, notice how you feel. Lighter? Hungrier? No different? Calmer? Then try it again next week.

Stale Leftovers for Couch Potatoes

Tamasic food is considered impure, and includes anything stale, old, aged, fermented, spoiled, overly processed, preservative-filled, or addictive. Some examples of *tamasic* food are:

➤ coffee, tea, cola, and other sources of caffeine (on this list, too, because they are both stimulating and addictive)

211

A Yoga Minute
Maybe you're wondering how caffeine can be both *rajasic* and *tamasic*. The stimulating quality of caffeine—that "buzz" that shifts you into high gear—is, indeed, *rajasic*, but there's more to caffeine than its stimulating nature. Coffee, tea, and cola are also addictive, and addictive substances are *tamasic*. The habitual nature of caffeine woos the *tamas*-natured; plus, the stimulating effect gets hard-to-move *tamas*-natured folks up on their feet and out the door to work. Yes, yes, we understand. You *love* your cup of coffee! (We love ours, too.) Fear not. Remember, it's what you do most of the time that counts. If the rest of your diet is basically sattvic, an occasional cup of coffee isn't going to hurt.

➤ alcohol, including wine and beer

➤ tobacco (We know, you smoke it, you don't eat it—but it still counts!)

➤ any food that's been sitting around too long, even if it still looks good (For example, produce that has been heavily sprayed and waxed so it can last through a journey across country and long periods of storage.)

➤ anything processed, packaged, frozen, or preserved, from that "lite" microwavable dinner to that box of snack cakes that would last in your pantry for five years

Tamasic foods dull your mind. They make you feel tired and sap your ambition and strength (just what the freezing process—*tamas*a-fying!—does to fresh, or *sattvic,* food). Too much *tamasic* food will drain away your energy and your vitality, eventually bringing on a lack of joy in life, if not serious illness. No matter how much coloring and how many preservatives are added to make the food look good, when our bodies ingest it, the "make-up" comes right off and the food's true quality is revealed. Unfortunately, many Westerners are addicted to *tamasic* food, especially sources of caffeine and alcohol. Also, we've been tricked into believing we don't have time for anything but preservative-laden "convenience" food. Our supermarkets are brimming with *tamasic* fare, but that doesn't mean you have to put it in your grocery cart. It is easier to keep a stock of canned tomatoes longer than a stock of fresh tomatoes, but it certainly isn't better, or worth the price!

Moderation in All Things (as if You Didn't Know!)

But wait! Just because you now know which foods are best for you doesn't mean you should throw down this book, run to the kitchen, and start indulging. Calm down, you *rajas*-natured ones. Don't plan your indulgent feast just yet, you *tamas*-natured folk. Cultivating *sattva* means more than shoveling in massive quantities of the "right" foods. It also involves a few principles of eating:

➤ Eat slowly. Chew each bite 50 times (or, if that's just too much to ask, start with 10 times and work your way up). Taste your food. Don't think about what you're going to eat next or what you need to do next. Give your meal some time.

➤ Eat with full attention to eating. That means no TV, no newspaper, and no trance-like gazing at the back of the cereal box, fascinating as it may be.

➤ Enjoy your food and savor the eating experience. Live in the moment of your meal!

➤ Don't eat too much. Try to leave the table with a little room left in your stomach.

➤ Don't eat too often. That means avoiding between-meal snacking, late-night binges, and 3:00 a.m. Dagwood sandwiches.

If food is too important to you, it'll control you. If you have a food addiction, you already know what it's like to be controlled. Food is meant to keep you alive and to enhance your existence; food isn't meant to fill emotional voids.

Wise Yogi Tells Us

If you've got habitual *tamasic* tendencies—to food, cigarettes, caffeine, or whatever—we recommend the forthcoming *Complete Idiot's Guide to Breaking Bad Habits*. Check it out!

Overindulgence taxes your body, and it's been suggested that regular and consistent undereating (not undernourishment—an important distinction) increases longevity. That means more time on this earth for practicing yoga, and more time to enjoy the improved you. Remember the old and familiar adage (did your parents ever tell you this?): "Moderation in All Things." This is a seriously important concept. Live moderately and you'll live well.

Sometimes the best way to let food work for you is to give your body a rest from food. Moderate eating is great, but sometimes even the moderate eater should give his or her body a break with a short juice fast. Occasional one-day juice fasts (nothing but fresh fruit and vegetable juice) are excellent system cleansers. However, fasting should not be overdone.

Another great and easy way to fast is to eat a healthy breakfast, a hearty lunch, and an early, light supper, then not to eat anything but juice and water after 5:00 p.m. (Some people prefer to fast after 3:00 p.m., an effective weight-loss and system-cleansing tool if you don't mind skipping dinner.)

If you fast too often or for too long, or fast while only drinking water, you're committing violence to your own body (and that isn't following the *yama* of *ahimsa,* or non-violence!). Before altering your diet or performing a fast, consult your physician or a licensed dietitian to come up with the best nutritional plan for your individual health and fitness needs.

Ouch!

If you are fasting and experience headaches, dizziness, or other discomfort beyond mild hunger, give yourself a break, practice non-violence, and have something to eat. Fasting is not about hurting yourself. When breaking a fast, make sure you begin eating gradually again. Start with soup, bread, a salad, or something equally light.

If you do suffer from food addictions, breaking them can be extremely difficult. Maybe you can't even imagine shelving your life-sustaining coffee mug. Maybe you binge on cookies every weekend or are seemingly incapable of passing a fast-food restaurant without driving through for a double cheeseburger and fries.

We've got a nice little secret for you: You don't have to feel guilty. You don't have to deprive yourself (just yet!). All you have to do is practice all the *other* aspects of yoga: the postures, the breathing, the meditation. Here's where yoga works its magic. Yoga is transformative. It changes you. If you diligently practice it, within a few weeks or months, you'll be able to enjoy a cup of coffee without needing more or feeling addictive. Or maybe you won't want it at all. You won't feel the need for the caffeine. Fresh fruit will seem far more luscious than a bag of processed, store-bought cookies. And fast food will seem downright...barbaric? The point is, you don't really need to try to change your habits. You don't need to suffer and strive. If you're disciplined in the other areas of yoga, yoga will help you with the rest.

C'mon, Vegetarian?

Okay, we'll say it again: Here's where yoga works its magic. Yoga is transformative. It changes you.

Westerners are funny about vegetarianism. They seem to fall into two camps. There's the "Of *course* I'm a vegetarian. Aren't *you*?" camp, and the "You aren't *actually* one of those *vegetarians*, are you?" camp. Even if you're a vegetarian and don't judge meat-eaters, or a meat-eater who doesn't judge vegetarians, most people who don't share your views about meat will assume you're in the "opposite camp" and will be on the defensive.

We aren't sure why this antagonistic scenario has developed in the West, but it has. If you're a vegetarian or have tried without success to quit eating meat, you have surely encountered "the attitude." Also, if you eat meat but know a lot of vegetarians, you may have felt similarly maligned.

So let's all try, just for a minute, to let go of all that. Let's be objective, as far as that's possible. Do you like meat? Could you do without it? Aside from what anyone else in the world might think, does the idea of a vegetarian diet appeal to you? Although some yogis are *vegans* and some are *fruitarians,* the most common yogi diet is a *lacto-vegetarian* diet. What exactly *is* a vegetarian, then, you ask? You never knew there were different *kinds* of vegetarians. Check out this vegetarian primer and you'll be an expert on the variety and range of vegetarian diets!

➤ *Lacto-vegetarians* don't eat any meat, poultry, fish, or eggs. Their diets consist primarily of fruits, vegetables, whole grains (like rice, oats, and wheat), pasta, nuts, seeds, pulses (dried beans, peas, and lentils), milk, and milk products.

➤ *Lacto-ovo-vegetarians* are the same as above, but also eat eggs.

➤ *Vegans* eat no animal substance of any kind, including all dairy products. Diligent vegans even avoid eating things like gelatin (made from animal cartilage) and wearing leather or other clothing made from animals.

➤ *Fruitarians* eat primarily fruit, but also some vegetables. The primary rule for fruitarians is that all food must be consumed raw. Yes, that means avoiding *all* cooked foods!

There are a lot of great reasons to practice a vegetarian diet:

➤ A vegetarian diet is in harmony with *ahimsa,* the *niyama* of non-violence.

➤ A vegetarian diet is healthier for your heart because it's extremely low in cholesterol and saturated fat.

➤ If you want to be a vegetarian but all day long you dream about hamburgers, we suggest eating the hamburger so you can move on. Snap out of it! Yoga is not about guilt and judgment.

➤ According to many wise yogis, when an animal is slaughtered, it's filled with intense fear and anxiety. Eating that meat transfers the terrible fear to you.

➤ A vegetarian diet makes many people feel lighter, more energetic, and healthier. Physical activity becomes less of an effort, and food becomes less of an obsession.

But what if your answer to the question of whether you could eat from the lacto-vegetarian menu is a resounding "No way!"? As we said before, don't force yourself to do anything you aren't yet ready to do. You can certainly be committed to yoga without being committed to vegetarianism. In fact, many yoga teachers don't encourage vegetarianism or any dietary modification, especially to their Western students. These teachers know that yoga will do that job on its own.

Wise Yogi Tells Us

Some meat-eaters feel guilty eating meat in front of vegetarians, and some vegetarians feel guilty because they don't want their meat-eating friends to feel guilty. The true yogic way is not to judge others or yourself harshly. Yoga is a path of loving acceptance. No guilt, no condescension. Pure joy.

Many yogis start out without any intention of becoming vegetarian, but the more yoga transforms them, the less interested they are in meat until finally, one day, poof! another vegetarian is born. Simply deciding to become a vegetarian will not magically grant you a kind heart. Plenty of mean-spirited vegetarians are walking around out there in the world! Vegetarianism doesn't make you a yogi—yoga leads you to non-violence, which may eventually lead you to vegetarianism.

Maybe this day is in your near future, and maybe it's a long, long way off. It's your journey. What's right for you is unique and only you can truly determine your own course. So consider vegetarianism, be open to the idea, but if it just isn't "you" (or at least, the "you" you are today), let it go. Maybe it'll come back to surprise you when you're ready for it.

Vegetarian or not, do try to eat a healthy, fresh, primarily *sattvic* diet. Everyone can agree that fresh, whole, unprocessed food is a delight to eat. A diet of *sattvic* food makes living so much nicer, yoga practice so much easier, and may even make this wonderful life of yours a little bit longer, and a little bit more wonderful.

The Least You Need to Know

➤ Different types of foods—*sattvic, rajasic,* and *tamasic*—have different effects on you.

➤ Fresh, whole, unprocessed food helps you to think more clearly. Stimulating food can agitate you, and stale or preservative-filled food can sap your energy.

➤ Moderation in all things is best!

➤ A lacto-vegetarian diet has many health-related and spiritual benefits.

Chapter 21

Rx: Yoga

In This Chapter

➤ Your body has many layers, or levels of existence

➤ How yoga can help your nagging complaints

➤ How yoga can help when your condition is more serious

If you're human (which we assume you all are?), chances are you've experienced illness and/or pain in your lifetime. Even if you've never been seriously ill, you've certainly had a cold, the flu, maybe insomnia, possibly indigestion, an occasional headache, an aching back. Our human bodies are far from perfectly functioning, especially considering how much and how vigorously we use them. But pain and discomfort aren't necessarily par for the course in the life of a yogi. The yogi has a few tricks, and you, as a novice yogi, are privy to this health-inspiring information. Read on for how to help prevent, relieve, and sometimes even cure your health problems.

What Makes You Sick?

Theories abound concerning the cause of illness and pain, but many yogis believe that although illness can be caused by physical factors such as viruses, bacteria, and accidents, illness can also be brought on or encouraged by:

➤ Insufficient *prana,* or life force, within the body

➤ Too much *rajasic* (causing agitation) and/or *tamasic* (causing lethargy) food

➤ Lack of cleanliness

➤ Unhappiness

➤ Pessimism and negativity

➤ An imbalance within the physical body or the mind, which can be caused by any of the above factors

One of the characteristics of traditional, or *allopathic,* medicine is that it tends to pinpoint and isolate a problem or symptom and treat it, and it alone, which is sometimes just what the body needs. The body is like a machine that occasionally requires specific repair. Holistic medicine tends to first look at the "big picture," or the whole person. What are you doing that could be causing your illness (*roga*), pain, or disease (*vyadhi*)? Who are you? How is your general health (*svasthya*)? What is your health history? How is your posture? What is your attitude? What is your view of life? Holistic medicine seeks the answers to all these questions in an effort to find the source of a problem, rather than merely treating the symptoms of a condition or illness.

Yoga, too, takes this holistic approach to your health. Yoga treatments are great when used in conjunction with traditional health care because such an approach results in an all-encompassing treatment. Yoga works on your body and your mind to free them of impurities and imbalances that could cause health problems for you later.

Body Beyond the Body: The Five Sheaths of Existence

In Chapter 8, we briefly mentioned the Five Sheaths of Existence, but they're worth touching on again here because they're intimately connected with the state of your health. The first sheath consists of your physical body. The second is the vital body, made of *prana,* the life force. The third sheath is your mind, including your emotions and thoughts. The fourth sheath is your higher intellect and the fifth sheath is the bliss sheath, filled with positive energy and inner peace.

Disturbances or imbalances in any of your body's sheaths, not just the physical layer, can result in illness. Neglecting your nutritional needs, for example, could cause an imbalance in your physical body, which could, in turn, result in an imbalance of *prana,* which could make you feel uncomfortable and stressed. When you don't feel good, maybe you begin to think more negatively, causing an imbalance in your third sheath of existence. Pretty soon, you're all out of whack!

Disturbances of the third, or mind, sheath can also arise when strong feelings distort your inner balance. Maybe you're fixated on your dislike of a colleague at work. You spend a lot of time fuming about what he said or what she did. Pretty soon, you aren't breathing productively and your second sheath becomes disturbed. Then you get a cold and your first sheath is unbalanced.

Even positive behavior can cause an imbalance when taken to an extreme. Perhaps you absolutely love running—normally, a healthy activity—so much that you spend all your time running at the expense of all other activities and interests. Your mind becomes obsessed with running and loses interest in other aspects of life. You lose friends because everyone is tired of hearing about running. Your body begins to suffer because you lose too much weight or injure your legs or feet. See how it's all connected?

The "Moderation in All Things" adage comes into play in health as well as in diet. Anything you do to an extreme will cause an imbalance in your body and mind, or in your first three sheaths of existence. Remember *ahimsa,* or non-violence? Practice it by refusing to commit violence to your body with obsessive actions. Also, observe *santosha,* or contentment, by practicing satisfaction, peace, and tranquillity. You'll have a much easier time staying obsession-free.

Yoga for Those Nagging Complaints

When your physical complaints are relatively minor but persistent, yoga can be great therapy. You'll probably find that with a regular, consistent yoga practice, you'll suffer less often from minor complaints. If they do arise, however, try a few appropriate yoga *asanas* (postures) and stick with your yoga rules for living (*yamas* and *niyamas*) for effective relief.

Oh, My Aching Back...

Because we all walk around upright, our backs are bound to suffer. Our poor spines carry all that weight around and are continually jarred by the pounding of our feet, not to mention twisted and contorted by those of us with less-than-perfect posture. Weak stomach muscles are a common cause of back pain. Injury, too, to a disk or vertebrae can cause back pain. Yoga can help in either case. If you suffer from back pain, include the following exercises, which strengthen the stomach and/or tone the spine, in your yoga routine:

➤ Cobra pose (Chapter 14)

➤ Single leg lifts (Chapter 16)

➤ Boat pose (Chapter 18)

Ouch!
This book isn't meant to replace your doctor! If you're sick, injured, or the victim of any kind of chronic pain, seek medical attention from a licensed medical professional. Yoga can be a great complement to your physician's treatment plan. Ask your doctor how yoga fits in!

Ouch!
If you have a spine-related injury, be sure to check with your doctor before trying any yoga postures. Once your doctor gives the go-ahead, practice under the supervision of an experienced teacher to be sure you perform the pose correctly and don't injure yourself further.

A Yoga Minute
Back pain sufferers may need more calcium and magnesium. Great sources are milk, yogurt, cheese, dark leafy greens like collard greens and kale, almonds, tofu, broccoli, wheat bran, wheat germ, whole-wheat flour, dried beans, peanut butter, and dried apricots.

Oh, My Aching Head...

It's the rare individual indeed who can say he or she has never suffered from a headache. Unfortunately, it's often difficult to find the source of a headache. Headaches can be caused by a negative reaction to a certain food, air pollution, allergies, sinus problems, eyestrain, stress, and any number of other factors. Try eliminating suspected sources of regular headaches, such as caffeine, poor posture, or a particular food. If your headache is severe or your headache patterns change, see a doctor. For occasional, irregular head-aches, however, your best bet may be to step up your yoga practice to put your body in the best possible condition for curing itself.

For headache relief, try the following:

➤ Try the breathing techniques in Chapter 7.

➤ Gently rotate and flex your neck and toes.

➤ Practice inverted postures where your head is lowered briefly. These may help a headache because inverted postures increase the flow of oxygen to the brain.

➤ Make sure you maintain a balanced diet. Decrease your intake of nuts, aged cheeses, chocolate, caffeine, and food containing nitrates (like luncheon meats and hot dogs).

Why Am I So Tired?

Fatigue is a common problem in our overextended and fast-paced lives. Sometimes we simply wear ourselves out! Fatigue can also be caused by stress and extreme mental exertion, such as when you've been studying excessively, or when you're bothered by an emotional problem, such as depression or anxiety. A good holistic health care practitioner or therapist may be able to help you discover the underlying cause of your fatigue. If you notice unusual fatigue, however, even when you've gotten enough sleep, consult a physician.

Wise Yogi Tells Us

A few lifestyle modifications could be the answer to eliminating fatigue in your life. Try the following:

➤ Get off caffeine ASAP!

➤ Don't eat anything sweet before noon.

➤ Eat a low-fat diet. Too much fat slows you down and wears you out.

➤ Try to maintain a positive attitude. Don't sweat the small stuff!

For occasional bouts of fatigue during the day when you aren't in a position to take a cat nap, try the following:

➤ Practice *shavasana*, or the corpse pose (see Chapter 19), for five minutes.

➤ Do deep breathing exercises to replenish your *prana*.

➤ Any of the backbends in Chapter 14 will help to energize you.

Why Can't I Sleep?

On the other hand, we have the insomniacs. If you have trouble getting to sleep, common sense will probably tell you to lay off the caffeine, especially in the evening, and not to eat a whole pepperoni pizza at midnight. Stress is a common cause of insomnia, too. How can you sleep if your mind is abuzz with the worries of the day? Maybe you aren't purposefully sabotaging your body's ability to snooze, but if you nevertheless can't seem to catch even a few winks, try the following:

➤ Meditate. Evening meditation can calm and still your mind, making sleep easier. Remember, many wise yogis sit in full lotus in meditation so that if—or when—they fall asleep, they won't fall over!

➤ *Shavasana* is as good for insomnia as it is for fatigue. See Chapter 19.

➤ Forward bends quiet the body and mind. Try any of the poses from Chapter 18.

➤ To help you get to sleep, take a warm bath before bed and don't eat for at least six hours before bedtime.

What's Up with My Digestion?

The digestive system is tricky. Maybe you've noticed you can eat chili dogs, cotton candy, and ice cream all day some days and feel fine, while on other days, a few bites of an enchilada are all it takes to give you heartburn all night long. Part of the reason is that much of your digestive success depends on the manner in which you eat. If you eat slowly, concentrate on your food, and enjoy the experience, you'll have a better chance at digesting without a hitch. Rushed, stressed eating or eating when you aren't hungry or aren't feeling good will lead you down a short path to indigestion.

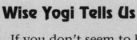

Wise Yogi Tells Us

If you don't seem to have a particular problem other than the simple presence of lots of stress, practice deep breathing to increase the production of endorphins in your system. Endorphins are the body's natural pain killers and will help to lower your blood pressure and heart rate.

Some people have chronic digestive problems, which can signal a number of problems. If you suffer from frequent heartburn, indigestion, bloating, gas, or stomach cramps after eating, see your doctor. Occasional cases can be alleviated by a few good yoga poses.

➤ Try *shavasana*. (See Chapter 19.)

➤ Poses that move the digestive area through compression and opening are good for improving digestion. Try the fish pose (Chapter 14), which lengthens the abdomen, followed by the child's pose (Chapter 18), which compresses the abdomen.

➤ The sun salutation (Chapter 16) is an excellent flowing series of poses to move and open the digestive process.

This Cold Won't Go Away...

Having a cold all winter long is frustrating as well as counter-productive to your happiness and well-being. If you can't get rid of your cold or keep getting colds back-to-back, consider where the virus is coming from. Are you washing your hands often enough? Do you frequently touch your face? Are you in contact with a lot of people all day long?

During the cold season, cold germs are everywhere, so be extra careful about hygiene. If you have kids, make sure they wash their hands before they eat and before they touch food others will eat. Remind them to wash their hands when they're away from home (at school or a friend's house) before eating and after touching anything that might not be sanitary, such as anything in a public bathroom.

Some colds have been known to turn into more serious problems like sinus infections, bronchitis, or even pneumonia, so it's in your best interests to do everything you can to prevent them. Increase your intake of vitamin C, preferably through real food such as fresh citrus fruit, fresh-squeezed juice, strawberries, and broccoli. Also:

➤ Do lots of *pranayama* to keep your breathing passages clear. Keep a tissue nearby! *Pranayama* techniques also work to increase and strengthen the immune system.

➤ If your cold comes with a headache, try the previously mentioned headache relief suggestions.

➤ Poses that open the chest can feel great when you are congested. Try the bow, fish, and cobra poses (all in Chapter 14).

When It's More Serious

Unfortunately, despite our best efforts, sometimes we get very sick. Competent medical care is crucial if you have a serious condition, but yoga can help, too. When your body is aligned, strong, and flexible, it will be able to fight off illness more effectively. When your mind is calm, peaceful, and optimistic, your body will be even better at battling the bad stuff. Keep your body filled with *prana* and positive thoughts, and don't give up hope. Hope is the best nurse of all.

Wise Yogi Tells Us

Even if you are unable to do yoga because of illness, injury, or chronic pain, visualizing yourself going through the postures has been known to improve *prana*, the life force. First visualize the pose, then visualize flowing into the pose, becoming one with the pose, flowing out of the pose, and releasing. Like Pavlov's dog, ultimately we can think "fish pose" and our body will receive all the benefits. We are more than our bodies, and must learn to work with whatever body we are given.

Yoga can be excellent for serious conditions, but *don't practice without a good teacher* if you:

➤ have recently had surgery.

➤ are pregnant (take one of the excellent pre-natal yoga classes offered in many cities).

➤ have cancer, diabetes, epilepsy, heart disease, high blood pressure, HIV, multiple sclerosis, or any other serious condition.

➤ have a debilitating physical handicap.

AIDS

Because the AIDS virus attacks the immune system, yoga can be of great benefit in extending life expectancy by encouraging the immune system to rally. Practice your regular yoga routine diligently and include the following:

➤ *Pranayama* techniques (Chapter 7) and relaxation techniques (Chapter 19) both boost the immune system.

➤ The general and gentle, non-violent practice of *Hatha Yoga* will increase your overall circulation and the delivery of oxygen throughout your body.

Arthritis

Chronic joint pain—including such common joint problems as TMJ, tennis elbow, and carpal tunnel syndrome—can be seriously debilitating. If you suffer from arthritis in particular or joint pain in general, relaxation is key to easing your distress. Yoga can be a great help, but if you have arthritis, it's important not to push yourself beyond what your body can do. Don't exercise joints that are inflamed.

However, many people with arthritis drastically decrease activity due to pain. Your joints should periodically be mobilized to keep them limber and clean. Yoga encourages you to keep moving, gently. As long as the following postures don't hurt, include them in your regular practice:

➤ *Vinyasa* routines (Chapter 16), such as a slow sun salutation, are excellent for maintaining your mobility.

➤ Try self-massage to bring warmth and circulation to painful areas.

➤ *Pranayama* (Chapter 7) increases your circulation and helps with pain.

Asthma, Allergies, and Respiratory Problems

When your breath is disturbed, your *prana* delivery system is disturbed, and that's a big deal. You don't want to mess with the life force! If you suffer from asthma, allergies, or other respiratory problems, you know how frustrating, let alone dangerous, breathing difficulties can be. Try the following to keep your breath flowing freely:

➤ Practice poses that open and stretch the chest: tree and warrior poses (Chapter 13); fish, bow, and cobra poses (Chapter 14). Be careful not to hold your breath while holding these poses.

➤ Two deep breaths while holding a pose are better than ten shallow breaths.

➤ Eat a healthy diet!

Cancer

In 1931, Dr. Otto Heinrich Warburg won the Nobel Prize in Medicine for his discovery that sub-optimal oxygenation of tissues and cells is the underlying cause of cancer. Translation? Give your body oxygen! Yogis discovered thousands of years ago that the quality of one's breath has a direct and profound influence on the quality of one's life. *Pranayama*, therefore, is one of the best things you can do to keep your body filled with oxygen (and *prana!*).

In addition, evidence is building to support the claim that you can prevent many cancers by changing lifestyle habits like smoking, drinking, and high fat intake. However, knowing this doesn't help the person already afflicted with cancer, and may even make you feel worse. If you have cancer, don't blame yourself or waste time thinking about what you might have done differently. Instead, focus on your future and getting well.

Many cancers are curable, and even advanced cancers have been cured. Several studies have shown that cancer survivors tend to take charge of their illness by learning all they can about it (*svadhyaya*—see Chapter 6) and by taking a positive attitude. Believe in yourself, the healing power of your body, and the healing power of your treatment regimen. Cultivate your own spirituality. Meditate, fill your lungs and body with *prana* through breathing exercises, and include the following *asanas* in your yoga routine (never do any poses that are too difficult or cause you pain):

➤ Practice that *pranayama!* Keep your body filled with the life force.

➤ Practice your *Hatha Yoga* routine slowly, steadily, and consistently to improve your circulation and overall strength.

➤ Eat a diet consisting of pure, whole foods.

Cardiovascular Disease

Your heart is the pump that keeps your body running. When it begins to lose efficiency or fails, your life is in immediate jeopardy. The best course of action is to prevent heart disease by eating a healthy, low-fat diet and by exercising regularly, but even perfectly healthy individuals are sometimes struck by cardiovascular disease. Maybe it's a matter of genetics. Sometimes, the reason is a mystery. The treatment needn't be mysterious, however. In addition to your regular medical care, remember the following:

➤ Yoga can help you to make the lifestyle changes you need for a better, happier heart. Yoga will decrease stress and increase circulation.

➤ The fastest way to reduce stress is to alter the breath. Deepen it. Inverted postures (Chapter 15) take pressure off the heart because it doesn't have to work as hard to pump blood to the extremities. More oxygen is pushed through the wall of the lungs, purifying the blood—but get your doctor's permission to practice inversions, first.

➤ Yoga *asanas* in general stretch the major blood vessels, keeping them open and elastic.

Diabetes

If you have diabetes, your blood has too much sugar and you may need to take insulin, which reduces blood sugar levels. Diabetes can be extremely serious if it isn't treated, but when treated, people with this condition can live virtually unencumbered by health problems.

For the diabetic, dietary control and weight control are crucial. Yoga is great for both and is, therefore, an excellent addition to the regular routine of anyone with diabetes. Yoga also helps with stress and improves the function of the pancreas, the organ that regulates blood sugar by producing insulin. Include the following in your routine:

➤ Obviously, you'll need a healthy diet. Yoga builds your confidence, concentration, and willpower, enabling you to want to stick with healthy eating habits.

➤ Since circulation in the extremities is important for those with diabetes, try resting your legs up against a wall as you lie back and relax. A slow, steady *vinyasa* routine will also help you balance your weight.

➤ Practice *pranayama* (Chapter 7) and meditation to help you gain focus and control.

Illness, disease, and pain don't have to keep you from a fulfilling yoga practice. With your doctor's and yoga teacher's guidance, progress at a pace that is right for you and let yoga help your body to help itself.

The Least You Need to Know

➤ Your body consists of five bodies: the physical you; the you containing *prana,* the life force; the emotional you; the intellectual you; and the blissful, peaceful you.

➤ Yoga can help with your minor health complaints such as colds, minor back pain, and fatigue.

➤ With the approval of your doctor, yoga can also help more serious problems, such as diabetes, cancer, and migraine headaches.

Chapter 22

Yoga for Two

In This Chapter

➤ How yoga is different when practiced in pairs

➤ Great postures for partners

➤ How yoga can make all your relationships—even sexual—more spiritual

➤ Meditation for two

Why practice yoga with anyone else? Isn't yoga a solitary and self-reflective pursuit? Yes, it is. But the journey can also involve spiritual communion between two bodies and two souls. Also, postures you can perform alone can be modified or performed more deeply or intensely when someone else helps you. Plus, practicing yoga with a friend, partner, or spouse can deepen your relationship because you'll be undertaking at least certain legs of your yoga journey hand in hand.

Double Your Insight

Finding wholeness and balance within yourself is important. However, because you probably aren't a hermit living alone in a cave or on a mountain top, it's also important to find wholeness and balance in your relationships. Practicing yoga with a fellow yogi can expand your sense of balance and improve your relationship, not only with your yoga partner but with all your fellow earthlings.

Double yoga helps to unfold your awareness, so it blankets your entire household, community, country, and planet. It gives you insight into the journeys, desires, suffering, and joys of others. It helps you to understand that every human being is as complex, interesting, and beautiful as you are.

Postures for Partners I

So let's try a few! Grab (non-violently, of course!) your spouse, partner, child, or friend, and try this set of postures for partners.

Be a Mountain Range

A first and easy posture to try is the mountain pose, but since there are two of you, let's make it a mountain range.

(1) Face your partner and close your eyes. After you're both centered, hold hands. Take some time to become aware of your partner across from you (keep your eyes closed). Feel your partner's form and energy, then feel the energy flow between you as it traverses the bridge made from your joined hands.

(2) Next, connect with the grounding energy of the earth. Feel how it pulls you towards its center. Feel your feet and legs connecting and becoming one with the earth.

(3) Let the earth's energy move through your body, from toe to head and beyond, and through your joined hands so that you and your partner are joined with the earth like mountains.

228

Warrior 2 Pose for 2

This pose will help you find balance with a partner. In the process, you'll both become stronger.

(1) Stand with one of you in front (Partner A) and one behind (Partner B). Each perform the warrior 2 pose (Chapter 13). Once you are both in position, Partner A balances the extended arms and hands on top of the back of Partner B's extended arms.

(2) Partner B keeps Partner A's arms and hands at shoulder height.

(3) Switch sides. Now Partner A holds Partner B's arms up. Breathe. Try to increase the length of time holding the pose. Encourage each other to hang in there.

Stretch and Pull

Both partners receive a nice spine stretch in this pose for two.

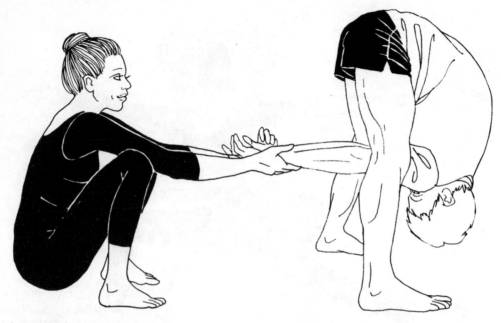

(1) Again, stand with one partner in front (Partner A) and one behind (Partner B). Partner B squats with heels on the floor. Partner A performs a forward bend, keeping the knees straight or slightly bending them and folding the torso forward at the hips. Partner A should be able to see Partner B between his/her legs. (Peek-a-boo!)

(2) Partner A reaches both hands between the legs and Partner B grasps Partner A's wrists, pulling slightly to help Partner A stretch.

(3) At the same time, Partner B bends down into a full squat, stretching the back.

(4) Hold and take some breaths.

(5) Switch places and do it again.

Lengthen Your Spine Together

Continue to lengthen the spine—maybe even grow an inch with this one!

(1) Hold hands, then each take a big step away from each other.

(2) Bend at your hips, but don't clunk heads! Be sure to step far enough away from each other that you don't collide.

(3) Bring your tailbones up and out. Take turns pulling on each other to lengthen your spines.

(4) Then find a balance—pull—and both come down into a squat. Keep your heels on the ground. Stretch that spine.

(5) Slowly come back up, balancing and stretching all the way back to standing.

The "S" in Sex Stands for "Spirituality"

Practicing yoga with your partner can deepen all aspects of your relationship, even your physical relationship. When practicing "couples yoga" with your partner or spouse, don't simply hold the positions. Take full advantage of your partner's proximity. Feel your partner's energy, body shape, and movement.

Truly connecting with your partner on a spiritual level is a much more blissful experience than mere physical connection. It can even be a bit alarming if you aren't used to really knowing someone on this level, because souls are much more sensitive than bodies. This is a goal you can work towards when practicing yoga with your partner.

A Yoga Minute
Mae West once said, "Sex is an emotion in motion." How true! One of the benefits of the fourth *yama, brahmacharya* (see Chapter 6), is that it teaches you to separate lust from a purer, spiritual connection. When you're fraught with emotional desire for the physical, you cannot perceive a deeper reality. Transcending intense emotions permits the spirit to manifest.

✳ Ouch!
When you're helping someone else stretch (or he or she is helping you), keep the lines of communication open. You can't feel when someone else is starting to hurt (unless you're extremely attuned), so let each other know when you're being pushed or pulled just far enough.

Problems in your relationship may surface, too, as you work together in different postures. You should be prepared for this possibility. Your bodies can reflect your minds, so when you have difficulty with a double posture, look into what's wrong and see if you can't find what's happening on a deeper level. Working through the barriers in your physical partnership can reveal the barriers in your spiritual partnership. Take the lessons you learn about each other into your hearts and memorize them. They're lessons in true love!

Postures for Partners II

Double yoga is a fun way to exercise your relationships. Let's try a few more poses for two.

Massage Your Spines Together

This pose will help your partner to connect to the muscles alongside the spine. A flexible spine = a youthful body. Help your partner loosen up his or her spine.

(1) Partner A sits in child's pose (Chapter 18).

(2) Partner B stands behind Partner A and places a palm on either side of the spine at the lower back. Gradually walk your hands up to the neck and back down to the lower back. Keep as much of your palm on your partner's back as you can at all times, pressing gently. Don't press on the spine, only on either side.

Forward Bend Together

This pose starts to look complicated, but it really isn't. It's only two poses in one. Partner B helps Partner A lengthen the spine by pushing down on Partner A's hipbone. Conversely, Partner A helps Partner B lengthen the hamstrings by pushing down on Partner B's heels.

Ouch!
Be sensitive to your partner's limits when practicing any partner poses.

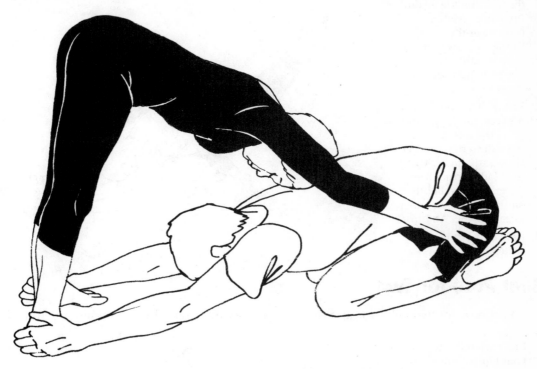

(1) Partner A gets into child's pose (Chapter 17).

(2) Partner B stands in front of Partner A. Partner A holds Partner B's ankles as Partner B assumes the downward facing dog posture (Chapter 18) over the top of Partner A, placing the hands on either side of Partner A's hips, palms facing in.

(3) Partner B helps Partner A lengthen the spine, while Partner A helps Partner B lengthen the hamstrings.

(4) Hold as long as is comfortable, then switch positions.

Forward Bend and Backbend Together

Try this one with a partner who is about the same size as you are. If one of you is much larger, he or she should be Partner A, and the positions shouldn't be reversed.

(1) Partner A sits on the floor a few feet from a wall with the back to the wall and the feet in front and together. Bending at the waist, Partner A brings the chest towards the thighs. Bend your knees if needed.

(2) Partner B lies on Partner A's back, facing up, and props the feet against the wall so that the feet are slightly higher than the head. Partner B's fingers can rest lightly on the ground on either side of Partner A's hips.

(3) Hold for a while, then switch.

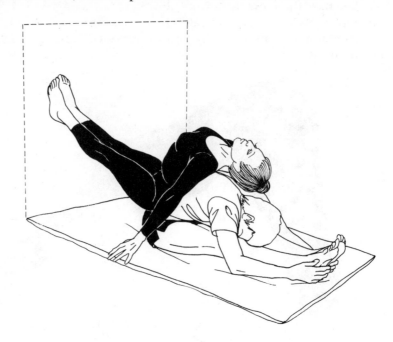

Boat Pose for Two

Boat pose for two helps to calm the rocky waters and strengthens tummies, too (or, two!).

• Face each other so that your hips are three to four feet apart. Both partners assume the boat pose (Chapter 18). Place your feet sole to sole and grasp hands on the outsides of your legs. Now you look like a schooner!

Wise Yogi Tells Us

Try double heart gazing to connect your heart *chakras*. Sit facing each other in any meditative pose with your knees touching. Look into each other's eyes. Really look, past the surface. Place your right hand on your partner's heart, and have your partner place his/her right hand on your heart. Then, each partner covers his/her own heart (and partner's right hand) with the left hand. Feel the energy flowing between your hearts' *chakras,* connecting you to each other. Close your eyes.

Don't miss out on the great physical, emotional, and spiritual benefits of yoga for two. This type of workout is completely different from solo yoga, and can be very fulfilling (although it isn't meant to replace a strong and steady personal *Hatha Yoga* practice). Vary your solitary communion with one of fellowship now and then. Partner yoga will increase your joy.

The Least You Need to Know

➤ Practicing yoga with a partner is fun and can deepen your relationship, including your sexual relationship.

➤ Practicing yoga with a partner can help you stretch further than you could alone.

➤ Yoga with your partner or spouse can make all aspects of your partnership—physical, emotional, and intellectual—more spiritual.

For Women Only

This chapter is for all you female yogis (yoginis) out there! Being a woman means certain things biologically and certain things culturally, too. We experience menstruation as our first rite of passage into womanhood, many of us experience childbirth, and eventually we experience menopause. We're also raised in a culture obsessed with beauty, youth, and the female body. Women have many unique challenges, and yoga can help with all of them by helping to keep us fit, strong, clear-thinking, and joyful.

The Truth About Beauty

Beauty really isn't skin-deep. In fact, it has nothing to do with your skin—not really. Beauty begins much deeper, so it's no wonder that many beautiful women don't believe they're beautiful. If you haven't found your inner self and aren't in touch with who you are, you won't be able to perceive your true beauty. Your inner beauty has nothing to do with your hair color or facial wrinkles or cellulite or breast size. These are transitory features of your soul's container. These aren't you.

The most important first step any woman can take in dealing with the issue of beauty is to practice *ahimsa,* or non-violence. Non-violent acceptance of yourself, not only physically but mentally and spiritually, too, is yoga's dictum. Don't commit violence to your body, either physically, by trying to force it to conform to some cultural ideal, or mentally, by hating it or obsessing over it. Remember that your body is a tool. Keep it well maintained so it doesn't interfere with the real you—keep it clean, strong, and flexible, but also keep it in its place.

The true you is much deeper, more complex, and more spectacular than your body. You're a manifestation of the universe. Finding yourself through yoga means finding the beautiful, spiritual you and bringing it out for everyone to see. Loving yourself means loving the universe, and loving the universe means loving yourself, because you're one and the same: You're both exquisitely radiant.

Kiss PMS Good-Bye

When you're suffering from PMS, however, you probably don't feel very radiant. PMS, or premenstrual syndrome, is a condition that affects a lot of women before the onset of their menstrual periods. Symptoms are as diverse as overall discomfort, bloating, backache, headache, irritability, food cravings, depression, acne, painful or swollen breasts, insomnia, fatigue, even uncharacteristically violent or suicidal behavior. Many women get a little emotional, uncomfortable, and hungrier, but everyone is different, and each woman may experience different symptoms from month to month—some may even experience no symptoms at all.

Wise Yogi Tells Us

When you're feeling particularly PMS-y (a new adjective?), lie on your back with your buttocks against a wall. Put your legs up against the wall, separate them a bit, and lie there for a while—very relaxing.

PMS commonly occurs during the week or two before the start of your period and can last until menstruation starts. Symptoms are generally attributed to the production of hormones related to the menstrual cycle. You may not care about the cause so much as a good remedy when you're in the throes, however.

How can yoga help? Be dedicated to your regular yoga routine during PMS. Your hormone-wracked body will appreciate the familiar routine and the exercise. The triangle pose (Chapter 13), sitting poses to open the hips, and twisting poses for lower back stiffness are all excellent for PMS. Although all the *asanas* activate the body, poses that stimulate the glandular and reproductive systems are good to practice during PMS, such as the cobra, bow (both in Chapter 14), and bridge (Chapter 15) poses.

Also, step up your *pranayama* practice (Chapter 7). As your body sheds its uterine lining, support it by cleansing the rest of your body through *pranayama* (deep breathing exercises). *Pranayama* also eases irritability, depression, and moodiness. *Mantra* work, too, can be of great benefit when your emotions are changing rapidly (see Chapter 3). The steady flow and vibration of a *mantra* soothes your nervous system and can help transform negative outbursts into outbursts of pure inspiration!

Wise Yogi Tells Us

Herbs known to help relieve the symptoms of PMS, such as bloating, pain, and depression, are dong quai, blessed thistle, cayenne, raspberry leaves, sarsaparilla, and Siberian ginseng. Look for these herbs in your local health food store, and take as directed.

And no matter how bad PMS is, stress only makes it worse—just one more reason to keep practicing yoga! All of the stress-reduction yoga performs on the human body can also help to lessen the effects of PMS. Don't forget *shavasana* (the relaxation pose in Chapter 19)—do it as often as you can. When you are feeling physically or emotionally uncomfortable, you'll welcome *shavasana's* utterly relaxed state, especially when you get so relaxed that you don't even feel your body anymore!

Meditation, too, can be helpful when you are uncomfortable but in a good frame of mind. Meditation, including *shavasana,* can help you to move beyond your physical body for awhile, to give yourself a break from the aches and pains.

Going Full Cycle: Celebrating Menstruation

Some women are pleased by the arrival of their menstrual period each month, but most of us are a little miffed. *"This* again?" we think. "Why do I have to go through this every month!" Do you really want to know?

Technically speaking, menstruation is part of your body's fertility cycle. About every month, from puberty to menopause, your womb first builds up nourishment for a potential embryo and, after ovulation, if pregnancy has not occurred, sheds this tissue in a self-cleansing process before beginning to prepare anew for next month's cycle. All of this happens due to the work of your hormones, which fluctuate throughout the month but seem to cause the most trouble in terms of discomfort during the premenstrual period.

Ouch!
PMS can literally be a big pain, and eating certain foods just before you expect PMS symptoms can make it worse. Even if you crave them, try to avoid chocolate, anything with caffeine, alcohol, excess salt, red meat, sugar, and overly processed foods, which seem to aggravate PMS symptoms in some women.

239

But that's not really what you mean when you wonder why you have to go through menstruation—we know that. We're just trying to remind you what it's all about. Your menstrual cycle sets you apart as a woman. (Well, it isn't the *only* clue, but it's certainly an unmistakable clue!) Menstruation is a monthly marker of your fertility and one of the few biologically imposed rituals we have.

Women have often been compared to the moon, probably because both operate in cycles. Study the moon for a few months, watching it nightly as its lighted section swells then shrinks each month. Feel a kinship with the moon. See if you can notice its effect on you. Do you feel different during a full moon than during a new moon? How does your menstrual cycle synchronize with the moon's cycle? Pay attention to the beautiful regularity of the moon's waxing and waning, then carry that reverence over to your own body. Your cycle is similarly splendid—even if it doesn't always feel that way.

Wise Yogi Tells Us

Rather than fighting gravity, yoga makes a friend of gravity. So, during those times when we want to encourage movement out of the body, such as during menstruation, it's counter-productive to work against gravity by practicing inversions like the headstand or the plough (Chapter 15). Thank gravity for helping your body with its monthly "out with the old, in with the new" process and stay right-side-up.

Incorporating yoga into your menstrual ritual is a nice way to make the experience even more positive. You can do any yoga posture you normally do (except for inversions—skip the headstand and shoulderstand during this week), but you might enjoy creating a special yoga routine for the week of your menstrual period. Try the following variations of poses for your menstrual cycle sessions.

An extra-long *shavasana* (Chapter 19) is the perfect way to end your yoga practice during your menstrual cycle.

You may also want to experiment with the triangle (Chapter 13), the cobra (Chapter 14), the bow (great for cramps if you're up to it, Chapter 14), the wheel (also great for cramps, Chapter 14), the bridge (Chapter 15), the butterfly, the lotus (all in Chapter 17), and the moon salutation (Chapter 16) poses. These are all just suggestions to help make this cycle a comfortable one.

(1) Sit in the hero pose, butterfly pose, or lotus pose (all in Chapter 17). Place a few pillows stacked on top of each other directly behind you. Lie back on top of the pillows. Extend your arms over your head. This position opens the Venus *chakra* and is also a good variation to perform during pregnancy.

(2) Sit with your feet in front of you, widely separated. Place a few pillows stacked on top of each other in front of your naval. Bend forward, bringing your hands towards your feet.

So, You're Having a Baby!

Pregnancy yoga is slightly different than regular yoga, and perhaps even more wonderful. Yoga helps you to develop a greater awareness of your body so you can respond better to your body's subtle signals (such as, "You're doing too much today" or "You need to get up and move today" or "You could really use a hearty serving of broccoli today").

Because yoga gets you moving, you'll be in better shape for the hard work of labor. Recovery and getting back to your pre-pregnancy shape will be easier, too. Taking a prenatal yoga class can be a lot of fun. You'll get to meet other, similarly-minded pregnant women, you'll get qualified instruction on the safest and most beneficial yoga poses, and you may be more motivated to keep up your workout. Plus, in the last month or two when baby is getting big, he or she may be able to move more freely as you open your body in a stretch. A few caveats are in order first, however. Take the following precautions when practicing pregnancy yoga:

➤ Tell your doctor you are practicing yoga, and get his or her consent for all poses you plan on practicing. If your doctor isn't familiar with yoga, show her or him pictures of the poses you'd like to do.

➤ Avoid extreme stretching positions and any position that puts pressure on or contracts your uterus. Skull-shining breath may be too jarring for baby, and full forward bends will probably be uncomfortable for you and baby, too.

➤ Avoid backbends and full forward bends—maintain that abdominal space. Give that little him or her a little room in there!

➤ Keep standing poses to a minimum and never jump into them.

➤ Remember that your center of balance is completely different than it was. Be careful doing balance poses. If you fall, the baby is well cushioned in your uterus, but you could injure yourself.

➤ Don't lie on your stomach for any pose.

➤ After the 20th week, don't lie on your back for any pose. The weight of the baby can hinder your blood flow.

Wise Yogi Tells Us

After the 20th week, practice *shavasana* with lots of pillows, lying on your left side instead of your back.

The following are suggestions only. If any pose feels uncomfortable or strenuous, stop at once. If you experience dizziness, sudden swelling, extreme shortness of breath, or vaginal bleeding, see your doctor immediately. Your best approach to these postures is to listen to your body and don't take it where it doesn't want to go.

➤ *Tadasana* (Chapter 13). Focus on tilting your lower back in to prevent the weight of the baby from pressing against the lumbar. Bend your knees slightly and place your hands on top of your knees. Tighten your thigh muscles and watch your kneecaps lift up. Straighten your legs and try to lift your knee caps.

➤ Hero pose (Chapter 17) (see figure on page 178). Sitting in this pose helps to reduce swelling in your ankles, reduces fatigue, and improves circulation in your legs. Place a stack of pillows behind you and lean back. Bring your hands alongside your body to push yourself back up.

➤ Child's pose (Chapter 18). See illustration below for further instruction.

• Support your body with a stack of pillows placed between your knees, or stand on your knees and cross your arms over the back of a chair and lean forward. You might want a pillow or blanket under your knees as well, to protect and cushion them.

➤ Simple hamstring stretches (your hamstrings are tendons at the back of your knee) relieve pressure on your lower back. Be gentle when you stretch.

➤ Twisting poses should be performed gently. When not pregnant, the focus should be on twisting the entire spine. During pregnancy, however, most of your twisting will be in your neck, shoulders, and head. Lift your spine as you inhale, twist as you exhale.

➤ Use chairs for support whenever you can. For example, try the warrior 2 pose or side angle stretch (Chapter 13) seated on the center of a chair. It is more freeing and takes the weight off your legs. See illustration below for the side angle stretch variation.

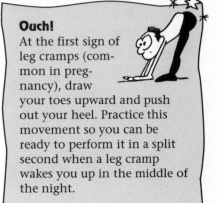

Ouch!
At the first sign of leg cramps (common in pregnancy), draw your toes upward and push out your heel. Practice this movement so you can be ready to perform it in a split second when a leg cramp wakes you up in the middle of the night.

Side angle stretch variation during pregnancy.

➤ Another way to use a chair is to try the downward facing dog while standing and using the back of the chair for support. (See the following illustration.) What a wonderful stretch and release for the spine! Holding onto the chair takes some of the pressure off the legs in this pose, too. You'll feel freer, and so will your little passenger.

➤ Learn some inspirational *mantras* to practice during childbirth. They'll be much more productive than yelling and swearing at your partner, midwife, or doctor. Let your baby experience the transcendent vibrations of a *mantra*. If nothing else, transform your "AAAAHHHHHHH!" into "AAAAUUUUMMMM!"

Downward facing dog variation during pregnancy. If you don't have a steady, firm chair to use, place your hands against a wall and stretch this way.

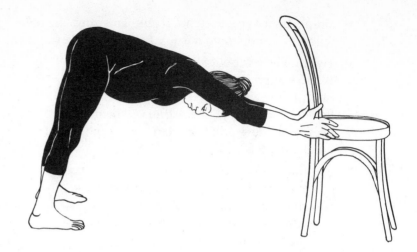

New Mama Yoga

Once you're home with your new little bundle, you may be a bit incredulous that you could have any time for yoga. You don't even have time to sleep! The first few weeks of transition are stressful, but also joyful. You may feel alternately ecstatic and despairing, frustrated and overflowing with love.

Practicing yoga now is important because you need the energy. Filling your body with *prana* through breathing exercises and 10 minutes daily in *shavasana* will recharge you and make the little sleep you do get more productive. Your body also needs all its resources to heal itself after childbirth.

You probably need some mental maintenance, too. Your hormones may be making you extra emotional or a little depressed right after childbirth. Add to that the fact that your entire life has changed and will never be the same. Pile on top of that the fact that your jeans look hopelessly small and even though you aren't pregnant anymore, all you may be able to wear are your old maternity clothes. Remember that it takes time to adjust to any major life change. It will also take your body time to readjust to a non-pregnant state. Be patient. Be kind to yourself. It took you nine months to get to childbirth, so give yourself nine months to get back. You have just accomplished something magnificent and it has changed you. Accept the change lovingly and with joy.

Give yourself time to practice yoga each day, either when your baby is sleeping or when your partner, a family member, or a friend can play with the baby. Consider it pampering time, and a well-deserved reward.

Wise Yogi Tells Us

A high-sugar diet will make you feel tired any time, but especially in the early weeks after childbirth. Sure, you deserve a treat now and then, but a diet based on whole grain foods like whole wheat bread and brown rice, sufficient iron (best sources are dark, leafy greens, wheat germ, and meat), and lots of vegetables is the best diet to combat fatigue.

With your doctor's approval, you can usually start gentle yoga postures two weeks after delivery, a few weeks longer if you had a cesarean section. Hold off on inverted poses for at least six weeks.

All women have postnatal bleeding for a few weeks after pregnancy. Watch this flow for signs that you're going too fast. If the bleeding gets heavier or brighter red, you need to slow down and give your doctor a call. Start with just a few poses, and gradually work back to your regular routine as your body lets you know it's ready.

The most beneficial pose for you right now is *shavasana* (Chapter 19), which you can even do the day you give birth (but you will want to listen to your doctor during the actual birth!). Any chance you get, lie down and practice this revitalizing pose. You'll handle all your new challenges with greater inner strength and energy. The following poses are also wonderful for a gentle post-pregnancy routine:

➤ *Tadasana,* the mountain pose (Chapter 13). Take some time to stand in the mountain pose and notice how your center of gravity has shifted yet again. Let *tadasana* help you reacquaint yourself with your body.

➤ The butterfly pose (Chapter 17), with pillows under your knees. Notice how this pose feels differently than it did when you were pregnant.

➤ Child's pose (Chapter 18). Let yourself be the child for a few minutes each day.

➤ The postpartum (the period after childbirth) time is a good time to read the Yoga Sutra or other yoga texts. Keep them on a bedside table or end table, to read while nursing your baby or while baby is sleeping.

More important than any postures at this point is your attitude. Being a new mother isn't easy. If you're feeling frustrated or unhappy and think you must be a bad mother, give yourself a break! All new mothers feel like that sometimes. Remember *ahimsa*—treat yourself non-violently. Your feelings are completely normal. Don't be afraid to talk to your partner, your close friends, or a counselor about your feelings. Just remember that you're entering an exciting new leg of your life journey.

Easing Through Menopause

Menopause is the time of life when a woman stops ovulating. Although the age at which it occurs varies greatly, it commonly occurs around age 50. Yet menopause means much more to women than this simple biological definition. The thought of menopause is daunting to many, and it's no wonder! Our culture puts so much emphasis on youth and beauty, especially for women, that aging is difficult enough.

Because women are finally beginning to share their experiences of menopause and more information is available, this transition from fertility to the next stage of life is easier to prepare for. Far from being the end of life, menopause signals a period of life during which spiritual growth can soar. Women who have passed through menopause often feel stronger, more in charge of their own lives, and more intimately acquainted with their own souls than ever before. Age brings wisdom, and once a woman is no longer a child-bearer, her body can focus on its own journey. An increasing number of strong, vibrant, amazing older women have become important figures in our culture. Look to these women as examples for your own life. This next stage of your journey may be the most thrilling yet. It's certainly full of possibilities.

But first, you have to get through the menopause, and that isn't always pleasant. A hot flash is still a hot flash (you could call it a recharge!), whether it signals an exhilarating life transition or not. Menopause comes with lots of other physical complaints beyond the often cited hot flashes. Dizziness, depression, heart palpitations, decreased sex drive, and shortness of breath are all symptoms of decreased estrogen levels. Considering menopause can last for five years, you'll probably want to do everything you can to minimize the unpleasantness.

Yoga balances the endocrine system and can ease the difficult transition by stabilizing hormone levels. Inverted postures are particularly helpful for hot flashes because they cool the body and fill it with *prana*. *Pranayama,* too, is cooling to the body.

As you work through menopause, incorporate the following into your yoga routine:

➤ The headstand, and other inversions like the shoulderstand and plough (all in Chapter 15). If you've never mastered the headstand, now's the time to try. The headstand may reduce your hot flashes. All the inversions will make you feel more vital, too, because they replenish and rejuvenate your body.

➤ Downward facing dog (Chapter 18) and other forward-bending postures such as standing head to knees and *yoga mudra* (all in Chapter 18). These forward-bending poses help you to focus inwardly, an important process right now. Rather than shunning your body or feeling it has betrayed you, embrace it, get to know it all over again, and let it work for you, leading you to a higher spiritual plane.

➤ Sun salutation (Chapter 16). Celebrate how your body has moved beyond moonlike cycles and catapulted like a rocket on towards the sun. Make the sun your newest ally. If you're up to it, start rising at dawn to practice yoga. Notice how, although the earth moves and turns and changes, the sun burns steadily and luminously in the center of our solar system. Meditate on how your body has become sunlike and strong, glowing with newfound steadiness and bliss.

➤ Any weight-bearing postures and activities. A drop in your estrogen levels can cause you to lose bone mass, but you can easily counter this by exercising your bones. Postures that put stress on your bones, such as inversions, standing postures, and downward facing dog, all increase bone mass. Light weight lifting is great for your bones, and so is walking. Take a walk in the fresh air every day to keep your bones strong, your lungs full, and your heart light.

➤ Place a folded blanket or pillows about nine inches high against a wall. Support your lower and midback on the blanket, stretch your legs up the wall, and let your shoulder blades and head rest on the floor. Rest in this pose for 10 minutes with your eyes closed; focus on your breathing. This pose is cooling and therapeutic for any pelvic or abdominal problems.

➤ Start regular meditation. You're in an excellent time of life to begin meditation. You have a better sense of yourself than ever before. Take advantage of your wisdom and experience and reap the benefits of meditation.

Most importantly, know that your life is far from over. You're a strong, vibrant woman with much to offer the world. Cultivate your soul like a garden and find your place in the universe.

The Least You Need to Know

➤ Beauty has nothing to do with your physical appearance. If you care for your body and radiate inner bliss, you'll be beautiful.

➤ Yoga can help reduce symptoms of PMS and menstruation.

➤ Yoga can be tailored to accommodate pregnancy and new motherhood.

➤ Yoga can ease the transition of menopause.

Yoga for the Rest of Us

Don't worry, we haven't forgotten the rest of you who don't happen to be women between adolescence and the golden years. People of all ages and both sexes can be yogis, and each group has its unique characteristics and problems. If the "For Women Only" chapter didn't happen to be directed at you, we hope you'll feel not only included but warmly welcomed in this chapter.

Mucho Macho

This section is for all you guys out there. Sure, we know lots of you have enrolled in yoga classes, and lots more are wondering what it's all about. Lots more of you, however, are probably just a little suspicious. We hope that so far, many of your questions have been answered, but here are a few more things to think about—you know, *guy stuff.*

Isn't Yoga for Chicks?

Maybe you've picked up this book because yoga interests you, but you just aren't sure yoga is a "guy thing." Isn't it sort of like home economics class or going to the ballet? Granted, if you took a survey today, you would probably find that in any given city, there are more women taking yoga classes than men. For some reason, women seem to be more comfortable taking exercise classes. But the imbalance is quickly shifting. Why should women get all the fitness benefits of yoga? And why should men miss out on the camaraderie and guided instruction of a class? And why should *anyone* miss out on the mental clarity and inner peace yoga can offer?

Plus, men played an important part in developing yoga into what it is today. Although yoga originated long before recorded history—so there's no telling whose *idea* it actually was—men were certainly instrumental in its refinement and philosophical evolution. Many, many men throughout history have devoted their lives to becoming sagacious yogis, and today, many of the major schools of yoga—*Iyengar Yoga, Sivananda Yoga, Bikram's Yoga*—were started by men. So why not give yoga a try? It can only make you healthier, stronger, and more flexible. Plus, what a great way to meet women!

Where's the Team?

You guys who've left that locker-room attitude back in high school gym class can skip ahead to the flexibility section. But let's face it: A lot of guys are very comfortable being athletic in a team situation. Football teams, basketball teams, baseball teams, hockey teams, soccer teams—these are all familiar scenarios for the average American guy. Two teams compete, and one of them wins. No wonder yoga seems a little strange and unfamiliar. No team, no points, no scoring method, and no winner is proclaimed and carried around on everyone's shoulders. Heck, there isn't even a coach on the sidelines on whose head you can pour your cooler of water when the workout is over!

Or so it would seem. Think of it this way: You and everyone else in your yoga class, or your circle of friends and family, or even the world, are a team. You're all seeking a common goal: fitness, happiness, and eventually, self-actualization.

Who's the other team? Let's rephrase that: *What's* the other team? The other team is a surly bunch of characters: self-doubt, negative thoughts, jealousy, hate, violence, illness, pain, and suffering. Formidable opponents! But your team can beat them, and it's up to you to set an example for your team members. Follow yoga's principles, practice the exercises, learn deep breathing, even try meditation. You'll be learning about yourself and learning how to live in the world, too, which is really the same as learning how to be a great team player.

But How Do You Win?

And best of all, with yoga, everybody wins. No, that's not some sappy cop-out. One of the most difficult things for some men to accept about yoga is the idea of non-competitiveness. Yoga isn't one-up-manship, so it would be against yoga's principles to say that the achievement of each new posture is another "point" for you. On the other hand, the achievement of each new posture *is* like a point against the other team—the suffering, illusion, and illness team. If you can see yoga as a competition against negativity rather than a competition against another person (because that would be like competing with your own team members), then maybe you can fit your competitive nature comfortably into yoga after all.

Although you may not be one of them, some men (and women) get discouraged easily when they aren't immediately skilled at an activity. If yoga is difficult for you at first, the hardest part of all may be adjusting your thinking. Don't compare yourself to anyone else. Even though you're on the same "team" as your fellow yogis, in another sense, you are alone in your journey. Only you can determine what your body can do now, and what it'll be able to do after further progress. Don't punish yourself or criticize yourself for being unable to accomplish any exercise. Cultivate patience with yourself and your body, and your body will respond in ways you never thought it could.

And when your workout is over, especially if it's a hot summer day, why not pull out all the stops, fill up a bucket with water, and pour it over your own head! You deserve it! (But you might want to go outside, first.)

> **Wise Yogi Tells Us**
>
> Guys: Maintaining balance is crucial for health. So, if you're very strong but not very flexible, spend more time on exercises that challenge your flexibility and less on strength-training exercises. If you're flexible but get out of breath easily, spend less time on stretches and more time on *pranayama* (deep breathing exercises).

These Muscles Don't Stretch

Another problem men commonly have with yoga is their lack of flexibility. From an early age, men are often encouraged to gain strength, but strength without stretching causes muscles to shorten, even if they gain bulk. The strongest man in the world may not be able to touch his toes.

"But the strongest man in the world looks great!" you may protest. "And who needs to touch his toes, anyway?" Flexibility is important for men for several reasons:

➤ Flexible bodies are most resistant to injury. Tendons and muscles become more elastic and can bend further without tearing.

➤ Getting up in the morning is a lot easier and your body is less stiff when you have good flexibility.

➤ Adding flexibility to your workout gives you a three-pronged approach to physical fitness: strength training, cardiovascular training, and flexibility training. This approach is more holistic, developing all aspects of your physical body and maintaining a healthier balance.

➤ If you're ever forced to sit on the floor for a long period of time, you won't mind as much.

251

➤ A flexible body encourages a flexible mind.

➤ Flexibility can make sex a lot more fun! (Isn't *that* reason enough, all by itself?)

Just remember that yoga can do great things for your health and your life. The exercises will tone and strengthen your body in ways that are both different and complementary to your other physical activities, or, if you're sedentary, yoga is a great way to move into a physical lifestyle. Yoga's deep breathing exercises and meditation can also be new ways for you to discover the limitless possibilities of your body and mind. Give it a try—and welcome to the team!

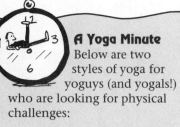

A Yoga Minute
Below are two styles of yoga for yoguys (and yogals!) who are looking for physical challenges:

➤ *Ashtanga Yoga* literally means the Eight Limbs of Yoga, as defined by Patanjali in his Yoga Sutra. However, it has come to be seen in our society as a *Hatha Yoga* practice that includes an intense *vinyasa* workout (see Chapter 16).

➤ *"Power Yoga"* (see Beryl Bender Birch's book of same name) is a specific, highly athletic form of yoga that is based on the Western conception of *Ashtanga Yoga*. It includes high-intensity, choreographed sequences of postures combined with breath, and is quite popular among athletes and others seeking a physically demanding workout.

Good yoga exercises for yoguys:

➤ Those that require cardiovascular exertion. (Look for "Power Yoga" or *Ashtanga* classes in your area, or invent some challenging *vinyasa* for yourself—see Chapter 16.)

➤ Sitting postures that increase flexibility in the legs and hips such as the hero and butterfly pose (Chapter 17).

➤ Standing postures to increase your confidence when it seems like you can't get your body to do anything, such as the mountain; warrior 1, 2, and 3; and lightning bolt (Chapter 13).

➤ Inversions, to replenish and balance your entire body, such as the bridge, shoulderstand, headstand, and handstand (Chapter 15).

➤ *Shavasana* (Chapter 19). The corpse pose may be incredibly challenging for you because, ironically, it *isn't* challenging! (Well, not in the typical sense.) Practicing *shavasana* may be the one time in your day when you can completely release challenges and simply "be." Completely relaxing your body and mind isn't as easy as it sounds. Even if you love a good challenge, remember that you need to maintain inner balance. Life isn't always challenging, nor should it be. Maybe you yearn for a space in your life without challenges. *Shavasana*—indeed, all of yoga—can be that space.

➤ Any others that look interesting or fun to you!

And gentlemen, no matter how self-sufficient you are, consider taking a yoga class because a yoga class is a place where you can go just for yourself. A lot of men are used to exercising in groups, but yoga lets you move, breath, and think without reference to anyone else. Taking a class will give your practice structure, plus the chance to really learn about yourself, not in terms of how others see you, but in terms of who you really are.

Yokids

Kids take naturally to yoga because it's so much fun. Getting the whole family involved in a yoga routine is a great way to keep you motivated. When your whole family practices yoga together, the family bond is strengthened. Everyone learns more about the other family members—what they can and can't do, what they like and dislike, how they like to play. Love is built on intimacy like this, and yoga offers the perfect environment to cultivate and nurture family intimacy.

Turn Off the TV and Play!

Kids today watch a lot of television and play a lot of video games. Sure, some television is stimulating and offers children valuable information. But healthy kids are built from exercise, nutritious food, and imaginative play. Encourage your kids to turn off the tube and get moving, using both their bodies and their minds more actively. Interacting with you and with each other (other siblings or friends) builds children's social skills and teaches them much more about the world than any half-hour sitcom or 60-minute talk show.

Finding Your Animal Nature

So what kind of yoga should you do with your kids? Try the following fun yoga activities (most aren't "classic" yoga postures, but modified yoga-esque kid-friendly fun), which are based on the imitation of animals or other elements of nature. Experiment to find the exercises your kids enjoy the most. Then add a new exercise or two each week to your family's yoga repertoire until you feel your kids are ready to start learning the classic yoga postures. (The teenage years are an appropriate time for this.)

Although you may be silent during your regular workout, encourage your kids to talk, respond, and flex their imaginations while practicing yoga (except during meditation, which should be quiet and focused for all). They'll get more out of the poses, and you'll have a better idea of how they're doing, what they do and don't understand, and how you can best progress with them.

➤ Mountain's Majesty. Stand as in the classic mountain pose (Chapter 13). Ask your kids what it feels like to be a mountain. What kind of mountain are they? Rocky and imposing? Volcanic? Rounded, green foothills?

➤ A Roar, and More! Everyone get on the hands and knees, sit back on the heels, stick the tongue out as far as possible, and look up. You're all lions, so everybody roar!

➤ Hop to It! Everyone squat down on the floor and hop around like frogs. A few "ribbits" offered up to the heavens never hurt anyone.

➤ Be the Tree. Everyone stand firmly rooted with both feet on the ground (unlike the classic tree pose—note the difference). Now let your kids feel how the weather is gradually changing: from sunny and still to windy to blustery to an all-out thunderstorm. How do all the trees shift and move with the weather? Have everyone make appropriate wind and leaf-rustling sounds.

➤ For the Birds. Everyone choose a type of bird, then practice standing, hopping, and flying like "your" bird. Notice how a sparrow is different from a great blue heron, a mockingbird different from a vulture, a hummingbird different from an eagle. (And remind your kids—birds don't bump into each other!)

➤ Dog Days. Have a dog party! Everyone chooses a dog, whether Poodle or St. Bernard. Run, play, pant, play, roll over, play, and play like the dog you have chosen.

➤ Pretty Kitties. Now be a bunch of cats. Notice how cats move differently than dogs. Lie down. Stretch out. Stand up. Streeeeetch! Try to feel the way a cat feels and move the way a cat moves.

➤ Flower Power. Everyone curl up on the ground like seeds, then imagine you're being watered and the sun is shining. Slowly expand, then rise up out of the ground. Slowly, now! Gradually get taller and taller until your head, face, and arms open up into a beautiful bloom.

➤ Invent your own nature poses. The possibilities are endless.

➤ Kids can also learn breathing exercises, but keep it simple. Have kids rest their hands on your stomach to feel how your stomach moves gently when you bring your breath lower. Then have them try this on each other. Ask them if they remember when they were sleeping in the crib and their tummies moved up and down. Ask them to pretend they are in the crib now.

➤ Kids can even meditate! Have kids sit quietly and focus on a pleasant object, like a flower, a small figurine, or a toy. At first, rather than stressing the absence of thought, suggest that your kids focus on one single feeling, such as love, happiness, or peacefulness. When thoughts arise, re-focus on how the feeling *feels*, instead.

The Lessons Yoga Teaches Kids

Yoga teaches kids valuable lessons about life. You'll probably teach your children all of the following in one way or another, but yoga can deepen and reinforce all of these healthy and life-affirming ideas:

➤ Exercise is fun!

➤ Exercise = active play.

➤ When the body and the mind combine into imagination, there are no limits.

➤ Stuff that's good for you doesn't have to be unpleasant—it can actually be the highlight of your day!

➤ "Feeling" like different animals and objects such as trees makes children more sensitive, not only to their own bodies, but to all our fellow inhabitants of the earth.

➤ Families that play together understand each other better.

➤ The earth and all its creatures have a lot to teach us about how to move and how to live.

➤ Sometimes it's fun to be quiet, still, and reflective.

➤ Kids can learn to be patient, too.

➤ Your body is your friend, ally, and instrument.

Ouch!
If you start to hear whines and complaints or sense any reluctance, boredom, or frustration in your kids during your yoga practice, either adjust activities immediately or stop. You don't want to make yoga a negative experience for kids. Fun yoga now could mean a lifetime love of yoga. Yoga that is boring or authoritarian may turn kids off for good. Never push a child into a pose. To kids, poses are play. You might want to try this with your own yoga practice, too! Have fun!

Yoldies but Goodies!

Senior yogis are often the wisest yogis of all, even if they're new to yoga. When you've walked the earth for a while, you understand a little more about yourself and about life, suffering, and joy, simply because you've seen more of it. If you haven't practiced yoga before, now is a wonderful time to start.

Seniors are perfect candidates for meditation. Your brain is so full of experiences, information, memories, and ideas that it can really use a break. For a few minutes each day, take some time to yourself to reflect on something beautiful, then let this beautiful reflection gently melt into the breath until breath and peace are all that remain.

A Yoga Minute

Deficiencies of vitamins B$_6$, B$_{12}$, and folic acid can aggravate or even imitate symptoms of memory loss, Alzheimer's disease, and other forms of senile dementia. Get enough of all three through vitamin supplements and/or food sources such as spinach, broccoli, Brussels sprouts, bananas, carrots, liver, salmon, leafy greens, asparagus, oranges, orange juice, and fortified breakfast cereals.

But maybe you want to get moving, first. Great! Any poses you enjoy will be good for your soul, but consider including poses that build bone strength. Add the following to your routine (check with your doctor before starting any new exercise program):

➤ Standing poses (Chapter 13) are great for developing strength and physical control. Try the mountain pose, the three warrior poses, and the lightning bolt pose to start.

➤ Balance poses (Chapter 13) are excellent for building strength and, once you've mastered them, confidence. The tree pose is a good balance pose to start with. Be patient with yourself. Balance poses will become easier with practice. Don't worry about holding any pose for a long time. Use a wall or chair for support at first if it helps you, then move a few inches away, once you feel secure. Other poses can be practiced while sitting in a chair. Use your imagination and do what your body tells you it can do.

➤ Practice downward facing dog (Chapter 18) each day. It builds upper and lower body strength, and also has many of the advantages of the inversions. Keep your knees bent. Increase the time in the pose by increasing your breaths. For example, "This week I'll hold the pose for two deep breaths. Next week (or month) I'll take three deep breaths in the pose."

➤ If your legs tend to be weak, try standing in front of a sturdy chair (preferably one without arms) and practicing the lightning bolt pose (Chapter 13). See the following illustration.

➤ You might also find inversions strengthening and empowering. Once you feel steady and strong in the mountain pose (Chapter 13), move to the bridge, then the shoulderstand, then the plough, and then the headstand (all in Chapter 15). The headstand isn't as hard as you might think, once you are centered and strong. Don't try it before you feel ready, but once you've done it, do it as often as you can. It will help you to feel rejuvenated. Get your doctor's okay on this. Once he or she sees how strong yoga practice is making you, your doctor may want a few yoga lessons!

➤ Practice the sun salutation (Chapter 16) each morning and reflect on the sun's power and beauty.

➤ Lie still in *shavasana* (Chapter 19) every day for at least 10 minutes. This pose teaches your body and your mind how to release their tensions and troubles. Everything will work better after a little *shavasana!*

- Each time you try the lightning bolt variation for seniors, come down just a little bit lower. If your legs start to feel weak or shaky, sit down in the chair and take a smile break. Stand up and try again. Slowly develop your thigh and ankle strength this way. If you have trouble reaching your arms over your head, place your hands in *namaste* (prayer) position.

Overall, keep in mind your particular areas of strength and weakness, then tailor your yoga program to balance both. Having lived on the earth for an impressive number of years should not keep you from attempting yoga. In fact, many yogis live to be over 100 years old and still practice each day. Don't forget breathing exercises and meditation, as well as adherence to the *yamas* and *niyamas* (Chapter 6). Practice outside whenever you can and pay attention to the natural world around you. Your fitness program, as well as your life, will be whole, balanced, peaceful, and filled with bliss.

The Least You Need to Know

➤ Men can be great yogis—why not take a class?

➤ Kids can do yoga and can learn to love it for a lifetime.

➤ Yoga is an excellent way of life for seniors.

Yoga Sessions for the Time You Have

Here are some great ideas for routines to begin your yoga practice, based on the yoga classes that Joan teaches to her students. Whether you need a relaxing five-minute break in the middle of the workday, or an invigorating full-hour session at home to get you energized, toned, and ready for anything, Joan has suggestions for you. Each sequence of yoga postures helps you focus on something specific; for example, one sequence can hone in on improving your physical sense of balance, while another one has to do with releasing anger and negative feelings. Other examples include toning internal organs, building upper-body strength, or increasing lung capacity. You'll want to choose the one that's right for you. And remember, it's not important *how much* yoga you do, but that you keep practicing, doing as much as you can whenever you can. Yoga moves at *your* pace, in the time *you* have!

Every Day is a New Opportunity to Grow

Every time you practice yoga, try to view it as the *first* time. Study what your body is doing, and don't take anything for granted. Yoga is a new experience every day! Let's say you've learned mountain pose, *tadasana,* but you think it's an easy pose and you don't concentrate on it very much during your practice. Your performance of the pose becomes unaware and your yoga practice is likely to be unproductive. Every time you enter this mountain pose, enter it fully. Feel your thigh muscles strong and engaged, reach through your fingertips toward the ground where each toe is securely planted, lower your shoulders and feel your head and neck rise upward; you are a mountain!

Also, put aside any preconceived ideas you have about being a "beginning student," "intermediate student," or "advanced student." Sure, some postures might be beyond your reach right now, but yoga is a *personal* journey. The length of time that poses are held in comfort—whatever their degrees of complexity—and how grounded you are in the poses are the closest things to "advancement" in performing *Hatha Yoga*. The evenness and strength of your breath are also a reflection of the depth of your study. Approach your body as a new and special friend with every yoga class...sensitively and kindly, and your yoga practice is sure to prosper.

Let's get started!

5-Minute Yoga Sessions

These sessions are good at home or at work—anytime you need a quick lift or a refocusing boost to help find your center!

Session 1

Try 5 minutes of breathwork doing alternate nostril breathing. The time will fly by and you will begin to feel quietly balanced (*ha - tha*).

Session 2

Stand in mountain pose and bend over into triangle pose. Hold triangle on the right side for five breaths, then do the left side for five breaths. Go back into mountain pose and study your alignment.

Session 3

Face a wall and reach your arms out to place your palms on the wall at shoulder height. Take a big step back and bend at the hips toward the wall. Lengthen your spine. Wall-downward facing dog! Hold this position for 5 minutes. This is a great way to energize the body and open those stiff shoulders.

15-Minute Yoga Sessions

The 15-minute practice is great when you're in a rush and don't have too much time to spare. It may be hard at first to find the time, but we bet you'll end up cherishing this quarter-hour as your indispensable yoga haven! Hold every pose for at least five breaths. Try flowing into each consecutive posture.

Session 1

This sequence builds strength and is a quick way of releasing anger that has turned inward. Use it to help purge negative feelings.

Mountain pose, warrior 1 pose (both sides), warrior 2 pose (both sides), side angle stretch (both sides), mountain pose.

Session 2

This sequence is good for relaxing, calming, and quieting down. It tones the internal organs of the chest and abdomen.

Lying down spinal twist, leg lifts, *shavasana.*

Session 3

This session focuses on meditation and internal reflection.

Yoga mudra, camel pose, meditative pose (pick the one you feel most comfortable in).

Session 4

This session uses *pranayama* techniques to open the heart *chakra,* deepening our feelings of love and opening the chest with the breath.

Alternate nostril breathing, OM exhalation, *shavasana.*

30-Minute Yoga Sessions

Build up to 30-minute sessions at least one or two times per week. Try to hold each pose for six full breaths. If you can, reserve a regular time and place for these nurturing yoga sessions. You deserve it!

Session 1

This session is an upper-body workout performed mostly on the floor, opening the chest and the heart with downward facing dog pose to balance the sequence.

Shavasana, bridge, plough, fish, child's pose. Repeat this twice. Continue on to cobra, child's pose, downward facing dog, child's pose, repeating the sequence twice. Finish in a return to *shavasana.*

Session 2

Energize and strengthen your body with this invigorating session.

Child's pose, single leg lifts, double leg lifts, lying down spinal twist. Bring your knees to your chest, hold there, and pause. Turn over and go into cobra three times; each time holding the pose a bit longer. Move into downward facing dog. Step one foot forward, straighten your legs, turn to the side and come up into triangle! Do triangle on both sides, then move into lightening bolt. Come back down into child's pose. Repeat the entire sequence of poses two times. Rest in *shavasana.*

Session 3

The Mars *chakra,* the *chakra* of action located at the center of the body, is stimulated in this session, catapulting the body to energy!

Three slow full rounds of sun salutations. Follow with camel and boat. Rest in *shavasana.*

Session 4

The Mercury *chakra,* the *chakra* of communication located at the throat, is activated in this session to help us improve our interactions with others.

Half spinal twist, shoulderstand, plough, bridge. Rest in *shavasana.*

Session 5

This session concentrates on the Jupiter *chakra* and helps to balance your sexual energy.

Yoga mudra, hero, mountain, triangle, eagle, cow, yoga mudra. Rest in *shavasana.*

Full-Hour Yoga Sessions

Congratulations! You're about to luxuriate in a full hour of yoga practice. We bet you'll find that this one hour devoted to centering, strengthening, and fostering the yoga mind/body connection will make the other hours in your day far more productive and fulfilling!

Session 1

➤ Stand tall in mountain pose, toes spread, knees lifted, and shoulders relaxed down. Do head and shoulder rolls.

➤ Like a rag doll, reach your hands to the ceiling and let them fall to the floor; keep your muscles loose and don't worry about touching your toes. Rag doll helps you warm up, increasing alertness by bringing blood to the brain and overcoming stiffness in the spine and legs. Return to mountain pose to regain focus.

➤ Jump your feet about a yard apart for triangle pose. Perform triangle on both sides. Return to mountain pose.

➤ From mountain pose, bend your right knee out and place the right foot on the left thigh to move into tree pose. Bring the palms together in front of your heart and then raise them over your head while retaining your balance. Return to mountain pose.

➤ Walk to a wall in the room and place your hands on the wall at shoulder height. Take a giant step backward. Slowly bend at the waist, keeping the natural alignment of the spine to lengthen into downward facing dog against the wall. Return to mountain pose.

➤ Turn around to face away from the wall. Jump your feet apart about a yard. Place your hands on your hips and bend forward slowly with a flat back. The legs stay active and the back retains its natural alignment. You are a table top! Move into downward facing dog and hold for five breaths.

➤ Move into child's pose. Rise into downward facing dog. Repeat three times, holding downward facing dog for a longer period in each repetition.

➤ Rest in *shavasana*.

Session 2

➤ Begin in *shavasana*. Concentrate on breathing from the diaphragm. Let go of all thoughts and relax each part of your body from toes to head.

➤ Prepare for leg lifts by lifting one knee to your chest, hugging it, and raising your head toward the knee. Hold for three seconds. Repeat with the other leg. This pose is called *pavana-maktasana* in Sanskrit; it is a wind-relieving pose, which massages the intestines. Now, perform single and double leg lifts.

➤ Move into hero pose and follow with cow pose. Hero benefits the knees and tones the thighs. Cow stimulates the nerves at the base of the spine, preventing calcifying and aging. Cow also stimulates the nerves in the feet.

➤ Now, move into butterfly pose to stretch the inner hips and thighs, a revitalizing pose.

➤ Stand erect in mountain pose—shins in, femurs out!

➤ Jump your feet three to four feet apart for warrior 2. Perform on both sides.

➤ Return to mountain pose.

➤ Jump your feet out again, this time for warrior 1. Reach toward the heavens, but stay grounded on earth.

➤ Return to mountain pose.

➤ Move into standing head to knees pose, a forward bend. Hold for as long as you can comfortably.

➤ Rest in *shavasana*.

Glossary

This glossary is divided into two sections to help you find the terms you need quickly and efficiently. The first section includes all of the Sanskrit yoga terms you've learned in *The Complete Idiot's Guide to Yoga*. The second section of the glossary includes more terms related to yoga and health that you'll want to remember. Use both sections of the glossary as quick reference tools and easy ways to look up whatever you need to know.

Sanskrit Terms

abhinivesha   survival instinct

adho mukha shvanasana   downward facing dog; a forward bend

adho mukha vrksasana   the handstand; an inversion

ahimsa   one of the *yamas;* non-violence

ananda-maya-kosha   The bliss sheath and fifth sheath of existence

anna-maya-kosh   the physical body and first sheath of existence

apana   a type of *prana;* the vital energy of excretion that flows downward and out of the body, ridding it of impurities

aparigraha   one of the *yamas;* non-greed

asanas   the postures, or exercises, of yoga, designed to help you master control of your own body

Ashtanga Yoga   literally referring to the Eight Limbs of Yoga, this type of yoga, in our culture, has come to mean a *Hatha Yoga* practice that includes an intense *vinyasa* workout

asmita   ego or individuality

asteya   one of the *yamas;* non-stealing

avidya   incorrect comprehension

baddha konasana   the butterfly; a sitting posture

baddha padmasana   the bound lotus; a meditative pose

bandha   literally "to bind" or "to lock," *bandhas* are muscular locks used during postures and breathing exercises to intensify the energy of *prana* so it can eliminate impurities from the body

Bhagavad Gita   one of India's most beloved and famous sacred texts, it is the epic story of Arjuna, a warrior-prince, who confronts moral dilemmas and is led to a better understanding of reality through the intercession of the god *Krishna*

Bhakti Yoga   sincere, heartfelt devotion to the divine is the primary focus of this type of yoga

bhastrika   literally "bellows," *bhastrika* is a breathing technique that imitates the action of a bellows

bhramari   also known as bee breath, this breathing technique imitates the sound of a bee

bhujangasana   the cobra; a backbend

brahmacharya   one of the *yamas;* chastity or non-lust

brahman   the absolute, or divinity itself

buddhi   the intellect

chakras   centers of energy that exist between the base of your spinal column and the crown of your head

chakrasana   the wheel; a backbend

chandra namaskara   moon salutation; a *vinyasa*

dandasana   the staff; a sitting posture

dhanurasana   the bow; a backbend

dharana   orienting the mind towards a single point

dhyana   meditation, or the process of quieting the mind to free yourself from preconceptions and illusions

duhkha   pain, suffering, trouble, and discomfort; a mental state during which limitations and a profound sense of dissatisfaction are perceived

dvesha   refusal

garudasana   the eagle; a balance posture

ghee   clarified butter, or butter from which all solids have been removed, leaving only the oil; a traditional Indian food

gomukhasana   the cow; a sitting posture

gunas   the three primary qualities existing in the universe, *sattva, rajas,* and *tamas;* they can apply to the mind and to influences on the body such as food

guru   literally "dispeller of darkness," a guru is a personal spiritual advisor who helps direct the yogi toward enlightenment

halasana   the plough; an inversion

Hatha Yoga   a type of yoga primarily concerned with mastering control over the physical body as a path to enlightenment; *Hatha Yoga* combines opposing forces to achieve balance

Hatha-Yoga-Pradipika   a 14th-century, comprehensive guide to *Hatha Yoga*

ida   a channel on the left side of the spine through which *prana* moves

ishvara-pranidhana   one of the *niyamas;* centering on the divine

jalandhara bandha   a *bandha* that locks the throat

janu shirshasana   sitting one leg; a forward bend

japa   the process of repeating a *mantra* over and over for the purpose of clearing the mind

Jnana Yoga   this type of yoga emphasizes questioning, meditation, and contemplation as paths to enlightenment

Jupiter chakra   located on the spine near the genitals, this energy center involves water, sexuality, passion, the creation of life, and taste

kali yuga   the fourth of four ages (*yuga* means "age"), and the age in which we are now living; the shortest of all the ages, *kali yuga* is 432,000 years long

kapalabhati   a cleansing ritual for the respiratory tract, lungs, and sinuses; also called skull shining

karma   the law of cause and effect, or the movement towards balanced consciousness; everything you do, say, or even think has an immediate effect on the universe that will reverberate back to you in some way

Karma Yoga   selfless action and service to others are emphasized in this type of yoga

koshas   the five sheaths of existence that comprise the body

Krishna   a popular Hindu god

Kriya Yoga   the yoga of action and participation in life

kundalini   literally "she who is coiled," *kundalini* is a psychospiritual energy force in the body that is often compared to a snake lying curled at the base of the spine, waiting to be awakened; when fully awakened, it is said to actually restructure the body, allowing the yogi control over previously involuntary bodily functions

Kundalini Yoga   this esoteric and mystical form of yoga is centered around awakening and employing *kundalini* energy

kurmasana   the tortoise; a forward bend

mandalas   beautiful, usually circular, geometric designs that draw your eye to the center and are used as a center of focus in meditation

mano-maya-kosha   the mind sheath and third sheath of existence

mantra   a sound or sounds that resonate in the body and evoke certain energies during meditation

Mantra Yoga   the chanting of *mantras* characterizes this type of yoga

maricyasana   the half spinal twist; a twisting pose

Mars chakra   located on the spine behind the naval, this energy center is associated with digestion or "gastric fire," your sense of self, and physical actions

matsyasana   the fish; a backbend

Matsyendra   a Hindu sage and one of the first teachers of *Hatha Yoga*

Mercury chakra   located in the throat, this energy center governs communication

moon chakra   located behind your head at the base of your skull, the moon *chakra* complements the sun *chakra*; energy enters the moon *chakra*, travels down to the Saturn *chakra*, then rises up and exits the sun *chakra*

mudhasana   child's pose; a forward bend

mudras   hand gestures that direct the life current through the body

mula bandha   an anal lock

nadi shodhana   a breathing exercise in which nostrils are alternated for inhalation and exhalation

nadis   subtle vibratory passages of psychospiritual energy

namaste mudra   a *mudra* in which the hands are placed together in prayer-like fashion to honor the inner light

naukasana   the full boat; a balance pose

nauli   a cleansing ritual for the inner abdomen

niyamas   five observances or personal disciplines, as defined by *Patanjali* in his Yoga Sutras; the *niyamas* are *shauca, santosha, tapas, svadhyaya,* and *ishvar-pranidhana*

OM   a sacred syllable commonly used as a *mantra* during meditation and representative of the absolute or oneness of the universe; a rough approximation of the sound of the universe's vibration

padma shirshasana   the lotus headstand; an inversion

padmasana   the lotus pose, a meditative posture in which the legs are crossed and each foot is placed on the opposite thigh; the pose is said to resemble the perfection of the lotus flower

parshvakonasana   the side angle stretch; a standing posture

pingala   a channel on the right side of the spine through which *prana* moves

prana   a form of energy in the universe that animates all physical matter, including the human body; the vital energy of respiration and the soul of the universe

prana-maya-kosha   the vital body and second sheath of existence

pranayama   breathing exercises designed to help you master control of your breath

pratyahara   withdrawal of the senses

purvottanasana   the hands to feet pose; a variation of the plough; an inversion

raga   attachment

Raja Yoga   also known as The Royal Path, this type of yoga emphasizes control of the intellect to attain enlightenment

rajas   the quality of high activity and agitation; a *guna*

Rig-Veda   literally "Knowledge of Praise," the Rig-Veda consists of 1,028 hymns and is the oldest known reference to yoga, and possibly the oldest known text in the world

roga   sickness

samadhi   the state of meditation in which ego disappears and all becomes one; it is a state of absolute bliss

samyama   when in a state of *samyama,* the yogi has investigated, concentrated on, meditated upon, and contemplated an object or subject until everything about it is known and understood

santosha   one of the *niyamas;* contentment

sarvangasana   the shoulderstand; an inversion

sattva   the quality of clarity and lightness; a *guna*

Saturn chakra   located just above the anus at the base of the spine, this energy center involves elimination and your sense of smell

satya   one of the *yamas;* truthfulness

setu bandha sarvangasana   the bridge; an inversion

shat kriyas   purification rituals

shauca   one of the *niyamas;* purity, or inner and outer cleanliness

shavasana   also known as the corpse pose, this pose is meant to bring the body and mind into total, conscious relaxation

shirshasana   the headstand; an inversion

shodhana   yogic cleansing rituals

sitali   a breathing technique involving rolling the tongue, then inhaling through it like a straw; a cooling technique

sukha   lightness and comfort

sukhasana   easy pose; a meditative pose

sun chakra   located in the middle of your brow, this energy center is also known as the third eye, or center of unclouded perception

surya namaskara   sun salutation; a *vinyasa*

sushumna   a hollow passageway between *pingala* and *ida* that runs through the spinal cord, and through which *kundalini* can travel once it is awakened

svadhyaya   one of the *niyamas;* the process of inquiring into your own nature, the nature of your beliefs, and the nature of the world's spiritual journey

svamin   a title of respect for a spiritual person who is master of himself rather than others

svasthya   health

swami   the Anglicized form of *svamin*

Swami Vivekananda   a *guru* from India who addressed the Parliament of Religions in 1893, and quickly became a popular figure; he was followed by a number of other *swamis* who came to the United States to teach and guide Westerners along the eastern path of yoga

tadasana   the mountain; a standing posture

tamas   the quality of heaviness and inactivity; a *guna*

Tantra Yoga   this type of yoga is characterized by certain rituals designed to awaken the *kundalini*

tapas   one of the *niyamas;* self-discipline

thousand petaled lotus chakra   located at the crown of the skull, this energy center is the core of self-realization, perspective, unity, and enlightenment

Transcendental Meditation   Also known as TM, this form of meditation involves the mental repetition of a *mantra*

trikonasana   the triangle or happy pose; a standing posture

uddiyana bandha   a *bandha* that locks the abdomen

ujjayi   a breathing exercise that produces sound in the throat with the inhalation; literally, "she who is victorious"

Upanishads   scriptures of ancient Hindu philosophy

urdhvamukha shvanasana   the upward facing dog; a backbend

ushtrasana   the camel; a backbend

utkatasana   the lightning bolt; a standing posture

uttanasana   standing head to knee; a forward bend

uttanatavasana   leg lifts

vajrasana   kneeling pose; a meditative pose

vasisthasana   the arm balance; a balance posture

Venus chakra   located behind your heart, this energy center is the seat of your compassion

vidya   correct understanding

vijnana-maya-kosha   the intellect sheath and fourth sheath of existence

vinyasa   a steady flow of connected yoga *asanas* linked with breathwork in a continuous movement; a particularly dynamic form of yoga

virabhadrasana   the warrior; a standing posture

virasana   the hero; a sitting posture

vrikshasana   the tree; a balance posture

vyadhi   disease

yamas   five abstinences that purify the body and mind, as defined by Patanjali in his Yoga Sutras; the *yamas* are *ahimsa, satya, asteya, brahmacharya,* and *aparigraha*

yoga mudra   a forward bend

Yoga Sutras of Patanjali   the source of Patanjali's Eightfold Path, this collection of succinct aphorisms has largely defined the modern concept of yoga

Yogi   someone who practices yoga

Yogini   a female yogi

More Terms You'll Want to Know

adrenal glands   a pair of glands located just above the kidneys (in mammals); these glands secrete epinephrine (a stimulant) and certain steroids

afferent nerves   the nerves that carry messages from the body to the brain

allopathic medicine   the traditional medicine of Western culture, which focuses on a specific disease or problem and treats it

Alzheimer's disease   a degenerative brain disease most common in the elderly

astral body   the vehicle of the spirit, corresponding with the mind; higher than the physical body, but below the causal body

causal body   the subtlest body, it houses the spirit; higher than the physical and astral bodies

circadian rhythms   the physiological rhythms people experience throughout the course of a 24-hour day

deltoids   muscles that lift and rotate the arms

diaphragm   a large, flat muscle at the base of the thoracic cavity that controls breathing

estrogen   several hormones that produce sexual changes in female mammals

fruitarians   a form of vegetarianism in which no animal products whatsoever are consumed, and all foods must be consumed raw

holistic medicine   an approach to medicine in which the patient's entire lifestyle, environment, and personality are considered in the treatment of disease

intercostals   muscles that expand the ribs

lacto-ovo-vegetarianism   a form of vegetarianism in which no meat, poultry, or fish is consumed, but eggs, milk, and milk products are consumed

lacto-vegetarianism   a form of vegetarianism in which no meat, poultry, fish, or eggs are consumed, but milk and milk products are consumed

larynx   the area of the throat containing the vocal cords

ligaments   a band of tissue connecting bones to bones or holding organs in place

menopause   the period in a woman's life, usually somewhere between the late thirties and the early sixties, when menstruation ceases

Occident   the West (Europe and the Americas), as opposed to the Orient

Orient   the East (Asia), as opposed to the Occident

patella   the kneecap

pectorals   chest muscles that pull in and rotate the arms

physical body   the lowest of the three bodies, the physical body is the body we see; the other bodies are the astral body and the causal body

pituitary gland   a gland attached to the brain that secretes hormones affecting growth

PMS   an acronym for premenstrual syndrome

postpartum depression   a condition experienced by at least half of new mothers characterized by depression, anxiety, drastic mood swings, and spontaneous weeping in the week after childbirth

premenstrual syndrome   a syndrome experienced by some women one to two weeks before the onset of menstruation; symptoms may include irritability, depression, restlessness, back pain, bloating, and swelling

sartorius   muscle that twists the thigh and bends the hip and knee

scapula   the shoulder blade

sciatic nerve   a long nerve that starts in the hip and runs down the leg

sciatica   a painful condition felt in the hip or thigh and down the back of the leg, resulting from inflammation of the sciatic nerve

sensory nerves   the nerves that carry messages from the brain to the body

sprain   an injury to a ligament

sternum   the breastbone, a flat bone to which the ribs are attached

strain   an injury to a muscle or its tendon

tendon   tough, connective tissue attaching muscles to bones

thoracic cavity   the cavity containing your lungs and heart

thyroid gland   located near the trachea, this gland secretes hormones that affect growth

tibia   the inner and thicker bone of the two bones of the lower leg

tibialis anterior   muscles that raise the foot

trachea   the passageway through which air travels after inhalation

ulna   the larger of the two bones of the forearm

veganism   a form of vegetarianism in which no animal products of any kind are consumed

vegetarianism   a diet in which no meat is consumed

Further Along the Yoga Path: Suggested Reading

Welcome! Now that you've begun your yoga practice with *The Complete Idiot's Guide to Yoga,* no doubt you'll want to read more about the many aspects of yoga, find out how to incorporate yoga into your everyday life, and enhance your yoga practice. Here's a great list of books to help guide you on your yoga path!

Balch, James. F. and Phyllis A. Balch. *Prescription for Nutritional Healing.* Garden City Park, New York: Avery Publishing Group, Inc., 1990.

Bender Birch, Beryl. *Power Yoga.* New York: Simon & Schuster, 1995.

Bhagavad Gita, multiple translations.

Budilovsky, Joan. *Fat-Free Yoga.* Oak Brook, Illinois: YOYOGA!, 1997.

Budilovsky, Joan. *The Little Yogi Energy Book.* Oak Brook, Illinois: YOYOGA!, 1997.

Budilovsky, Joan. *Yoga for a New Day.* Oak Brook, Illinois: YOYOGA!, 1996.

Carper, Jean. *Jean Carper's Total Nutrition Guide.* New York: Bantam Books, 1987.

Chopra, Deepak. *Ageless Body, Timeless Mind.* New York: Harmony Books, 1993.

Choudhury, Bikram. *Bikram's Beginning Yoga Class.* New York: G.P. Putnam's Sons, 1978.

Christensen, Alice. *The Easy Does It Yoga Trainer's Guide.* Sarasota, Florida: American Yoga Association, 1995.

Couch, Jean. *The Runner's Yoga Book.* Berkeley, California: Rodmell Press, 1990.

Desikachar, T.K.V. *The Heart of Yoga: Developing a Personal Practice.* Rochester, Vermont: Inner Traditions International, 1995.

Farhi, Donna. *The Breathing Book: Good Health and Vitality Through Essential Breath Work.* New York: Henry Holt and Company, 1996.

Feuerstein, Georg. *The Shambhala Guide to Yoga*. Boston: Shambhala Publications, Inc., 1996.

Feuerstein, Georg. *The Yoga-Sutra of Patanjali, A New Translation and Commentary*. Rochester, Vermont: Inner Traditions, International, 1979.

Gunther, Bernard. *Energy Ecstasy and Your Seven Vital Chakras*. North Hollywood, California: Newcastle Publishing, 1983.

Hanh, Thich Nhat. *Peace is Every Step*. New York: Bantam Books, 1991.

Hanna, Thomas. *Somatics*. Reading, Massachusetts: Addison Wesley, 1988.

Hewitt, James. *Teach Yourself Yoga*. Lincolnwood (Chicago): NTC Publishing Group, 1993.

Hittleman, Richard. *Yoga for Health: The Total Program*. New York: Ballantine Books, 1983.

Iyengar, B.K.S. *Light on Yoga*. New York: Schocken Books, 1979.

Japananda, Swami K. *Yoga, You, Your New Life*. Chicago: The Temple of Kriya Yoga, 1981.

Kabat-Zinn, Jon Ph.D. *Full Catastrophe Living: Using the Wisdom of Your Body and Mind to Face Stress, Pain, and Illness*. New York: Delta, 1990.

Kriyanada, Goswami. *Extraordinary Spiritual Potential*. Chicago: The Temple of Kriya Yoga, 1988.

Kriyanada, Goswami. *The Laws of Karma*. Chicago: The Temple of Kriya Yoga, 1995.

Kriyanada, Goswami. *The Spiritual Science of Kriya Yoga*. Chicago: The Temple of Kriya Yoga, 1992.

Kriyananda, Sri (J. Donald Walters). *Yoga Postures for Higher Awareness*. Nevada City, California: Crystal Clarity, 1967.

Lasater, Judith Ph.D. *Relax and Renew*. Berkeley, California: Rodmell Press, 1995.

Lerner, Michael. *Choices in Healing: Integrating the Best of Conventional and Complementary Approaches to Cancer*. Cambridge, Massachusetts: MIT Press, 1994.

Levitt, Atma JoAnne. *The Kripalu Cookbook*. Stockbridge, Massachusetts: Berkshire House Publishers, 1995.

Living Yoga: A Comprehensive Guide for Daily Life. Edited by Georg Feuerstein and Stephan Bodian with the staff of *Yoga Journal*. New York: Jeremy P. Tarcher/Perigee Books, 1993.

Mehta, Silva and Shyam Mihra. *Yoga the Iyengar Way*. New York: A.A. Knopf, 1990.

Monro, Robin, R. Nagaranthna, and H. R. Nagendra. *Yoga for Common Ailments*. New York: Fireside, 1990.

Moyers, Bill. *Healing and the Mind*. New York: Doubleday, 1993.

O'Brien, Paddy. *Yoga for Women: Complete Mind and Body Fitness*. London: Thorsons, 1994.

Prabhupada, A.C. and Swami Bhaktivedanta. *Bhagavad-Gita As It Is.* Los Angeles: Bhaktivedanta Book Trust, 1968.

Rieker, Hans-Ulrich. *The Yoga of Light: Hatha Yoga Pradipika.* Middletown, California: The Dawn House Press, 1971.

Rig-Veda, multiple translations.

Rush, Anne Kent. *The Modern Book of Yoga.* New York: Dell Publishing, 1996.

Scaravelli, Vanda. *Awakening the Spine.* New York: Harper Collins Publishers, 1991.

Schatz, Mary Pullig M.D. *Back Care Basics.* Berkeley, California: Rodnell Press, 1992.

Schiffmann, Erich. *Yoga: The Spirit and Practice of Moving Into Stillness.* New York: Pocket Books, 1996.

Sivananda Yoga Vedanta Center. *Learn Yoga in a Weekend.* New York: Alfred A. Knopf, 1995.

Sivananda Yoga Vedanta Center. *The Sivananda Companion to Yoga.* New York: Simon & Schuster, 1983.

Sivananda Yoga Vedanta Center. *Yoga Mind Body.* New York: Dorling Kindersley, 1996.

Stewart, Mary and Kathy Phillips. *Yoga for Children.* London: Webster's International Publishers, 1992.

Tigunait, Pandit Rajmani. *Inner Quest: The Path of Spiritual Unfoldment.* Honesdale, Pennsylvania: Yoga International Books, 1995.

Upanishads, multiple translations.

Vishnudevananda, Swami. *The Complete Illustrated Book of Yoga.* New York: Bell Publishers, 1960.

Yogananda, Paramahansa. *Autobiography of a Yogi.* Los Angeles: Self-Realization Fellowship, 1946.

Yogi Bhajan, Ph.D. *Kundalini Yoga, The Flow of Eternal Power.* Los Angeles: Time Capsule Books, 1996.

Yukteswar, Swami Sri. *The Holy Science.* Los Angeles: Self-Realization Fellowship, 1949.

Index

Enjoy a selection of quality yoga books and tapes by Joan Budilovsky!

SPECIAL OFFER FOR READERS OF THE COMPLETE IDIOT'S GUIDE TO YOGA!

Breathworks   Only $6.50!

30-minute audiotape of yoga deep-breathing exercises. Breath is the key to opening the life force, what yoga calls *prana,* within you.

Additional Audiotapes

Total Relaxation...with Shavasana $10.00

This tape will help you to let go of all tensions and stresses. It will help you come to your center of peace and tranquillity through the yoga process of *shavasana.* Let Joan guide you on this journey of pure serenity.

Beginning Yoga with Joan $10.00

Joan guides you through an hour of relaxing yet invigorating yoga postures and breathwork.

Sun-Salutations!...with Joan $10.00

Joyful and empowering, this is a faster moving series of continuous yoga postures forming the salutation to the sun. For an aerobic yoga workout, Joan will be sun-saluting with you step-by-step!

The Art of Massage Made Simple $10.00

This tape is a perfect complement to your yoga practice. Also a nationally certified massage therapist, Joan guides you and a partner through a complete one-hour full-body Swedish massage.

Books

Fat-Free Yoga $7.00

An introductory book for beginning yogis, this is a simple, fat-free look at the basic yoga principles correlated to beginning yoga postures.

Yoga for a New Day $10.00

This intermediate level book is packed full of information and further discourse on the basic philosophy of yoga observances and abstentions, with an extensive series of beginning yoga postures with detailed explanations.

The Little Yogi Energy Book $7.00

Small in size, but grand in energy. This book contains advanced yoga postures, correlating specific, challenging postures with the seven major *chakras.*

Come visit Joan at her Web site: http://www.yoyoga.com

Order form on back

7/4

YES, send me my copies of Joan's yoga audiotapes and books:

Audiotapes:

❏ SPECIAL OFFER Breathworks $6.50
❏ Total Relaxation...with Shavasana $10.00
❏ Beginning Yoga with Joan $10.00
❏ Sun-Salutations!...with Joan $10.00
❏ The Art of Massage Made Simple $10.00

Books:

❏ Fat-Free Yoga $7.00
❏ Yoga for a New Day $10.00
❏ The Little Yogi Energy Book $7.00

Add $2.75 shipping/handling charge to your total order: _____

Add an additional $5.00 shipping/handling charge if
your total order is $40.00 or over: _____

Subtotal: _____

Illinois Residents add 6.7% sales tax: _____

TOTAL: _____

Payment to be made in U.S. funds. Prices and availability are subject to change at anytime without notice.

❏ Check or Money Order enclosed.

I would like to charge to: ❏ MasterCard   ❏ Visa

Acct. #: _____

Exp. Date: _____

Signature: _____

Send this order form with your check, money order, or charge information to:

Yoyoga, Inc., P.O. Box 5013, Oak Brook, Illinois, 60522.
Fax: (630) 963-4001

Allow 4-6 weeks for delivery.

Ship to:

Name:_____

Address:_____

City/State/Zip:_____

Telephone:_____